Public Policy

An Evolutionary Approach

THIRD EDITION

JOSEPH STEWART, JR.
Clemson University

DAVID M. HEDGE
University of Florida

JAMES P. LESTER
Late, Colorado State University

THOMSON ™

WADSWORTH

Australia • Brazil • Canada • Mexico • Singapore • Spain
United Kingdom • United States

THOMSON
WADSWORTH

Public Policy: An Evolutionary Approach, **Third Edition**
Joseph Stewart, Jr.; David M. Hedge; James P. Lester

Publisher: Michael Rosenberg
Managing Development Editor: Karen Judd
Technology Project Manager: Yevgeny Ioffe
Marketing Manager: Karin Sandberg
Marketing Communications Manager: Heather Baxley
Senior Content Project Manager: Josh Allen

Art Director: Linda Helcher
Print Buyer: Linda Hsu
Permissions Editor: Mardell Glinski Schultz
Production Service: International Typesetting and Composition
Cover Designer: Laurie Anderson
Text and Cover Printer: West Group

Printed in the United States of America
1 2 3 4 5 6 7 11 10 09 08 07

Library of Congress Control Number: 2007927800

Student Edition:
ISBN-13: 978-0-534-57494-9
ISBN-10: 0-534-57494-7

Instructor's Edition:
ISBN-13: 978-0-495-38159-4
ISBN-10: 0-495-3819-4

Thomson Higher Education
25 Thomson Place
Boston, MA 02210
USA

For more information about our products, contact us at:
Thomson Learning Academic Resource Center
1-800-423-0563

For permission to use material from this text or product, submit a request online at
http://www.thomsonrights.com.
Any additional questions about permissions can be submitted by e-mail to
thomsonrights@thomson.com.

To James P. Lester
1944–2000

Brief Contents

Contents

7   Policy Implementation   106

Preface

M uch has happened in America since the first edition of this text was published in the mid-nineties. On the political front, both the presidency and the Congress have changed partisan hands, one president survived attempts to remove him from office through the impeachment process, and not a few members of Congress have been indicted and convicted of crimes including influence peddling and violation of campaign finance laws. Public policy has changed as well. Congress passed major welfare reform during the Clinton presidency, and the Bush administration worked with a Republican Congress to pass major tax cuts, a prescription drug plan for the elderly, and a new round of federal mandates for local schools. On the foreign policy front, the nation has been involved in no less than three major military actions in the last ten or so years—Bosnia and Kosovo and, in the wake of the 9/11 attacks on America, wars in Afghanistan and Iraq.

Our understanding of the process and substance of public policy has changed as well. In recent years policy scholars have conducted systematic assessments of important policies including education, welfare, and environmental policy so that we now have a much better sense of which policies and programs have worked and under what circumstances those policies achieve their goals. The last several years have also witnessed considerable effort to develop and test our best theories of an evolving policy process. Most notable in that regard are the gains made in understanding policy change both in the long run and in the short term.

Not surprisingly, much remains to be done. Policy makers are faced with a never-ending set of problems that beg some form of public solution, whether it relates to global warming, health care, immigration, or the United States' place in a rapidly changing global community. For their part, policy scholars need to continue developing and testing theories of how governing proceeds and adapt those efforts to reflect changes in the policy process, including a greater reliance on market mechanisms to do the business of government and a blurring of lines between the various stages of the policy process.

In the pages that follow we look at the process and substance of public policy in America. In doing that we offer what we believe is a unique approach to introducing students to policy studies by focusing on how our understanding of the policy process and several substantive areas of public policy has evolved over the past several decades.

The book is organized into four parts. Part I considers how the field of policy studies, and policy and politics in the United States, have evolved in recent decades. It also discusses alternative approaches to policy analysis, what we mean by "models," and the means by which we evaluate those models. Part II considers how research and thinking about various aspects of the policy cycle have changed in the past several years. In doing that, we outline numerous models that attempt to account for, among other things, agenda setting, policymaking, implementation, and policy change. We also consider how different phases of the policy process have changed over the years. Part III of the book examines the evolution and impact of three substantive areas of public policy in America—education, welfare, and the environment. Part IV begins by looking more closely at how and why policy analysis is (and often is not) utilized by those in and out of government. In the final chapter we summarize the major changes that have occurred in how America governs itself and consider the implications of those changes for doing and understanding public policy in the years ahead.

TO THE INSTRUCTORS USING THIS BOOK

The following discussion provides what we hope is some useful advice to professors adopting this book. We have found that an old Chinese proverb provides much insight into how students learn and how professors might approach this course. The old Chinese proverb says, "*Tell* me and I will forget . . . *Show* me and I might remember . . . *Involve* me and I will remember." As the proverb suggests, students learn in at least three ways. First, all students need some basic *information* about the topic. They also need some type of *experience* with the topic at hand. Finally, they need to *reflect upon and apply* what they have been told or were exposed to that week. Therefore, one could adopt three separate activities directed toward the students. First, each week might begin with a brief *lecture* on the topic for that particular week. Students are expected to come to class prepared to discuss the assigned readings for that week's topic within the context of a large group. The second meeting each week could then be devoted to a *videotape* (or guest lecture or even a "field trip") to provide the students with some *experience* with the topic. Finally, the week may end with a small-group *discussion* for reflection on and application of the material presented during that particular week. These three sets of activities are mutually reinforcing, and they provide the student with multiple kinds of learning activities that hold their interest and make the course more stimulating and engaging. Guest lecturers and small-group discussions represent powerful alternatives (as well as supplements) to the traditional lecture format. By augmenting large class meetings and lectures with these other activities, teachers can share some of the responsibility for instruction with their students. The students thus become more active participants in this learning context—unlike in the traditional, more passive approach wherein they are constrained by listening and note taking.

ACKNOWLEDGMENTS

Many individuals have helped to make this book a reality. First, we owe an enormous intellectual debt to numerous scholars who, over the past two decades, have contributed greatly to our own intellectual development. Among these are (alphabetically): James Anderson, Ann O'M. Bowman, Charles Bullock, Richard Cole, Peter DeLeon, William Dunn, Malcolm Goggin, Richard Hofferbert, Helen Ingram, Hank Jenkins-Smith, Michael Kraft, Dean Mann, Peter May, Daniel Mazmanian, Paula McClain, Eugene Meehan, Kenneth Meier, Terry Moe, Henry Nau, Walter Rosenbaum, Paul Sabatier, Anne L. Schneider, Robert Stoker, Harvey Tucker, Richard Waterman, and David Webber. By their prolific writings, and often their willingness to provide constructive comments on our work, they have contributed directly to whatever success this book enjoys. We are very grateful for their help. Second, several external reviewers or adopters of this book offered their constructive criticisms and advice on one or more editions; they include Les Alm, Brian Cook, Charles Davis, Malcolm Goggin, Jeffrey Greene, Bernie Kolasa, John Piskulich, James Sheffield, Andrew Skalaban, and James Wunsch. We are especially grateful to Robert Blair of the University of Nebraska-Omaha, June S. Speakman of Roger Williams University, and William Parle of Oklahoma State University for their suggestions regarding this edition. We adopted many of the reviewers' suggestions, and the book is much improved as a consequence. We extend our sincere thanks to all of them for their helpful advice.

We are also grateful for the encouragement and assistance we received from Thomson Wadsworth. Several individuals, including Mardell Glinski Schultz, Joshua Allen, Christianne Thillen, and Deepti Narwat, provided a great deal of help that made this book much better than it otherwise might have been. We are especially grateful to Karen Judd, whose tenacity combined with patience kept the revisions more or less on schedule. Special thanks go to Hyun Jung Yun at the University of Florida for her help in preparing some of the figures that appear throughout the chapters. As always, we are indebted to our families for creating an environment within which we were able to work. We are also appreciative of the support and encouragement we have received over the years from our students in public policy studies. It is our hope that this book will further enhance their perspectives and understanding about American public policy.

Finally, we dedicate this book to our coauthor and friend, James Lester, who passed away shortly after the second edition was released. Jim was an outstanding scholar whose contribution to this book, his discipline, and pursuit of public policies that matter are huge.

Joseph Stewart, Jr. and David M. Hedge

The Context of Public Policy Studies

1

The Nature of Public Policy

"The farther backward you can look, the farther forward you can see."
SIR WINSTON CHURCHILL

Every day we are reminded of the many policy issues confronting leaders at all levels of government. At the national level, the attack on America on September 11, 2001, propelled national security to the forefront of the nation's policy agenda. Should we have invaded Iraq? What is the best way to protect our borders? Does a war on terrorism require that we rethink the civil liberties of the American people? How should the United States respond to instability elsewhere in the world? Domestic issues loom large as well. Can social security be reformed before the trust fund runs out? What, if anything, should government do to limit the outsourcing of jobs? Should stem cell research be funded with federal dollars when embryonic cells are used? What can be done to ensure that more Americans have access to quality health care? Is it time that America acknowledges gay and lesbian unions, at least as legal unions?

Across the American states, lawmakers continue to wrestle with how best to educate our children, take care of the elderly and poor, and protect the environment. One emerging issue is whether the private sector can do a better job of teaching our children and delivering welfare services. Are vouchers and competition between private and public schools the solution to what many perceive as a failure of public education? Should private profit and not-for-profit organizations play a greater role in administering welfare and child services? What about faith-based organizations? State governments face new challenges as well. As a result of the welfare reforms enacted by the U.S. Congress in 1996, state officials now have more leeway in deciding who will receive welfare and under what conditions. In the absence of federal initiatives, a number of states have also enacted or are considering ways to address the problems of CO_2 emissions and global warming. In a related fashion, some states (and for that matter, local communities) have created programs that provide subsidized health insurance to the working poor. And, while Congress debates stem cell research, some states have passed legislation allowing such research to be conducted within their state.

At the local level, the "devolution revolution" of the 1980s and 1990s has made the policy debates even more important as jurisdictions struggle to decide which programs should be cut and which should be retained. Should taxes be raised to cover the costs of environmental and other programs that experienced cutbacks under the "new federalism" and the decentralization of social programs? Should funds be shifted from low-priority areas to those of higher priority? Should programs be cut? If so, which ones? Local governments also must deal with what are ostensibly national issues. While the nation debates immigration policy, local governments must decide how to provide (or not) local services to an increasing illegal immigrant population. In the wake of 9/11 local communities have had to add the prevention of and responses to possible acts of terrorism to their already crowded public safety agendas.

As the examples illustrate, finding answers to these and other policy questions is never easy. In large part this is because many of the policy issues governments face often touch on the most basic ethical issues facing society. The ongoing debate concerning abortion and more recently stem cell research are first and foremost questions of when life begins and the respective rights of embryos, fetuses, and women. More recently the passage and reenactment of the so-called Patriot Act pitted two long-standing American values—national security and civil liberties—against one another and forced national policy makers to find a balance between the two.

Fashioning policy solutions is also made difficult by serious disagreements over whether the alleged "crisis" actually exists and, if so, the sources of the problem. Was the United States under the imminent threat of an attack by Iraq in 2002? Is the outsourcing of jobs really a problem or just a natural consequence of globalization? Does allowing gay and lesbian couples to join in legal unions threaten the sanctity of marriage and the family? Nor is there much agreement as to what causes many of the problems Americans face. Take education for example. For decades politicians and citizens alike have concluded that America's schools are in trouble. But why? Is it simply a lack of funding, particularly for those schools in the poorest parts of our nation's cities and states? Or is the failure of America's schools a more fundamental problem of how we organize and govern education? Are we asking schools to do too much? Too little?

Even when there is consensus about what values should be pursued or what problems should be addressed, there is still uncertainty and conflict about how best to address those problems. Again education provides an excellent example. In recent years, state, federal, and local policy makers have considered and debated a range of alternative solutions to the problems of education—including an increase in standards for both teachers and students, privatizing education through vouchers and charter schools, and relying on state- or district-wide testing to determine which schools are doing their jobs and which schools should be punished or rewarded. And, of course, disagreements and uncertainty do not end once policies have been adopted and implemented. As the reader will see when we look at educational policy, there are serious disagreements among the ranks of policy scholars as to whether vouchers and charter schools actually improve the quality of education.

The goal of this book is to provide students with the knowledge and analytic skills necessary to understanding how governments and their citizens address these and other pressing policy issues. That same information can also be used to help fashion policy solutions, sort out competing claims about what the sources and solutions of public problems are, and assess the viability of government policies already in place. The need for these kinds of information is obvious. As the reader knows, few areas of our lives are untouched by governments at some level. The air we breathe, the food we eat, the schools we attend, the health care system we use, and our very security as a nation are dependent upon someone in government doing the "right thing." Moreover, the issues governments address are often the most complex and intractable issues facing their citizenry. In many cases governments are asked to tackle the very problems that other elements of society cannot (or will not) adequately address—including poverty, pollution, crime, workplace safety, and in some cases social injustice. Not surprisingly, those are often the problems that have the most complex causes and consequences. For those and other reasons, scholars and policy actors alike have pointed to the need for reliable information, produced in a timely manner, on which critical policy choices can be made. While politics-as-usual may have been sufficient for governing a century ago, as Quade and McCarter (1989) note, "Technology and events move so rapidly that natural trial-and-error and give-and-take processes can become too catastrophe prone for comfort before approaching completion—not only war but population pressures, resource shortages, and environmental deterioration are in this category."[1]

In the chapters that follow, we attempt to provide some of the information citizens and governments alike need to do "the right thing." In Chapters 5 through 9, we walk the student through the stages of the policy process to illustrate how governments typically operate in addressing (or not) policy issues. Chapters 10, 11, and 12 consider how governments at all levels deal with three policy issues that have received considerable attention in recent years—education, welfare, and the environment.

Before we can do all of that, however, we need to define our terms and to offer a framework for understanding both the process and substance of public policy in America. In the remainder of this chapter we begin by defining what we mean by public policy and outlining the stages of the policy process. Once that is done we look at how the field of public policy has evolved over the last three to four decades.

WHAT DO WE MEAN BY PUBLIC POLICY AND POLICY ANALYSIS?

Various authors have offered definitions of what is meant by the term *public policy.* Thomas R. Dye, for example, defines public policy as "what governments do, why they do it, and what difference it makes."[2] Harold Lasswell defines public policy as "a projected program of goals, values, and practices."[3] Finally, James Anderson defines the term as "a purposive course of action followed by an actor or set of actors in dealing with a problem or matter of concern."[4] What all these various definitions have in common is that they are talking about a **process** or a series or pattern of governmental activities or decisions that are designed to remedy some public problem, either real or imagined. The special characteristic of public policy is that it is formulated, implemented, and evaluated by authorities in a political system, for example, legislators, judges, executives, and administrators. Public policies are always subject to change on the basis of new (or better) information about their effects. In the chapters to follow, we describe in greater detail the roles of each of these actors in each stage of the policy process. Private policy, on the other hand, refers to actions taken by individuals or businesses to deal with problems for themselves.

Likewise, there are several definitions of *policy analysis.* Thomas Dye defines policy analysis as the description and explanation of the causes and consequences of government activity. His view is that public policy analysis should exhibit a primary concern with **explanation** rather than **prescription.**[5] That is, policy analysts should attempt to develop and test general propositions about the causes and consequences of public policy and to accumulate reliable research findings of general relevance. Grover Starling, on the other hand, thinks that policy analysis should be an interdisciplinary effort to facilitate the reaching of sound policy decisions.[6] Weimer and Vining further underscore the notion of relevance to day-to-day governing by arguing that "policy analysis is client-oriented advice relevant to public decisions and informed by social values."[7] Clearly, a difference of opinion exists about the purposes of policy analysis, ranging from the scientific to the practical. The result is two kinds of policy analysis—one that produces knowledge *of* the policy process, another that yields knowledge *for* the policy process. The former examines how the process of governing (policy making or implementation, for example) unfolds while the latter aims at producing research that policy makers can use to assess and improve public policies. Much of that applied research looks at the impact of substantive public policies. Social scientists—political scientists, sociologists, and economists—who analyze policy from an applied perspective often discover that the basic logic embodied in the original legislation is flawed or based on an incomplete understanding of a particular policy problem. At other times, administrators who are charged with policy evaluation or legislators engaged in oversight find that the policy simply does not work. Frequently the results of policy analysis indicate that the policy needs to be changed or terminated. In the United States, either designing new legislation to deal with a public problem or "fixing" previously designed policies that did not work as planned is a constant activity and policy analysis is often an integral part of that effort. In the last section of this book, we look more closely at how a changing understanding of public policy problems often leads to efforts to develop better (or more comprehensive) policies.

TYPES OF PUBLIC POLICIES

Many types of public policies exist. Some policies—for example, highway policies—seek to distribute, or cannot prevent distributing, benefits to everyone. Other policies seek to redistribute benefits from the "haves" to the "have-nots." Policies such as welfare for the poor would fit this category. Finally, some policies seek to regulate behavior, such as crime policies or environmental protection policies. Theodore Lowi termed these policies **distributive, redistributive,** and **regulatory** policies.[8]

Policies can also be "**liberal**" or "**conservative.**" Lowi and others argue that it is possible to define these two types of policies. Liberal policies are those in which the government is used extensively to bring about social change, usually in the direction of ensuring greater levels of social equality.[9] Conservative policies, on the other hand, generally oppose the use of government to bring about social change but may approve government action to preserve the status quo or to promote favored interests. In addition, liberals tend to favor a concentration of power in higher levels of government, whereas conservatives tend to favor decentralization of power and authority. This difference has colored much of the debate on new federalism since the 1970s and is due to the belief by liberals that an effective constituency exists at the national level and that regulatory and distributive capacities are stronger at the national level than at the state and local levels. Conservatives, on the other hand, believe that public policy problems should be solved at the level of government that is nearest to them; hence, they tend to favor state and local (or even neighborhood) governmental involvement, rather than national involvement, unless decentralization promotes uncertainties in markets. They fear the centralization of power in the national government that has developed over the past 200 years in the United States.

There are also "**substantive**" and "**procedural**" policies. Substantive policies are concerned with governmental actions to deal with substantive problems, such as highway construction, environmental protection, or payment of welfare benefits. An example would be the Clean Air Act of 1990, which sought to deal with air pollution. Procedural policies, on the other hand, are those that relate to how something is going to be done or who is going to take action.[10] An example would be the Administrative Procedures Act of 1946, which describes the rulemaking procedures to be used by agencies.

Policies can also be "**material**" or "**symbolic,**" depending on the kind of benefits they allocate.[11] Material policies either provide concrete resources or substantive power to their beneficiaries or impose real disadvantages on those adversely affected. For example, welfare payments, housing subsidies, and tax credits are material. Symbolic policies, on the other hand, appeal more to cherished values than to tangible benefits. Some examples of these policies are national holidays that honor patriots, policies concerning the flag, and religion in schools.

Finally, public policies can embody "**collective**" versus "**private**" goods. Collective goods are those benefits that cannot be given to some but denied to others. Some examples would be national defense and public safety. Private goods are those goods that may be divided into units, and for which consumers can be charged. For example, food is, for the most part, a private good in the United States. There has been a national debate for some time over whether to convert many of those goods historically treated as collective goods to private goods. Services such as trash collection and home security are sometimes purchased by consumers from private companies. This is called **privatization** of services, and it is based on a feeling that the private sector can do a better and less expensive job than government. There has also been a debate over the costs and benefits of **nationalization** of medical care, which would convert a private good to a public or collective good. This debate between privatization and nationalization of goods and services will likely continue well into the new century. It is thus important to understand the debate and the issues. We explore some of these issues in greater detail in Chapters 10 through 12, when we discuss alternative perspectives on education, welfare, and the environment.

THE POLICY CYCLE

Public policymaking is often viewed as a "conveyor belt" in which issues are first recognized as a problem, alternative courses of action are considered, and policies are adopted, implemented by agency personnel, evaluated, changed, and finally

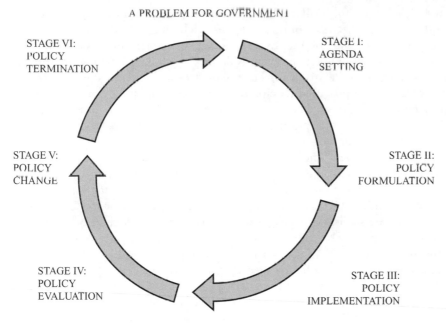

FIGURE 1.1 The Policy Cycle.

terminated on the basis of their success (actual or perceived) or lack thereof. Clearly this oversimplifies a complex process. Differentiating the consideration of alternatives from their adoption is not always easy. When vague pieces of legislation are adopted, it is often not known what the policy really is until the implementers promulgate rules and regulations. Despite this oversimplification, the policy cycle, or "stages heuristic," is a political process through which most public policies pass over the course of their lifetime.[12] Although the reality of the policy process is complex, thinking of it as a series of discrete stages such as those depicted in Figure 1.1 gives a framework for classifying the many activities that occur in public policymaking.

Over the past 30 years, substantial progress has been made in acquiring a better understanding of the policy cycle. For example, the first stage of the policy cycle—**agenda setting**—has been a subject of much recent research.[13] An agenda is, according to John Kingdon, "the list of subjects or problems to which government officials . . . are paying some serious attention at any given time."[14] For example, the list of items to be seriously considered at a public meeting of a city council or a legislature is a public agenda. Some problems never make it to the public agenda, whereas others are immediately acted on or at least considered at a later date. On some occasions, action items are deliberately kept off the public agenda by those who seek to delay or block responsive action to a public problem.[15] At first, agenda setting was described as "a set of political controversies that will be viewed as falling within the range of legitimate concerns meriting the attention of the polity," and it included both "systemic agendas" and "institutional agendas."[16] More recently, John Kingdon describes agenda setting as the result of three streams, including the problem stream, the policy stream, and the political stream.[17] The problem stream is essentially concerned with how the public problem is defined, including how it comes to the public's attention in the first place. The policy stream is concerned with the technical feasibility of a proposed solution to the problem and the public's acceptance of it, among other things. The political stream has to do with the national mood, public opinion, electoral politics, and all the factors that make the proposed solution a likely reality or not.[18]

The second stage of the policy cycle is **policy formulation** or policy adoption, usually defined as the passage of legislation designed to remedy some past problem or prevent some future public policy problem. During his first term in office, President George Bush, for example, was able to work Congress to pass tax cut legislation, a major initiative in education, legislation providing drug benefits, and the so-called Patriot Act. Because it is the first area of research in the policy cycle, the policy formulation stage has been the most heavily researched phase, and this has resulted in numerous conceptual frameworks that aid understanding of this part of the cycle.[19]

Originally, policy formulation was explained in terms of an elitist or pluralist model.[20] More recently, however, policy formulation is viewed as the result of a multitude of forces that affect policy outputs, such as historical/geographic conditions, socioeconomic conditions, mass political behavior (including public opinion, interest groups, and political parties), governmental institutions (including legislatures, courts, and the bureaucracy), as well as elite perceptions and behavior.[21] For example, historical or geographical conditions set the context for what may or may not happen in policy formulation, whereas socioeconomic conditions limit (or provide opportunities for) policy outputs. Mass political behavior may affect elite decisions or government institutions independently from socioeconomic conditions. Finally, governmental institutions and elite responses exert a substantial influence on policy outputs.[22]

Policy implementation is the third stage in the policy cycle. It has most often been described as "what happens after a bill becomes a law."[23] Simply enacting legislation is no guarantee that action will be taken to put the law into effect or that the problem will be solved. Law must be translated into specific guidelines so that the federal, state, or local bureaucracy can see to it that the intent of the legislation is achieved at the point where the policy is to be delivered. According to various scholars, implementation may be described as a process, an output, or an outcome.[24] The implementation process can be defined as a series of governmental decisions and actions directed toward putting an already decided mandate into effect. The term *implementation outputs* refers to the means by which programmatic goals are pursued (expenditures by a state toward some problem, for example), whereas implementation outcomes are the changes in the larger societal problem that the program is intended to rectify (e.g., have crime rates been reduced?).[25]

Policy implementation may well be the most important part of the policy cycle, yet it is often overlooked by those who simply assume that policies will implement themselves. Clearly, they do not. For example, Congress passed the

Hazardous and Solid Waste Amendments of 1984, which mandated that all small firms generating at least 100 kilograms of hazardous waste a month safely dispose of this waste. Yet there was no real mechanism (other than voluntary compliance) by which this would, in fact, be carried out. Since that time, Congress has been paying much more attention to the implementation process when it formulates policy. Nonetheless, the recent failure by the Federal Emergency Management Agency (FEMA) to respond in a timely and effective manner to Hurricane Katrina and the devastation and misery it visited on New Orleans and other coastal communities illustrates how problematic implementation continues to be.

Policy evaluation is concerned with what happens as a result of the public policy—that is, what happens after a policy is implemented. It is concerned with the actual impacts of legislation or the extent to which the policy actually achieves its intended results. For example, the evaluation question might be: "Does increasing the level of per pupil educational expenditures bring about an increase in student performance or learning?"[26] Or, one might be concerned with an evaluation of the multiple impacts, if any, of the 55-mile-per-hour speed limit. Does it save lives by reducing highway fatalities? Does it reduce property damage and conserve fuel? These are the kinds of questions that policy evaluation studies seek to answer.

Prior to the 1960s, little rigorous evaluation was done. The War on Poverty and the Great Society programs of the late 1960s played a major role in the development of policy analysis and evaluation research. Currently, policy evaluation takes place at all levels of government, within universities, and in scores of think tanks and other private organizations. The result is a substantial body of research findings across a variety of substantive policy areas that policy makers and others can draw upon as they consider and reconsider policy options and solutions. We will consider much of that research in the chapters on education, environmental, and welfare policy.

Policy change is the newest conceptual development in the study of the policy cycle. Largely "discovered" by Paul Sabatier and his colleagues in the mid-1980s,[27] policy change absorbs several stages of the policy cycle, including policy formulation, policy implementation, policy evaluation, and policy termination. As an analytical concept, policy change refers to the point at which a policy is evaluated and redesigned so that the entire policy process begins anew. According to Sabatier, one must examine public policy over a period of a decade or more so that one can begin to appreciate the evolution of policy through time. The basic unit of analysis is the policy subsystem composed of competing advocacy coalitions, or the interaction of actors from many different institutions and levels of government interested in a policy area.[28] Sabatier's model of policy change has been applied in several empirical settings in recent years, and there are likely to be many more such studies in the future.[29] Chapter 9 describes policy change in greater detail.

Policy termination is a means of ending outdated or inadequate policies. Some programs are found to be unworkable and thus need to be abolished, whereas other programs are often scaled back due to a shortage of resources or for purely nonrational or symbolic reasons. Essentially, policy termination is the end point of the policy cycle. It can mean many things, such as agency termination, policy redirection, project elimination, partial elimination, or fiscal retrenchment.[30] There are several types of termination, including functional termination of a policy area, organizational termination, policy termination, and program termination. Terminations may occur with a "big bang," meaning a sudden authoritative decision, or a "long whimper," meaning a long-term decline in resources necessary to run a program.[31] At the present time, research on policy termination is relatively scarce. Scholars in this area are developing the concept and building up a body of case study materials that will help them eventually to develop a comprehensive analytical framework for more systematic study of policy termination.[32]

THE EVOLUTION OF POLICY STUDIES

Policy studies have clearly come of age. Since the late 1960s, the policy studies subfield has developed into a well-organized body of work with courses, curricula, schools of public policy, organizations, journals, textbooks, conferences, panels, summer institutes, awards, funding sources, research institutes, and job opportunities.[33] During the last four decades there has been enormous growth in the subfield through courses offered, papers presented at national or regional meetings, graduates from public policy schools, and dissertations. For example, an examination of papers presented at the annual meeting of the American Political Science Association (APSA) illustrates the tremendous growth in policy studies over the past 30 years. In 1967, only four papers dealing with public policy were presented at the annual meeting of the APSA.[34] By the early 1990s, over 200 papers were delivered on the topic of public policy at the national APSA meeting.

Other evidence of growth of this subfield is exhibited by membership in various professional organizations. One of the oldest is the Policy Studies Organization (PSO). Founded in the 1970s, the PSO boasts 800 institutional members and a membership representing over 80 countries.[35] Operating out of its headquarters in Washington, D.C., the PSO publishes two key academic journals including the *Policy Studies Journal* and the *Review of Policy Research*. The Association for Public Policy and Management (APPAM) was founded at Duke University in the spring of 1979. Like the PSO, APPAM's membership is multidisciplinary and promotes research and teaching in public policy. Currently it has 2,000 individual members, 95 institutional members, and an operating budget of $600,000. APPAM provides a range of graduate fellowships and research awards, hosts annual teaching and research conferences, and publishes the *Journal of Policy Analysis and Management*.[36] A third association, the Organized Section on Public Policy, is the third largest section within the APSA with over 900 members. It cosponsors (with the PSO) the *Policy Studies Journal* and typically organizes some 20 or so policy panels at the annual meeting of the APSA.[37]

A number of changes in the character of policy studies have occurred over the last several decades. These changes involve what is studied, how researchers approach

T A B L E 1.1   The Evolution of Policy Studies, 1950–2000

	1950s	1960s–1980s	1990–Present
Phase of policy cycle addressed	Policy formulation	Policy implementation Agenda setting Policy evaluation Policy termination	Policy change Policy implementation Agenda setting
Dominant challenge	Prebehavioral	Behavioral (Positivism)	Post-positivism
Method of analysis	Case studies	Quantitative techniques	Mixed methods

the study of public policy, and the methods used in their analyses. Table 1.1 illustrates the evolution of policy studies during this time. In the 1950s and the early 1960s, the focus of policy studies tended to be on the problem of **policy formulation.** Various analysts attempted to explain why policies were formulated, using such explanatory models as the elitist, pluralist, and subgovernment models. Later, scholars developed alternative models to explain policy formulation, such as the rational and incremental models. The primary method used during this time was the **case study,** a detailed explanation of all the factors that influenced the formulation of public policy. The dominant approach was largely qualitative or **prebehavioral;** rigorous statistical analysis was rarely used. Evidence was drawn largely from detailed descriptions or anecdotal evidence.

Beginning in the mid-1960s, policy scholars began to use **quantitative statistical techniques** to assess the influence of various factors on policy formulation. Their new approach reflected **behavioralism (positivism)**—the view that public policy could be studied scientifically, that hypotheses could be formulated about these phenomena and then tested through rigorous statistical analysis. During this time period, policy scholars began to examine other aspects of the policy cycle, including **policy implementation, agenda setting, policy evaluation,** and **policy termination.** Clearly, this period witnessed tremendous growth in the field of policy studies.

Finally, the most recent period in the history of policy studies, from 1990 to the present, suggests another spurt of growth and evolutionary development. In this period, research continues on **policy implementation** and **agenda setting** as scholars seek to refine and extend earlier research as well as to develop the concept of **policy change.** Methods and approaches have also changed. A challenge to the positivist paradigm has occurred in the form of **post-positivism,** in which it is argued that many policy phenomena cannot be studied with scientific methods and rigorous statistical techniques. Post positivist scholars argue instead that concepts such as policy implementation require more intuitive approaches. This criticism of quantitative methods and the advocacy of more qualitative techniques have brought about a healthy reconciliation. Policy scholars now rely on **mixed methods,** or a combination of quantitative and qualitative techniques, in their analysis of public policy.

Some Tensions in the Subfield

Many evaluative comments on the subfield have been made by social scientists and others. According to Stuart Nagel, those comments include the following: (1) policy studies are a fad that will eventually wither away; (2) policy studies are too practical or too theoretical; (3) policy studies are too multidisciplinary or too narrowly focused on political science; (4) policy studies are too quantitative or too nonscientific in method; (5) policy studies are too little used or overutilized; and finally, (6) policy studies are too liberal or too conservative.[38] Each of these arguments is examined in turn.

Nagel argues that public policy reflects a long-term philosophical tradition in the social sciences that has existed since Plato's *Republic*. Although the field is clearly not a fad, it has changed considerably, in that practitioners today emphasize the idea of synthesizing the essentially normative philosophy (associated with Plato through Marx) and the scientific method (associated with Harold Lasswell and others).[39] Since the 1970s there have been a number of more specific trends in policy studies, such as the evaluation of alternative policies and the incorporation of new methods (both qualitative and quantitative) to achieve greater utilization of policy analysis by decision makers. More specifically, in the 1960s a great deal of emphasis was placed on public policy formulation, whereas in the 1970s and 1980s the emphasis was on public policy implementation. In the 1990s, the emphasis shifted to policy optimization studies or policy analyses that sought to answer the question, "What effects are we trying to achieve (i.e., what are the goals of public policy)?" For example, which policy among those being considered is best able to reduce environmental pollution? Which type of welfare policy will best reduce the level of poverty? Given the growth of policy studies over the past 30 years, it would be difficult to argue convincingly that it will eventually wither away from lack of interest.

On the second point discussed above, one may argue that policy studies are both practical and theoretical. Some policy analysts lean toward the theoretical (scientific) side, insofar as they avoid making policy recommendations that might improve policy performance. Rather, they are primarily interested in pursuing **pure science** as opposed to **applied science.** That is, they are more interested in scientific understanding than in improving policy performance. Others are more interested in the practical side of policy analysis, meaning that they are interested in providing information on the basis of their analysis to inform decision makers as to how to improve system performance. Yet, still others are interested in both the development of policy theory and the improvement of governmental performance and effectiveness. In fact, good theory is practical, so it is difficult to separate the two from one another. As William Glazer once said, "If the study of theory and fact do not fertilize each other, both will be barren."[40]

Sometimes, this dichotomy between the policy scientist's roles as a "pure scientist" and as an "expert" creates a role conflict that can lead to the prevention of scientific advancement as the scientist's role gives way to the demands for governmental "experts."[41] Pure science becomes neglected as demands for policy expertise take precedence. Nevertheless, policy analysis is both practical and theoretical.

Third, policy studies are by definition and nature interdisciplinary, with political scientists playing key roles. The type of policy under analysis often determines which disciplines are most involved. For example, economists are very likely to be involved in welfare policy evaluation, whereas political scientists are most heavily involved in defense policy analysis. An analysis of the field in the 1980s found that political scientists, followed by economists, continued to dominate the field, although there was a small increase in multidisciplinary authorship from 1975 to 1984.[42]

Fourth, policy analysis is concerned with both rigorous quantitative methods as well as simple, yet systematic, methods. For example, a study in the early 1980s found that only 43 percent of the articles surveyed on policy analysis were empirical and quantitative, whereas 57 percent were descriptive and rhetorical in nature.[43] The percentage of quantitative articles had dropped to 29 percent by the mid-1980s.[44] This change is related to the emerging consensus in policy analysis that multiple approaches are relevant and that the use of quantitative techniques is not the only valid approach to policy analysis. We discuss various approaches to policy analysis in Chapter 3.

In addition, Nagel notes that policy analysis is often criticized as being underutilized by emphasizing the many examples of policy analysis that have not been used in any way by policymakers. In one sense the argument that policy analyses are underutilized need not be a primary concern for the policy analyst. The primary job of the analyst is to do valid research. However, policy analysts would benefit from a better understanding of the factors that lead to nonuse. We will discuss the utilization of policy analysis in Chapter 13, as well as the factors that affect use of policy analysis by decision makers.

Finally, policy analysis is neither inherently liberal nor conservative. Nagel argues that studies that begin with conservative assumptions about human nature and/or conservative goals will likely produce conservative results. Likewise, liberal conclusions stem from liberal assumptions and liberal goals. Thus, given different goals and assumptions, some policy analyses will arrive at conservative conclusions and others will arrive at liberal conclusions. We suspect that the role of ideology in policy analysis is less than Nagel suggests. In the first place, policy analysts frequently uses methods that ensure a certain amount of objectivity. Moreover, to the extent that ideology plays a role in policy research it is more likely to be found in the choice of topics and in how empirical findings are interpreted. In the next chapter, we discuss several approaches to policy analysis, including liberal and conservative approaches and the assumptions of each.

THE PLAN OF THE BOOK

In this brief introduction we have discussed what we mean by public policy and the policy cycle, and we have identified various types of public policy. We have also looked at how the study of public policy has changed over the years. In looking at what policies are and how we study them, we are reminded of how useful an evolutionary approach is to understanding both the substance and process of governing. American politics and policy are in transition, with new developments in federalism, public opinion, political parties, and the fundamental values that shape public policy. Not surprisingly, our understanding of how those events have unfolded is evolving (and we think for the better) as well.

Accordingly, the thesis of this book is that by observing the changes in the past, one may obtain a better understanding of the present and perhaps a glimpse of what to expect in the future. In the chapters that follow, three questions are used to structure our discussion. First, where have we been in terms of our conceptual understanding of each phase of the policy cycle and, in the case of the substantive chapters, how has policy evolved over time? Second, what is our present understanding of each phase of the cycle? In the case of the substantive chapters, what is the predominant "vision" within each policy area? Where are we in our conceptual understanding of various aspects of the policy cycle or substantive policy prescriptions? Third, where are we going in terms of our conceptual understanding or, in the case of the substantive chapters, where are we likely to go over the next 20 years? In some substantive areas, it may be useful to describe alternative visions for public policy. This concern with the various prescriptions for the future allows discussion and evaluation of the normative implications of alternative policy choices. This reflects an emerging trend in the policy studies subfield.

In the first section of the book, Chapter 2 discusses the evolution of American politics and public policy in both the long and short term. Chapter 3 discusses several approaches to policy studies, ranging from the purely scientific to the political (or advocacy) use of policy studies. It also identifies two competing visions of public policy choices that are discussed in greater detail in the substantive chapters in Part III. Chapter 4 describes what we mean by a model and presents several criteria for evaluating models before we discuss several alternative models in the next few chapters.

In the second and third sections of the book, we examine the evolution of our understanding of the policy cycle and our understanding of the substance of American public policy in three areas. In Chapters 5 through 9, an evolutionary perspective is presented for each phase of the policy cycle, noting how our understanding has advanced from initial concept development to the present agenda for future research. Chapters 10 through 12 discuss three substantive areas of public policy—education, welfare, and the environment. We also use an evolutionary approach in these chapters so that the student can fully appreciate how much policy history can aid our understanding and help to predict the future in each of these substantive areas.

Finally, the last section of the book discusses the utilization of policy analysis by decision makers, and in the concluding chapter, we offer some observations and conclusions based on the previous chapters about trends in American public policy and its study from the past three to four decades. We also venture some predictions for the next few years. These conclusions and predictions are based on the idea that the past, under normal conditions, provides much insight into the future.

DISCUSSION QUESTIONS

1. What do we mean by "policy studies," and how does this area of inquiry relate to political science and other social sciences?

2. In training students for policy analysis, how much emphasis should be placed on theories, models, and concepts, as opposed to research methods and substantive knowledge about specific policy areas?

3. What trends can be identified in the evolution of public policy studies from the 1970s to today?

4. Are policy analyses inevitably biased toward either liberalism or conservatism? Is it possible for policy analysts to be objective?

5. Should policy analysts, as Nagel suggests, not worry that much about the use of policy analysis? Or do they have the added responsibility of ensuring that the information they produce gets to and is used by those in government?

SUGGESTED READINGS

Anderson, James E. *Public Policymaking,* Sixth Edition (Boston: Houghton Mifflin, 2006).

Dye, Thomas R. *Understanding Public Policy,* Tenth Edition (Upper Saddle River, NJ: Prentice Hall, 2002).

McCool, Daniel C. *Public Policy Theories, Models, and Concepts: An Anthology* (Englewood Cliffs, NJ: Prentice Hall, 1995).

Stone, Deborah. *Policy Paradox: The Art of Political Decision Making* (New York: W. W. Norton and Company, 1997).

NOTES

1. E. S. Quade and Grace McCarter. *Analysis for Public Decisions,* 3d ed. (New York: North-Holland, 1989), p. 3.

2. Thomas R. Dye, *Understanding Public Policy,* 7th ed. (New York: Prentice Hall, 1992), pp. 2–4.

3. Harold Lasswell, quoted in Grover Starling, *The Politics and Economics of Public Policy* (Homewood, IL: Dorsey Press, 1979), p. 4.

4. James Anderson, *Public Policymaking: An Introduction* (Boston: Houghton Mifflin, 1990), p. 5.

5. Dye, *Understanding Public Policy,* p. 4.

6. Starling, *The Politics and Economics of Public Policy,* p. 11.

7. David L. Weimer and Adrian Vining, *Policy Analysis: Concepts and Practice* (Upper Saddle River, New Jersey: Prentice Hall, 1999) p. 27.

8. Theodore J. Lowi, "American Business, Public Policy, Case Studies, and Political Theory," *World Politics* 16 (July 1964), pp. 677–715.

9. Ibid.; also Anderson, *Public Policymaking,* p. 18.

10. Anderson, *Public Policymaking,* p. 10.

11. Ibid., p. 15.

12. Deborah Stone, to the contrary, rejects this "production" model of policymaking, "whereby policy is assembled in stages, as if on a conveyor belt." See her book entitled *Policy Paradox and Political Reason* (Glenview, IL: Scott, Foresman, 1988), p. viii. In addition, Paul A. Sabatier and Hank Jenkins-Smith think that the "stages heuristic" has outlived its usefulness in teaching and research. See Paul A. Sabatier and Hank Jenkins-Smith, eds., *Policy Change and Learning: An Advocacy Coalition Approach* (Boulder, CO: Westview Press, 1993). We obviously do not agree with either perspective of the critics of the policy cycle approach. Instead, we believe that the stages heuristic has great value both for teaching about public policymaking and for research on the policy process.

13. See Roger W. Cobb and Charles D. Elder, "The Politics of Agenda-Building," *Journal of Politics* 33 (1971), pp. 892–915; Roger W. Cobb and Charles D. Elder, *Participation in American Politics: The Dynamics of Agenda-Building* (Baltimore: The Johns Hopkins University Press, 1972); John W. Kingdon, *Agendas, Alternatives, and Public Policies,* 2d ed. (New York: HarperCollins, 1995); Barbara Nelson, *Making an Issue of Child Abuse* (Chicago: University of Chicago Press, 1984); and Frank Baumgartner and Bryan D. Jones, *Agendas and Instability in American Politics* (Chicago: University of Chicago Press, 1993).

14. Kingdon, *Agendas, Alternatives, and Public Policies,* p. 3.

15. See Peter Bachrach and Morton Baratz, "The Two Faces of Power," *American Political Science Review* 57 (December 1962), pp. 947–952.

16. Roger W. Cobb and Charles D. Elder, *Participation in American Politics: The Dynamics of Agenda-Building* (Baltimore: The Johns Hopkins University Press, 1972), pp. 14–15.

17. Kingdon, *Agendas, Alternatives, and Public Policies,* pp. 90–164.

18. See also Baumgartner and Jones, *Agendas and Instability in American Politics.*

19. See Thomas R. Dye, *Understanding Public Policy,* 6th ed. (Englewood Cliffs, NJ: Prentice Hall, 1987), pp. 20–44.

20. See Thomas R. Dye and Harmon Zeigler, *The Irony of Democracy,* 5th ed. (Monterey, CA: Brooks/Cole, 1981); Floyd Hunter, *Community Power Structure* (Chapel Hill: University of North Carolina Press, 1953); G. William Domhoff, *The Higher Circles* (New York: Vintage Books, 1971); and Robert A. Dahl, *Who Governs?* (New Haven, CT: Yale University Press, 1961).

21. Richard I. Hofferbert, "Elite Influence in State Policy Formation: A Model for Comparative Inquiry," *Polity* 2 (Spring 1970), pp. 316–344.

22. Ibid., pp. 326–330.

23. See Eugene Bardach, *The Implementation Game: What Happens After a Bill Becomes a Law* (Cambridge, MA: MIT Press, 1977).

24. See Malcolm Goggin, Ann O'M. Bowman, James P. Lester, and Laurence O'Toole, *Implementation Theory and Practice: Toward a Third Generation* (New York: HarperCollins, 1990).

25. Ibid., p. 34.

26. See the report on student performance by Professor James Coleman in 1965–66 reported in Christopher Jencks, *Inequality: A Reassessment of the Effects of Family and Schooling in America* (New York: Basic Books, 1972); see also Kevin B. Smith and Kenneth J. Meier, *The Case Against School Choice* (Armonk, NY: M. E. Sharpe, 1995).

27. Paul A. Sabatier, "Knowledge, Policy-Oriented Learning, and Policy Change: An Advocacy Coalition Framework," *Knowledge: Creation, Diffusion, Utilization* 3 (June 1987) pp. 649–692.

28. Ibid., pp. 652–653.

29. See, for example, Hank Jenkins-Smith, "Explaining Change in Policy Subsystems: Analysis of Coalition Stability and Defection Over Time," *American Journal of Political Science* 35 (November 1991): 851–880; and Paul A. Sabatier and Hank Jenkins-Smith, "Evaluating the Advocacy Coalition Framework," *Journal of Public Policy* 14 (1994): 175–203; Michael Mintrom and Sandra Vergari, "Advocacy Coalitions, Policy Entrepreneurs, and Policy Change," *Policy Studies Journal* 24 (September, 1996), 420–434; Sato, Hajime, "The Advocacy Coalition Framework and the Policy Process Analysis: The Case of Smoking Control in Japan." *Policy Studies Journal* 27 (February, 1999), 28–44; Litfin, Karen T., "Advocacy Coalitions Along the Domestic-Foreign Frontier: Globalization and Canadian Climate Change Policy," *Policy Studies Journal* 28 (February, 2000), 236–252; and Margaret Mikkelsen, "Policy network analysis as a strategic tool for the voluntary sector," *Policy Studies* 27 (March, 2006), 17–26.

30. See Eugene Bardach, "Policy Termination as a Political Process," *Policy Sciences* 7 (June 1976), pp. 123–131; Peter DeLeon, "Policy Evaluation and Program Termination," *Policy Studies Review* (1983); and Robert Behn, "How to Terminate a Public Policy: A Dozen Hints for the Would-be Terminator," *Policy Analysis* 4 (Summer 1978), pp. 393–413.

31. Bardach, "Policy Termination as a Political Process," pp. 123–131.

32. Susan E. Kirkpatrick, James P. Lester, and Mark R. Peterson, "The Policy Termination Process: A Conceptual Framework and Application to Revenue-Sharing," *Policy Studies Review* 16 (Spring 1999), pp. 209–236.

33. Stuart Nagel, "Evaluating Public Policy Evaluation," *Policy Studies Journal* 16 (Winter 1987), pp. 219–233.

34. Susan B. Hansen, "Public Policy Analysis: Some Recent Developments and Current Problems," *Policy Studies Journal* (1983), pp. 218–220.

35. PSO website www.ipsonet.org/ accessed November 26, 2006.

36. APPAM website www.appam.org/about/index.asp accessed November 26, 2006.

37. In addition to the various associations of policy scholars, there are a number of professional associations of public administration scholars and practitioners. The most notable of these is the American Society for Public Administration.

38. Nagel, "Evaluating Public Policy Evaluation," pp. 219–233.

39. Ibid., p. 220.

40. William A. Glazer, "The Type and Uses of Political Theory," *Social Research* 22 (1955), pp. 275–296.

41. Edward B. Portis and Dwight F. Davis, "Policy Analysis and Scientific Ossification," *PS: Political Science and Politics* 15 (Fall 1982), pp. 593–599.

42. David M. Hedge and Jin Mok, "The Nature of Policy Studies: A Content Analysis of Policy Journal Articles," *Policy Studies Journal* 16 (Autumn 1987), pp. 49–61.

43. Janet A. Schneider et al., "Policy Research and Analysis: An Empirical Profile," *Policy Sciences* 15 (1982).

44. Hedge and Mok, "The Nature of Policy Studies."

2

The Evolution of Public Policy and Politics in America

"We must adjust to changing times and still hold
to unchanging principles."
FORMER PRESIDENT JIMMY CARTER

Politics and policy in America have changed dramatically over the last several decades. Coming out of the Great Depression and World War II, the party of FDR dominated government and politics for the next 50 years. Democratic majorities in the U.S. Congress joined with Democratic and Republican presidents alike in passing far-reaching legislation that substantially increased the reach of the national government into areas of the nation's life that previously had been the purview of state or local governments or the private sectors, including civil rights, poverty, environmental protection, workplace and product safety, women's rights, and education. The presidency of Ronald Reagan sought to "get government off the backs of the American people" by attempting to reduce the role and budget of the federal government. Concurrent with a desire to shrink the role of government was a renewed sense that the private sector and markets represented a better way of doing the people's business. In recent years, an increasing amount of governing has been outsourced to the private sector, including defense policy, welfare, and education. Nothing better illustrates the desire to use markets instead of governments than recent proposals to privatize social security.

The developments of the last 50 years (not to mention those that took place over the first 150 or so years of American history) underscore the need to take an evolutionary approach to understanding the process and substance of governing. We begin that exploration in this chapter by looking at the evolution of the American political system and public policy from both a near- and long-term perspective. Before we do that, however, we look briefly at what we believe are the core or central issues that governments at all levels and at all times must face. Not surprisingly, much of the changes that have occurred in American politics and public policy center on those issues.

THE CRITICAL ISSUES FOR GOVERNMENTS

At the risk of oversimplifying, much of the business of governing comes down to resolving four fundamental issues: ***Should government act? What values should governments pursue? What actions should government take? Which level of government should govern?*** As the discussion of the evolution of American politics and policy that follows will demonstrate, one or the more of those issues are typically at the center of a changing American government.

Should Government Act?

For most of the nation's history, the answer to this question has been no. At the very outset of the nation's history, the founding fathers included a number of provisions in the U.S. Constitution that would make it more difficult for government to act. These provisions included federalism, a separation of powers, and the Bill of Rights. Nonetheless, by the middle of the 19th century government had become a critical force in the life of the nation. A number of rationales have been offered to justify government action. In some instances, government action simply reflects a general **consensus** that collective action is necessary. Defense, criminal law, and public education are obvious examples. In other instances, government action is seen as necessary to resolve **conflicts** within society that cannot be easily resolved by private economic or social institutions. Litigation of contract disputes and child custody fights are just two examples of that view. Economists and others rely on the notion of **market failures** to explain and justify government intrusions into the economy. Put simply, governments should act when markets fail to achieve the conditions that justify *their* use—including competition, information, and choice. Much of what the U.S. Food and Drug Administration, the Department of Agriculture, the Federal Trade Commission, and other government agencies do is to ensure that consumers have the information they need to make informed choices about food and other products. The warning label on cigarettes, rules governing the use of the organic label on produce, and the system of grading meats illustrate those information strategies. In other cases, the existence of natural monopolies, like the provision of electricity or other utilities, warrants the government's setting prices and rules of production. Negative externalities (costs imposed on others without their consent), like air or water pollution, are another instance of the failure of the private sector and the need for government or collective action.

What Values Should Governments Pursue?

A large part of the rationale for government action is the promotion of those values that Americans hold dear. There is no shortage of values that governments can pursue. Many of these are built into our system of government, including free speech, the right to privacy, and the right to a fair trial. Others have had to be added to the public agenda over the course of the nation's history; these include racial and gender equality and an expansion of the "rights of the accused" in criminal proceedings. A critical and often contentious issue concerns which values should be added to that agenda. Efforts to make abortion illegal, for example, are an attempt to use government authority to achieve the moral values held by a substantial number of Americans. Conversely, the U.S. Supreme Court's landmark decision in *Roe v. Wade* (1973) relied on the notion of the right to privacy to guarantee the rights of women to choose to have an abortion within certain limits. Governments must also wrestle with finding the proper balance between important values. Environmental policies, for example, aim at achieving environmental protection without undercutting economic development. The U.S. Patriot Act attempts (some would argue unsuccessfully) to balance national security needs with the privacy rights of the American people.

Writing in the early 1990s, former Colorado Governor Richard Lamm and Robert Caldwell drew on polling data and other sources to assess how social values had changed in America between the 1950s and the 1990s.[1] The results are offered in Table 2.1 and represent an assessment that is surprisingly on target over a decade later. As the reader can see, Lamm and Caldwell note a dramatic shift in how Americans view a changing social, political, economic, and international landscape. Among other things, those authors note a shift from a "we" to a "me" society. In the "me" society, individuals fend for themselves, and America's middle class finds itself shrinking as the nation attempts to cope with a global economy and a shift from an exporting to an importing and service economy. Prophetically, Lamm and Caldwell anticipate the rise of terrorism and a changing view of what it takes to secure America from attack.

What Actions Should Government Take?

Once the decision is made to act, policy makers still have to decide which actions governments will take. Governments have a number of policy "tools" at their disposal. In some cases, government action takes the form of regulations, rules of conduct that promise some form of sanction for failing to comply with those rules. Federal environmental statutes, for example, subject firms and individuals to monetary fines for failing to meet emission standards. In other instances government

TABLE 2.1 Changes in American Values, 1950s–1990s

1950s	1990s	Consequences/Results
Saving	Spending	Federal debt; Trade deficit
Delayed gratification	Instant gratification	Narcissism
Ozzie and Harriet	Latchkey kids	71% high-school graduation rate
Certainty	Ambivalence	Marriage counseling
Investing	Leveraging	Low rate of productivity growth; Michael Milken
Unionization	Bankruptcy	Middle-class decline
Lifetime employer	Outplacement	Look out for #1; Alienation
Neighborhood	Lifestyle	Community failure; Single-issue politics; Age segregation; Ethnic conflict; Gentrification
Middle class	Underclass	Drugs; Gangs; Teenage grannies; Columbine
Export	Import	Acura; Infinity; Lexus; FAX; VCRs
Containment	Economic security	Trade sanctions; Managed trade
Deterrence	Terrorism	Metal detectors
Upward mobility	Downward mobility	The homeless; Shrinking middle class
Duty	Divorce	Despair
"We"	"Me"	"Them"
Sexual repression	Affairs	Celibacy
Equity	Renting/leasing	Balloon payments
Organized religion	Cults; TV preachers	Authoritarianism
Heroes	Cover girls	Cynicism
Internationalism	Isolationism	Personality politics; "Psychiatrization" of foreign leaders (Mikhail and Raisa Gorbachev as role models)
Public troubles	Private issues	Greed; Fear; Pessimism
Money	More money	Even more money
"Do what you're told"	"Do what you want"	"You do it"
Young	Middle age	Old
Public virtue	Personal well-being	Decline of polity; Voter alienation
Civil rights	Affirmative action	Quotas and "politically correct" thinking

TABLE 2.1 Continued

1950s	1990s	Consequences/Results
Press conference	Photo opportunity	*People* magazine
Achievement	Fame	Political polls
Manufacturing	Service	Mitsubishi buys Rockefeller Center; Sony buys Columbia Pictures
Value-added	Mastercard	Five-year car loans; Repossessions
Problems	Pathologies	Analysis paralysis
Hope	Happiness	Preference by L'oreal
Bomb shelters	Crack houses	Drug czar William Bennett
Organization Man	Murphy Brown	Androgyny
NATO; Godless communists	Commie capitalists	Trading blocs; New alliances
Psychoanalysis/neurosis	Support groups/serial killers	Big book sales
Cheeseburger, fries, shake	Cheeseburger, fries, shake	American cultural hegemony
USA	Japan	"Japanaphobia"
Regulation	Deregulation	Re-regulation
Cash	Credit	Cash

SOURCE: Richard D. Lamm and Richard A. Caldwell, *Hard Choices.* Copyright © 1991 by The University of Denver, Center for Public Policy. Reprinted by permission of the Center for Public Policy, University of Denver. The table was authored by Richard A. Caldwell.

action entails the direct provision of public services by government agencies. The most visible instance of direct provision is the system of public schools in America. Governments also provide cash subsidies to individuals and firms. These include cash grants, vouchers like food stamps, and low-interest loans. So-called tax expenditures are another popular form of government action. Tax breaks abound in the tax code and include deductions for the interest paid on mortgage loans, some educational expenses, and a variety of business expenses. Increasingly the discussion of policy tools centers on the use of **market mechanisms** to achieve public ends. Providing educational vouchers to parents to "purchase" their children's education from public or private schools introduces the concept of competition into the public sector. Similarly, environmental laws that allow firms to trade and sell the right to produce emissions are another example of using market forces to do the business of government.

Which Level of Government Should Govern?

An enduring issue in American politics is which level of government should be responsible for enacting and implementing public policy. As we have seen, the U.S. Constitution ostensibly outlines what should be the respective roles of national and state authorities; but the vagueness of the provisions that do so, various amendments to the constitution, and subsequent rulings by the U.S. Supreme Court guarantee that the balance between national and state interests will always be a critical and frequently contentious issue in governing. Historically, a number of developments—including the adoption and application to the states of the Fourteenth Amendment to the U.S. Constitution, the creation of the federal income tax, FDR's New Deal, and the preponderant role of the United States in international affairs—have meant an inevitable shift in the balance of power to the national government. Nonetheless, state governments continue to play a major role in governing America, and policy debates still consider the respective roles of each level. Most federal environmental regulation, for example, relies on state governments for implementation. Similarly, most criminal law originates in the states, which still are the predominant force in deciding, among other things, how our children will be educated, who is eligible for welfare and under what conditions, and what the role and responsibilities of local governments will be. And the U.S. Supreme Court continues to hear cases that pit national versus state and local governments. In the fall of 2006 the Court heard arguments—on behalf of a dozen states, three cities, and a U.S. territory—challenging the U.S. Environmental Protection Agency's refusal to regulate greenhouse gas emissions under the Clean Air Act (*Massachusetts v. EPA*). Nor are the states reluctant to pass their own legislation when national authorities fail to act. In recent years a number of states have passed legislation dealing with global warming, stem cell research, and gay marriage.

THE CHANGING FACE OF AMERICA'S POLITICAL SYSTEM

The American political system has several features that exert strong effects on public policy. Among these are federalism, separation of powers, political culture, pluralism, and public opinion and ideology. Not surprisingly, the character of each feature has changed considerably over the course of the nation's history. We discuss each one in turn.

Federalism

In crafting the U.S. Constitution, the founding fathers purposely sought to balance the powers of the new national government with the authority of the thirteen original states. The result is a federal system of government in which each level of government has its respective spheres of influence; but it is a system that also requires each level to interact with the others. There are both **vertical federalism** (intergovernmental relations among different levels, that is, federal-state-local) and **horizontal federalism** (relations between similar units—that is, state-state or local-local). Federalism today is very different from what it was in 1787, or even from what it was in 1960. Intergovernmental relationships are constantly evolving as different presidential administrations have very different visions of the "proper" relationship among the three levels of government. For example, before 1937, **dual federalism** was the dominant view of the relationship between the state and federal governments. From this perspective, each level of government had its own separate authority and areas of responsibility. The analogy often used was that of a layer cake. In this period, the U.S. Supreme Court interpreted the Constitution as requiring a hands-off relationship between the federal and state governments. In effect, each level of government had its own responsibilities and was at least somewhat independent of the others. The belief was that separate functional responsibilities for each level of government were in the best interests of all.

From 1937 to 1960, federalism evolved into what could be best described as a **cooperative** system in which the powers of these two levels of government were intermingled. The federal government occasionally intervened into state and local affairs. The three levels of government were no longer separate, as in the layers of a layer cake, but mixed together as in a marble cake. The separation between the states and the national government was seen as artificial. Before 1960, the typical federal assistance program did not involve an expressly stated national purpose; instead, the federal role was limited to providing federal technical assistance rather than control.

From 1960 to 1972, another vision of federalism evolved into what was called **creative federalism.** In this version, the federal role was believed to be necessary for the state and local governments to achieve its social objectives; state and local governments were perceived to be major constraints on responsible action to achieve national goals, particularly to improve the plight of the poor, minorities, and the environment. Creative federalism provided the basis for implementing national goals defined by Congress and carried out by the states. By way of grants-in-aid, control over programs resided with the federal government and Congress rather than the states. For example, the War on Poverty was a federal program directed from Washington, D.C., and carried out by the states, rather than the reverse. Essentially, power was shifted toward the national government, and the states provided an implementing role. The period of creative federalism has been criticized extensively by some policy analysts, who argue that the social programs of that era actually exacerbated, rather than alleviated, such problems as poverty.[2]

Finally, since 1972, the United States has sought a **new federalism,** in which states and cities are given much more authority than in the 1960s. This period began with President Nixon's shift of power and authority from the national government back to state and local governments. Essentially, he believed that the locus of authority should reside with those closest to the problems. The 1972 State and Local Fiscal Assistance Act (or General Revenue Sharing Act) provided the mechanism for "restoring" the balance among federal, state, and local governments that was seen as having been lost under creative federalism. The key difference between this version of federalism and the previous one was that the states and cities were given control over the resources that Washington provided (through revenue-sharing funds) so that they could decide which projects and programs would be funded and which would not be funded. In the 1980s, this version of new federalism was embraced by President Reagan, who continued the decentralization of power and authority but cut much of the federal support for these programs. Thus, under Reagan's version of new federalism, the states and cities had to make a choice among (1) cutting programs; (2) reprogramming funds from areas of low priorities to those with higher priorities; and (3) raising taxes to cover the costs of programs now under their control. Revenue sharing was terminated in 1986.

Presidents George H. W. Bush, Bill Clinton, and most recently George W. Bush have also supported greater devolution. President Clinton, for example, signed legislation in 1996 that gave state governments major control over welfare policies within each of their states. That support aside, the presidency of George W. Bush illustrates how other policy priorities often preempt the principles of devolution. President Bush's landmark education bill in 2002 undercut state control by imposing federal standards on local school districts. The president's support in 2004 for a constitutional amendment prohibiting gay and lesbian marriages also flew in the face of devolution by preempting state law in the area of marriage.

Separation of Powers

A second characteristic of American government and politics that affects public policy is **separation of powers.** This refers to the Founding Fathers' establishment of a system of checks and balances among the executive, legislative, and judicial branches. The president and members of Congress are elected separately, for terms of differing lengths, and have powers that are independent of each other. The Founding Fathers, exemplified by James Madison in **Federalist 10,** were fearful of a concentration of power in any one branch. One of his best-known quotes from **Federalist 51** is that "if men were angels, no government would be necessary." Clearly Madison held a constrained view of human nature and thus assumed that the abuse of power had to be controlled. By spreading power over the three branches, the Founders ensured that each branch was kept in its "proper" place.

Throughout history, the relative power of presidents and Congress has shifted periodically. Historians maintain that except for the presidencies of Jefferson, Jackson, and Lincoln, Congress had the upper hand through most of the 19th century.[3] It is only since the Great Depression, WWII, and the Cold War that there has been a clear tendency to concentrate power in the executive branch relative to the legislative and judicial branches. Nonetheless, Congress remains willing and able to assert its institutional will—witness the impeachment proceedings brought against Richard Nixon and the impeachment and trial of Bill Clinton.

Political Culture

In addition to being affected by federalism and separation of powers, public policy is affected by citizens' attitudes, beliefs, and expectations about what governments should do, who should participate, and what rules should govern the political game.[4] These attitudes, beliefs, and expectations are known as **political culture**, a term defined by Lucien Pye as the "set of attitudes, beliefs, and sentiments that give order and meaning to the political process."[5] Political culture is a mind-set, or a way of perceiving and interpreting politics. Daniel Elazar has identified three political cultures in America that exist side by side and have an effect on political behavior.[6] These three cultures are the moralistic, the individualistic, and the traditionalistic.

The **moralistic** culture emphasizes a "commonwealth" conception of politics in which politics is seen as a "search for the good society," or an effort to exercise power for the betterment of the commonwealth. Politics is viewed as a healthy enterprise in which those who govern strive to promote the public good in terms of honesty, unselfishness, and a commitment to the public welfare. States that exhibit this culture are characterized by an issue-oriented public, high levels of participation, respect for bureaucracy and government growth, rejection of party ties and patronage, and little corruption. Some examples include the New England states, California, Washington, and Oregon.

The **individualistic** culture, on the other hand, conceives of politics as a "marketplace" or a "business" (albeit a "dirty" one). In this mind-set, government is initiated for strictly utilitarian ends to handle only those functions demanded by the people it is created to serve; that is, government should be limited only to those functions that the people want it to perform. Government is a source of favors, rather than a source of pursuit of the common good. States where this culture is dominant are characterized by very little issue concern, limited participation, ambivalence about the place of bureaucracy in the political order, and corruption in government. Examples include Illinois, Indiana, and several other Midwestern states that were settled by English and German immigrants.

Finally, the **traditionalistic** culture emphasizes an "elitist" conception of politics and views the function of government as limited to preserving the status quo. Where this culture is dominant, there is likely to be a *noblesse oblige* attitude toward government in which there is a positive view of government, but its role is limited to preserving the status quo. In states where this culture predominates, the public views issues as of little importance. There is a lack of citizen participation, an antibureaucratic attitude, a view of political parties only as a source of favors (patronage), and what is thought of as a "conservative" position in the kinds of policies that are adopted. These states are largely those of the Deep South, where the landed gentry settled and established sugar and cotton plantations.

These three political cultures were transferred to America in the various waves of immigration to this country in the past two centuries. They originated in northern and western Europe and were carried to this country by the Yankee Puritans, the English, the Germans, the French, and the Scandinavians. They persist to this day and affect the kinds of policies that are likely to be adopted in various states. In effect, they provide a set of contextual inducements or constraints on public policies in the states. For example, liberal policies might fare better in moralistic cultures, whereas conservative policies would fare better in traditionalistic states.

Will the most recent waves of immigrants, particularly those from Latin America, alter the character of America's political culture? Will what has been the predominant culture change in the years ahead? Much will depend on how the new immigrants are integrated into American politics, the economy, and the nation's social fabric. How that will play out is hard to determine. Certainly, politics in states like California, Texas, and Florida will likely change as racial minorities make up a much larger proportion of the population and approach majority status. As this text is written, there is considerable debate over the conditions under which the millions of illegal immigrants currently working in the United States should be allowed to stay, and pressures have been placed on the federal government to strengthen its southern border. While national policy makers seek to resolve the issue, local governments are faced with demands on local services. A handful of cities have responded by declaring English their community's official language.

The latest wrinkle in the discussion of America's political culture is the recent debate among scholars, pundits, and politicians over whether the country is in the midst of a culture war—one that divides Americans almost evenly over social issues including abortion, gay rights, prayer in the schools, and other "family values." Pointing to the closeness of the most recent presidential and congressional elections and the apparent role social values played in each, America is depicted as consisting of "Red" and "Blue" states. The Blue states tend to be located on the East and West coasts, vote Democratic, and tend to be more progressive on social values. The Red states are found in the South and the Heartland of America, invariably vote Republican, and are generally conservative on so-called family values. This is the war over morality that Pat Buchanan referred to when calling upon Republicans to fight in his address before the 1992 Republican national convention. While mainstream Republicans, most notably George H. W. Bush, resisted Buchanan's call to arms, social issues and religious conservatives apparently played a critical role in the 1994 Republican takeover of the U.S. Congress and George W. Bush's victories in the 2000 and 2004 presidential elections.[7] But not everyone agrees that a culture war is in fact taking place, or that Americans are polarized along social issues. Based on an analysis of polling data, political scientist Morris Fiorina concludes:

> There is little evidence that Americans' ideological or policy *positions* are more polarized today than they were two or three decades ago, although their *choices* often seem to be. The explanation is that the political figures that Americans evaluate are more polarized. A polarized political class makes the citizenry appear polarized, but it is only that—an appearance.[8]

Pluralism

America's **pluralism** affects the making and implementation of public policies as well. The pluralism theory of government contends that power is group based. Adherents to this theory claim that because American government has multiple points of access, various groups in society possesses a near equal opportunity when competing with other groups for power and resources. According to the pluralist model, several inherent characteristics of the American political system give the role of interest groups special importance. First, because contemporary government is very complex, individuals must join interest groups as a way of participating in politics. Power thus becomes defined as an attribute of individuals in their relationships with each other in the process of decision making. Second, these power relationships are highly fluid. By this we mean they are formed for a particular decision; and once the decision is made they disappear, to be replaced by a different set of power relationships when the next decision is made. Third, there is no permanent distinction between elites and masses. That is, individuals who participate in decision making at one time are not necessarily the ones who participate at another time. Individuals move in and out of the ranks of decision makers simply by becoming active or inactive in politics. Fourth, multiple centers of power exist within a community; no single interest group totally dominates all decisions or is dominated by another interest group. Finally, there is considerable competition among various interests, so that the policy outcome is a result of bargaining and negotiation among competing groups.

The pluralist model is not without criticism. Critics argue that it creates a "leaderless society" in which all values are treated as equivalent interests, without an *a priori* hierarchy or ranking of values. Instead, pluralist structures are reactive and do not engage in rational planning or long-range planning. In addition, some argue that pluralist politics is inherently incapable of achieving justice; when one group wins, another loses. The problem is made worse because some groups have substantially more resources than others. Finally, pluralism, it is argued, is inherently corrupt because formal procedures have been replaced by informal bargaining in which the product is more likely to be a product of interest groups' strength, rather than a principled and reasoned outcome.[9]

Ideology and Public Opinion

Even though most groups and individual citizens lack a consistent ideological position, the majority of Americans are classified as "moderates" or "middle-of-the-road" in the ideological spectrum. Historically, Americans have always held this position on the spectrum. Figure 2.1 indicates the percentages of the American public that fall into different categories.

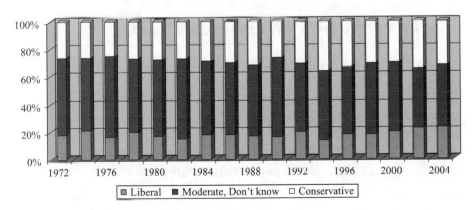

FIGURE 2.1 Ideology over Time.

SOURCE: calculated from data provided in American National Election Studies, http://www.electionstudies.org/nesguide/toptable/tab3_1.htm.

Although it is difficult to link these ideological positions to specific groups, some generalizations can be made about liberals and conservatives in society. For example, liberals tend to favor redistributive policies, government services, progressive taxes, strong government, and maximum citizen participation. Conservatives, on the other hand, tend to favor distributive policies, minimal government services (unless such services benefit their interests), regressive taxes, weak government, and limited citizen participation. At the same time, many conservatives favor an active role for government in morality policy—whether it be preventing abortion, allowing prayer in the schools, or regulating sex and violence in the media.

Thomas Sowell labels these ideological positions "visions," or competing perspectives, which he identifies as "constrained" and "unconstrained."[10] The **constrained vision** is a picture of egocentric human beings with moral limitations. The fundamental social and moral challenge, therefore, is to make the best of possibilities existing within that constraint, rather than to dissipate energies in a vain attempt to change human nature. By this logic, policy should be based on incentives, rather than dispositions, to obtain the desired behavior.[11] The prospect of rewards and the fear of punishment provide the incentives to obtain desirable behavior. Fundamentally, then, this results in a constrained view of human nature and leads to less-ambitious policy positions if it is assumed that the primary constraints come from within the individual rather than being imposed from the environment outside the individual.

The **unconstrained vision,** on the other hand, provides a view of human nature in which understanding and human dispositions are capable of intentionally creating social benefits. From this perspective, humans are capable of directly feeling other people's needs as more important than their own and, therefore, of acting impartially, even when their interests or those of their family are involved.[12] This view of human nature is often associated with the liberal view that human nature is no constraint; rather, the environment imposes constraints.

THE EVOLUTION OF AMERICAN PUBLIC POLICY

As American politics change, so too does the character of public policy. Those changes have occurred in both the long and near term. Not surprisingly, long-term trends are easy to depict. But as we shall see, accounting for policy changes in the near term is much more difficult and uncertain.

The Long-Term View: Some Recurring Patterns
in American Public Policy

If American public policy is observed over a longer time frame, of perhaps 100 years or more, a number of recurring patterns are found. Some observers argue that American public policy resembles a zigzag pattern in which the country pursues conservative policies for a time and then liberal policies (as a reaction) before eventually returning to conservative policies. More specifically, some argue that American public policy has evolved through four discrete periods.

The first period, during the late 19th century, was characterized by high levels of spending that largely benefited Northern white males, especially those who had served the North in the Civil War (1861–1865).[13] The Civil War pension system distributed benefits in a political way, in that one's political affiliation to the Republican Party was a major criterion for acquiring the pension. This form of political patronage later led to a backlash against the "radical Republicans" in the Deep South.[14] Then, during the Progressive Era of 1900 to 1930, there was an attempt to eliminate this patronage and corruption of the previous era by civil service reforms, the adoption of the merit system, child labor laws, women's hours legislation, and various health and safety laws. At this time, the Democrats became known as the "reform party" due to their opposition to the previous policies of the radical Republicans. In addition, the Democrats began to establish a sort of social democracy, which spilled over into the next era from 1930 to 1950.

During the New Deal period (1930–1950), the Democrats led the support for social insurance programs and welfare programs, fueled to a large extent by the Great Depression and a sense that the private sector had failed in fundamental ways that needed correction by government. The result was the beginning of a 50-year period of unprecedented growth in the role of the federal government that would not be seriously challenged until the 1980s. Until then major federal programs were enacted in education, workplace safety, poverty, the environment, health care for the aged, and civil rights for minorities and women. But almost immediately the sheer volume and depth of those new programs fueled a conservative backlash that would culminate in the election of Ronald Reagan in 1980. In contrast to the New Deal, the new paradigm of governing emphasized a renewed respect for the private sector, a sense that state governments were now able to govern, and a commitment to substantially reducing the role of the federal government. While the Reagan administration was only partially successful in realizing its policy goals, it appeared that the days of unchecked growth in the federal government had ended.

Did the presidency of Ronald Reagan usher in a new era of conservative government only briefly interrupted by the presidency of Bill Clinton? After all, Democrats lost control of the Congress in the 1994 election and suffered similar losses in state house after state house in the years that followed. The election and subsequent reelection of George W. Bush and congressional Republicans in 2000 and 2004 seemed to suggest that it had. But as the war in Iraq seemed less winnable and President Bush's public support declined to all-time lows, Democrats in the midterm election of 2006 were able to recapture the U.S. Senate and House after a dozen years of nearly uninterrupted Republican control.

The Near-Term View: America in Transition

Where does that leave us in the near term? Obviously, America is at a critical crossroads. Events over the next years, much like events over the last few years, will largely determine in what direction the nation's politics and policy will head. Writing in the late 1980s, historian Arthur Schlesinger suggested that America is headed in a liberal direction.[15] Professor Schlesinger argued that a 30-year conservative cycle would come to an end in the early 1990s, to be replaced by a liberal resurgence that would extend into the next century. Specifically, he argued that the rhythms of American politics dictate a fairly regular cyclical alternation between conservatism and liberalism in the national moods, or "swings back and forth between eras when the national commitment is to private interest as the best means of meeting our problems and eras when the national commitment is to public purpose."[16] He argued that this 30-year cycle corresponds to the span of a generation because people's political attitudes are formed by the ideals dominant during the years when they attain political consciousness, which is roughly between their 17th and 25th birthdays. Given this hypothesis, he predicted that the 1990s would usher in a new era of political liberalism in which government would be seen as an instrument of public welfare rather than a threat to people's liberties. That will be followed in the 2020s by a period of national conservatism as the mood of idealism and reform will have run its course and the public will turn once more to the view that, left to the unfettered market and the ethos of capitalism, America's problems will solve themselves. Each swing of the cycle, he argues, "corrects the excesses of the other so that the republic survives."[17]

Obviously Professor Schlesinger could not have predicted the 2000 presidential election, the attack on America a year later, and the decision to invade Iraq. Perhaps the 2006 midterm elections will usher in the liberal era he predicted in the late 1980s. Only time will tell. One thing is certain: America and the world are changing, and the nation's leaders will need to find new solutions that address those changes without, as President Jimmy Carter notes at the beginning of this chapter, altering our basic values.

SUMMARY

Our brief review of politics and policy in America underscores the value of an evolutionary approach to public policy. As we have seen, the values that Americans subscribe to, the major features of our political system, and the character of our public polices are constantly in flux. If there is a constant to all of that, it is the need for governments to attend to a core set of policy issues while working within the contours of the American political system. Invariably governments are called upon to choose among competing values and decide which levels of government should take which actions to achieve those values. Those decisions are shaped in large part by the major features of the American political system, including federalism, a separation of powers, political culture and public opinion, and ideology.

DISCUSSION QUESTIONS

1. Are American social and political values changing for the better or for the worse? Why? Discuss the implications of the value changes described in Table 2.1.

2. Which of the critical policy issues is likely to present the toughest decisions for governments in the next several years?

3. How do the major features of the American political system affect the kinds of policies governments adopt?

4. Is America in the midst of a culture war?

SUGGESTED READINGS

Bork, Robert H. *Slouching Towards Gomorrah* (New York: HarperCollins, 1996).

Carter, Jimmy. *Our Endangered Values: America's Moral Crisis* (New York: Simon and Schuster, 2005).

Fiorina, Morris P., with Samuel J. Abrams and Jeremy C. Pope. *Culture War? The Myth of a Polarized America* (New York: Pearson Longman, 2004).

Hunter, James Davison. *Culture Wars: The Struggle to Define America* (New York: Basic Books, 1991).

NOTES

1. Richard D. Lamm and Richard A. Caldwell, *Hard Choices* (Denver, CO: The University of Denver, Center for Public Policy, 1991).

2. See, for example, John Donovan, *The Politics of Poverty* (New York: Pegasus, 1967); Daniel P. Moynihan, *Maximum Feasible Misunderstanding* (New York: Macmillan, 1970); Charles Murray, *Losing Ground: American Social Policy, 1950–1980* (New York: Basic Books, 1986); and John E. Schwarz, *America's Hidden Success,* Revised Edition (New York: W. W. Norton, 1994).

3. See Congressional Quarterly, Inc., *Origins and Development of Congress* (Washington, D.C., 1976).

4. John J. Harrigan, *Politics and Policies in State and Communities* (New York: Harper-Collins, 1991), pp. 23–27.

5. Lucien Pye, "Political Culture," in *International Encyclopedia of the Social Sciences,* Vol. 12 (New York: Macmillan, 1968), p. 218.

6. Daniel J. Elazar, *American Federalism: A View from the States* (New York: Thomas Crowell, 1972).

7. See Hunter, James Davison. *Culture Wars: The Struggle to Define America* (New York: Basic Books, 1991); David Broder, "One Nation Divisible: Despite Peace,

Prosperity, Voters Agree to Disagree," *Washington Post,* November 8, 200?: A1; and Jill Lawrence, "Behind Its United Front, Nation Divided as Ever," *USA Today,* February 18, 2002: A1.

8. Morris Fiorina, *Culture War? The Myth of a Polarized America* (New York: Pearson Longman, 2004), p. 5.

9. Theodore J. Lowi, *The End of Liberalism* (New York: W. W. Norton, 1969).

10. Thomas Sowell, *A Conflict of Visions* (New York: William Morrow, 1987).

11. Ibid., pp. 19–23.

12. Ibid., pp. 23–25.

13. Edwin Amenta and Theda Skocpol, "Taking Exception: Explaining the Distinctiveness of American Public Policies in the Last Century," in *The Comparative History of Public Policy,* ed. Francis G. Castles (New York: Oxford University Press, 1989), pp. 292–333.

14. James W. Lamare, *Texas Politics: Economics, Power, and Policy* (St. Paul: West, 1981).

15. See Arthur M. Schlesinger, Jr., "America's Political Cycle Turns Again," *Wall Street Journal*, 10 December 1987, p. 28.

16. Ibid.

17. Ibid.

3

Approaches to Policy Analysis

"An appropriate choice of research strategy can only be made in light
of a particular set of research objectives."
GROVER STARLING

When we speak of approaches to policy analysis, we mean the various ways political and other social scientists go about "doing" policy analysis. Every policy analyst implicitly or explicitly adopts a research strategy that best suits him or her. Yet no one has perfect vision as to the "proper" approach to policy analysis. Rather, policy analysts take many diverse approaches to the analysis of public policy. These alternative approaches are often based on one's primary objectives for conducting policy analysis. At the broadest level, Cook and Vaupel discuss three basic "research styles" in policy analysis: (1) policy analysis, (2) policy research, and (3) applied social science research.[1]

Policy analysis, according to Cook and Vaupel's definition, refers to a staff memorandum on a narrowly defined problem. Such an analysis might take anywhere from days or weeks to prepare. The methods used in this instance are basic data collection techniques, including the compilation of readings and the synthesis of many ideas into a coherent course of action. For example, such an analysis might be done to advise the Health and Human Services Department as to whether it should recommend a particular type of welfare policy.

Policy research, on the other hand, refers to a monograph on a broad problem, such as the feasibility of natural gas deregulation. This type of analysis might take a year or more to prepare, and the methods used might include decision analysis, cost-benefit analysis, systems analysis, or other sophisticated techniques. This type of policy analysis might be carried out by several analysts at the Brookings Institution, or at the Urban Institute for decision makers at the Department of Energy, or perhaps at the White House.

Finally, **applied social science research** refers to a scholarly assessment of the effects of a policy intervention on some narrowly defined set of outcomes, such as analyzing the effects of using seat belts on traffic fatalities in the state of Oklahoma. The research might be carried out by university researchers on behalf of a state agency that is interested in requiring such a law or assessing the impacts of a seat-belt law. The techniques used might be quantitative, such as multiple regression, or even less-sophisticated techniques, such as case studies.

SPECIFIC APPROACHES TO POLICY ANALYSIS

As Table 3.1 suggests, there are many more specific approaches to policy analysis. For example, one may be interested in the analysis of either a part of the policy process (e.g., agenda setting, policy implementation) or a substantive area

T A B L E 3.1 **Approaches to Policy Analysis**

Type of Approach		Primary Objective
1.	Process approach	1.	To examine a part of the policy process
2.	Substantive approach	2.	To examine a substantive area
3.	Logical positivist approach	3.	To examine the causes and consequences of policy using scientific methods
4.	Economic approach	4.	To test economic theories
5.	Phenomenological (post-positivist) approach	5.	To analyze events through an intuitive process
6.	Participatory approach	6.	To examine the role of multiple actors in policymaking
7.	Normative or prescriptive approach	7.	To prescribe policy to decision makers or others
8.	Ideological approach	8.	To analyze from a liberal or conservative point of view
9.	Historical approach	9.	To examine policy over time

(e.g., environmental policy). One may rely on rigorous statistical approaches or more intuitive approaches. Finally, one may utilize prescriptive (what should be) or empirical (what is) approaches. In the following sections, each of these alternative approaches is discussed to give a better sense of the various options one has in approaching policy analysis. Of course, any one, or a combination, of these approaches can be adopted in an individual's own work in public policy analysis.

The Process Approach

Perhaps the most commonly adopted approach is to identify stages in the policy process and then to analyze the determinants of each particular stage. This perspective refers to the familiar conveyor-like concept of the policy cycle that was discussed in Chapter 1. As we mentioned there, it is called the **policy process approach.** In this approach, societal problems are first recognized as an issue for action, and then policies are adopted, implemented by agency officials, evaluated, and finally terminated or changed on the basis of their success or the lack of it. Certainly the process is much more complex than this rather simple image; but when we speak of the policy cycle, we are speaking about a political process through which most public policies pass. Although the reality of the policy process is complex, it can be better understood by thinking of it as if it went through a series of discrete stages such as those discussed in the first chapter. Over the past 30 years, policy analysts have made substantial progress in acquiring a better understanding of the policy cycle. Various authors have examined particular aspects of the policy cycle and have advanced the understanding of each phase. Some aspects of the policy cycle have been more heavily studied than others (e.g., policy formulation), whereas others are just beginning to be further developed by research that seeks to advance the concepts involved or test a series of hypotheses that explain a particular aspect of the policy cycle (e.g., policy change). For example, John Kingdon's work on agenda setting has provided a rich explanation of the central determinants of this phase. Future research will be directed to testing his model and other models of each phase of the policy cycle. Most recently, scholars have begun examining the politics of policy change.[2]

The Substantive Approach

Many policy scientists become **substantive** specialists in a particular area. For example, they might analyze the determinants of environmental policy formulation, implementation, or change.[3] Others become educational policy specialists, health-care policy specialists, energy policy specialists, crime policy specialists, or welfare policy specialists.[4] These individuals may stay within the context of a single substantive area for much of their professional careers; or alternatively, they may delve into policy in a particular area for a short time and later move on to yet another policy area. According to a study of articles published in leading journals of political science, the most often studied areas from a substantive perspective are economic policy (14.5%), science/technology policy (14.1%), and foreign policy (13.7%).[5] An earlier study, however, concluded that health and natural resources/energy/environmental policy studies were the most studied areas of interest during the period of 1975–1984.[6] However, the substantive areas that attract the most interest may well change over time.

Some policy scientists argue that expertise within a substantive area is highly desirable and gives a person much more credibility than that of a "generic" policy analyst who is a welfare policy specialist one month and a crime policy specialist the next. To acquire expertise in a substantive area often requires that one become familiar with both the technical and the political aspects of a policy area. For example, when Charles O. Jones wrote his classic book on air-quality policy in the 1970s, he had to become very familiar with the technical issues as well as the political issues associated with clean air.[7] By doing so, he was able to produce a fine book that combined policy analysis skills with substantive expertise.

On the other hand, some policy scientists argue that substantive knowledge is not necessary to be a good policy analyst; instead, they argue that one need only to be skilled in the process and methods of public policy; substance is relatively unimportant.[8] It is our belief that, to the contrary, substance is important; it can give one insight into what questions to ask in conducting policy analysis. This substantive knowledge is necessary, we think, to understand and to interpret one's empirical findings. At any rate, there will always be those who argue either for or against substantive knowledge in policy analysis. This is an area of individual choice for budding policy scientists.

The Logical Positivist Approach

The **logical positivist approach,** often called the **behavioral approach** or the **scientific approach,** advocates the use of deductively derived theories, models, hypothesis testing, hard data, the comparative method, and rigorous statistical analysis. *Scientific* in this context means several things. First, it means clarifying key concepts used in the analysis of policy. For example, concepts such as policy implementation must be defined more carefully than in the past. Previously, implementation was defined as a yes/no dichotomy rather than as a process of drafting guidelines, appropriating funds, monitoring performance, and revising statutes. Second, it means working from an explicit theory of policy behavior and testing hypotheses derived from the theory. Third, it means using hard data, developing good measures of various phenomena, and (ideally) examining various explanations across time.[9] This approach really began with the "behavioral revolution" in social science shortly after World War II. It has endured over 50 years and has become the dominant epistemological approach in political science.

The scientific approach is not without its critics, however, who argue that it misunderstands the policy process by treating it as a "rational project."[10] That is, the policy process is much more complex than this conveyor-like perspective; thus, it does not lend itself to highly sophisticated techniques of analysis. The criticism has taken the form of a post-positivist deconstruction of traditional behavioral methods and has argued instead for more intuitive or participatory approaches to the analysis of public policy. We discuss these latter approaches below.

The Economic Approach

The **economic approach,** sometimes called the **public choice approach** or the **political economy approach,** is primarily based on economic theories of politics in which human nature is assumed to be "rational," or motivated by purely personal gain. This approach assumes that people pursue their own fixed, weighted preferences regardless of collective outcomes.[11] An excellent example of this approach is the principal–agent model articulated by Terry Moe and others. This model has been used to account for a range of policy behaviors, including the relationship between voters and elected officials, the political control of bureaucrats, and the ability of the national government to shape the actions of state governments. According to Moe and others, much of what transpires in governing involves the efforts of political principals (e.g. voters, elected officials, superior levels of government) to control the behavior of their agents (e.g. politicians, bureaucrats, and subordinate governments). Faced with a divergence of values between principals and their agents and an information asymmetry that advantages the agent, political principals seek tools that will allow them to more closely monitor and control the actions of their agents.[12]

An economic approach has wide currency and respect in the policy sciences, although it has been criticized for being a somewhat narrow approach to policy analysis.[13] Specifically, some argue that this approach is not completely wrong, but that it is very incomplete in its assumptions about human nature and political power. Specifically, humans are also altruistic (not just rational or selfish) and are thus occasionally motivated to serve the public or collective interest.[14]

The Phenomenological (Post-Positivist) Approach

As noted above, recent years have seen a growing disenchantment with the utility of scientific methods (including logical positivism and econometrics) in the study of public policy.[15] Those who oppose the scientific (behavioral) study of public policy prefer an approach whereby *intuition* is more important than positivist/scientific approaches. This approach is called the **phenomenological, naturalistic,** or **post-positivist approach.**[16] Essentially, this approach argues that analysts need to adopt "a respect for the disciplined employment of sound intuition, itself born of experience not reducible to models, hypotheses, quantification, hard data," and the like.[17] Methodologically, these analysts treat each piece of social phenomenon as a unique event, with ethnographic and other qualitative indices becoming paramount.[18] This alternative view is described by its concern with understanding rather than prediction, with working hypotheses rather than rigorous hypothesis testing, and with mutual interaction between the inquirer and the object of study rather than detached observation on the part of the analysts. To gather "evidence," this approach favors the continued use of case studies, rather than more sophisticated techniques of analysis.[19] In short, it substitutes a concern for scientific rigor with intuition and total immersion in relevant information. Table 3.2 compares the positivist approach with the post-positivist (naturalistic) approach.

T A B L E 3.2 Contrasting Positivist and Naturalist Axioms

Axioms About	Positivist Paradigm	Naturalist Paradigm
The nature of reality	Reality is single, tangible, and fragmentable.	Realities are multiple, constructed, and holistic.
The relationship of knower to the known	Knower and known are independent, a dualism.	Knower and known are interactive, inseparable.
The possibility of generalization	Time- and context-free generalizations (nomothetic statements) are possible.	Only time- and context-bound working hypotheses (idiographic statements) are possible.
The possibility of causal linkages	There are real causes, temporally precedent to or simultaneous with their effects.	All entities are in a state of mutual simultaneous shaping, so that it is impossible to distinguish causes from effects.
The role of values	Inquiry is value-free.	Inquiry is value-bound.

SOURCE: Yvonna S. Lincoln and Egon G. Guba, *Naturalistic Inquiry* (Newbury Park, CA: Sage Publications, 1985), p. 37, copyright © by Sage Publications, Inc. Reprinted by permission of Sage Publications, Inc.

The naturalistic approach may be criticized for its lack of rigor and for its movement away from the scientific approach advocated by the behavioralists and economists. It is almost as if these post-positivist scholars want researchers to return to the pre-behavioral approaches of the 1940s and 1950s, in which descriptive, nonscientific, and intuitive studies characterized much of what passed for policy analysis.

The Participatory Approach

The **participatory approach,** associated with Peter DeLeon and others, is closely related to the post-positivist challenge and involves a greater inclusion of the interests and values of the various stakeholders in the policy decision-making processes.[20] It is presumably closer to what Harold Lasswell called the "policy sciences of democracy," in which an extended population of affected citizens would be involved in the formulation and implementation of public policy through a series of discursive dialogues.[21] It would involve extensive open hearings with a broad range of concerned citizens, in which these hearings would be structured in such a way as to prompt individuals, interest groups, and agency officials to contribute to policy design and redesign. The declared purpose of participatory policy analysis is to gather information so that policymakers can make better (i.e., more completely informed) recommendations and decisions. As an approach to analysis, it encourages consideration of a greater number of players and values in the policymaking process and thus provides a better catalog of the various perspectives being brought to bear on the policy under consideration.[22]

Critics of participatory approaches, on the other hand, often argue that increased citizen involvement will lead to an increase in group dissensus over program goals and procedures, that it will lead to needless delays in policy formulation and implementation, that the costs of policymaking and implementation will increase dramatically, and that disaffected interests will seek to obstruct programs through litigation or recourse to Congress.[23] Moreover, where such participatory experiments have been tried previously, confusion and conflict increase.[24]

The participatory approach may be more useful as a guide to agenda setting, policy formulation, and policy implementation than in analyzing other stages of the process. In some respects, it is more of a prescription for policy design or redesign than an empirical approach to understanding policy formation or implementation. The next section describes what we mean by a prescriptive approach.

The Normative or Prescriptive Approach

Still others adopt a **normative** or **prescriptive approach** and define their task as a policy analyst as one of defining a desirable "end state," perhaps arguing that this prescription is both desirable and attainable. They often advocate a policy position and use rhetoric in a skillful way to convince others of the merits of their position.[25] Some examples of this type of policy analysis would be the works of Henry Kissinger, Jeane Kirkpatrick, Daniel Patrick Moynihan, or, more recently, Paul Wolfowitz. Essentially, these analysts employ skillful argumentation and (sometimes) selective use of data to advance a political position and to convince others that their position is a desirable policy choice. Sometimes, this type of policy analysis leads to the charge that policy analysts often disguise their ideology as science.[26]

The Ideological Approach

Although not all policy analysts explicitly adopt a liberal or conservative point of view, they almost always have such a view embedded somewhere in their policy analysis. Thomas Sowell calls these ideological approaches "visions" and identifies two competing perspectives.[27]

The **"constrained vision"** is a picture of egocentric human beings with moral limitations. The fundamental social and moral challenge, therefore, is to make the best of possibilities existing within that constraint, rather than to dissipate energies in a vain attempt to change human nature. By this logic, then, one should rely on incentive, rather than dispositions, to obtain the desired behavior.[28] The prospect of rewards or the fear of punishments provides the incentives to obtain desirable behavior. Fundamentally, then, this results in a conservative view of human nature and will lead to more conservative policy positions if one assumes that the primary constraints come from within the individual rather than being imposed from the environment outside the individual.

The **"unconstrained vision,"** on the other hand, provides a view of human nature in which understanding and human dispositions are capable of intentionally creating social benefits.[29] Under this perspective, humans are capable of directly feeling other people's needs as more important than their own and therefore are capable of consistently acting impartially, even when their interests or those of their family are involved.[30] This view of human nature, then, is often associated with the liberal view that human nature is no constraint; rather, constraints are imposed by the environment outside the individual. Both of these visions are illustrated in the substantive chapters of this book.

The Historical Approach

Many public policy scholars are increasingly turning their attention to the evolution of public policies across time.[31] As one examines American public policies from the perspective of a hundred years or more, one begins to see certain patterns in the contours of public policy that were previously unrecognized due to rather short time frames of analysis (i.e., either cross-sectional analyses or analyses limited to a decade or less). Only by examining public policies from the standpoint of a longer period of time can analysts gain a more complete perspective about patterns that exist in the making of public policy in the United States.

Extant research along these lines suggests two rather opposing perspectives on the nature of American policymaking. The first is that American policymaking tends to follow a **cyclical** or **"zigzag"** pattern in which more conservative tendencies follow more liberal tendencies, and then this pattern is repeated across time.[32] This perspective suggests a reactive approach to policymaking that is repetitive and, in some respects, nonrational over time. Others suggest an evolutionary explanation, in which American public policy reflects policy learning as America evolves toward more thoughtful (and by implication more rational) policymaking.[33] Table 3.2 briefly describes each of these approaches.

Still Other Approaches

Other scholars have identified approaches that are quite similar to the above. For example, Dubnick and Bardes identify five distinct approaches, some of which overlap with our discussion above.[34] Their approaches, identified in Table 3.3, provide a comprehensive set of ways in which analysts approach their jobs.

Scientific policy analysts engage in the search for the "causes and consequences" of public policies rather than the prescription of policies. They use scientific rigor to analyze policies and work to develop and test general propositions and to accumulate reliable research findings of general relevance.[35] This approach, much the same as the logical positivist approach identified earlier, is represented by such analysts as William Gormley, Bryan Jones, Ken Meier, Hank Jenkins-Smith, Paul Sabatier, George Krause and many others.

The **professional** policy analyst is one who studies public policy to improve it. Austin Ranney, for example, describes this approach as the study of public policy that seeks to apply scientific knowledge to the solution of practical problems.[36] These analysts believe that policy studies will eventually develop a "policy science" that is capable of informing decision makers by (1) effectively defining and diagnosing policy problems, (2) proposing policy alternatives, (3) developing models that can aid in the achievement of desired ends and methods for testing those models, (4) establishing intermediate goals, and (5) estimating the feasibility of various policy programs.[37] This approach is represented by policy analysts trained at policy institutes (e.g., the RAND Corporation), who tend to practice in think tanks as opposed to universities.

TABLE 3.3 Dubnick and Bardes' Approaches to Policy Analysis

Type of Policy Analyst	Public Policy Problem	Motivation	Approach	Relevant Training
1. Scientist	Theoretic	Search for theory, regularities, "truth"	Scientific method, objectivity, pure analytics	Basic research methods, canons of social science research
2. Professional	Design	Improvement of policy and policymaking	Utilization of knowledge, strategic	Strategic; benefit-cost analysis; queuing, simulation, decision analysis
3. Political	Value maximization	Advocacy of policy positions	Rhetoric	Gathering "useful" evidence; "effective" presentation
4. Administrative	Application	Effective and efficient policy implementation	Strategic, managerial	Strategic; same as professional with stress on those talents useful in implementation
5. Personal	Contention	Concern for policy impacts on life	Mixed	Use of many models and techniques from other approaches; less sophisticated

SOURCE: Melvin J. Dubnick and Barbara A. Bardes, *Thinking About Public Policy: A Problem Solving Approach,* © 1983 by John Wiley & Sons. Reprinted with permission of Melvin J. Dubnick and Barbara A. Bardes.

The **political** policy analyst, on the other hand, sees the function of policy analysis as a mechanism to advocate the "right" policy position. The primary task, under this perspective, is to give credence to certain policy positions or to challenge others. Teaching policy analysis within this perspective would stress fundamental research skills and instruction in the rhetorician's methods of rationalization and argumentation.[38] It is much like the normative or prescriptive approach described above.

The other two categories of policy analysis Dubnick and Bardes describe are the **administrative** and the **personal** policy analysts. The administrative analyst is primarily interested in helping to achieve effective and efficient policy implementation and tends to adopt the methods and goals of the professional policy analyst. The personal policy analyst is reflected in the citizen and layperson's use of policy skills to "reach tentative solutions to some of the basic policy related problems."[39] In effect, this last category is a residual category involving laypersons who adopt policy analysis but who are not members of any other category, such as the scientific, professional, political, or administrative categories.[40]

In summary, approaches to policy analysis are numerous. In actual practice, scholars often cleverly combine several approaches in various ways. For example, an analyst might write a book that advocates the formulation of a type of employment policy that is clearly redistributive (liberal) in its intent, using (albeit selectively) empirical data that substantiates his or her position. In such a policy analysis, the approach combines the process, substantive, positivist, normative, and ideological or political approaches. By knowing these various approaches to public policy, one acquires the ability to recognize a type of policy analysis for what it is when one sees it. He or she may then evaluate it on its own terms, rather than by applying criteria that are inappropriate to a specific policy analysis or by failing to evaluate it at all. From this discussion, the student should know that there are many options in conducting policy analysis.

Although we do not support the view that there is one "correct" approach to policy analysis, we do believe that the student should nevertheless select an approach that he or she deems most appropriate to the objectives of the analysis. The approach to policy analysis that is selected should be one with which the analyst feels most comfortable, and this approach should be made explicit in the analysis. Each of these approaches is appropriate in certain contexts.

Periodically, attempts have been made to identify trends in approaches to policy analysis over time. These evaluations show that policy analysis is becoming more scientific (logical positivist) in approach, although there are continuing elements of prescriptive and qualitative research.[41] Although positivist (especially quantitative) policy analysis, according to studies by Schneider et al. and by Hedge and Mok, is increasingly characteristic of policy studies, it still represents the minority approach compared to more descriptive (qualitative) and rhetorical (prescriptive) approaches. Policy analysis is also becoming more multidisciplinary and includes more analysis of state and local policy, especially natural resource issues and taxing/budgetary issues.[42]

ON BECOMING A BETTER POLICY SCIENTIST

No matter which of these approaches one finally selects, there are several ways to become a better policy analyst. Political scientist Yehezkel Dror identifies some things that can be done over the course of one's professional career to become "more of a policy scientist."[43] First, he says that policy scientists should **gain historical and comparative perspectives.** He argues that "present and emerging realities cannot be understood and handled within thin slices of time-space."[44] An ignorance of history thus condemns policy scientists to misperceptions of reality and severely limits their understanding due to the insight provided by analysis over time. Therefore, reading extensively and broadly is a must. One should always, therefore, know the complete history of the policy area being researched. Such an understanding can aid in identifying trends over time and in predicting the future of policy in that substantive area. This recognition guides our chapters in the last section of this book.

Second, the policy scientist should **know policymaking realities.** Very distorted views of policymaking can be obtained from "popular" theories or theories not well related to practice. Here Dror is openly criticizing the reliance on the economic approach (public choice) to policy analysis. He is simply saying that it is not a good idea to become attached to a single approach to policy analysis, for there is the danger that such an approach could become dogmatic and therefore restrict one's capacity as a policy scientist to discover "objective truth."

Third, the policy scientist should **study his or her own society in depth.** "At the very least," says Dror, "predicaments must be understood within the broader context of societal problem-handling processes; main social institutions and their dynamics must be seen within historic configurations; and main facts of present situations must be known fully with alternative interpretations and within comprehensive alternative futures."[45] Sometimes, it is necessary to leave one's current operational context to more fully understand it. He encourages traveling to gain perspective on one's own country and its institutions and values.

Fourth, the policy scientist should **take up grand policy issues** and work on diverse issues.[46] All too often, Dror feels, policy scientists fail to take on grand policy issues, instead opting for "micro-issues" that easily fit into extant methods. He advocates taking on grand policy issues, such as those written about by Herman Kahn, Amitai Etzioni, and Robert Reich. In addition, to build policy skills, one must gain experience on a wide variety of issues and public policy problems. Specialization within a single substantive area may be desirable for a time, but over the long term, it is better to broaden one's expertise.

Fifth, the policy scientist should **move into metapolicymaking.**[47] By this Dror means that one should work on efforts to improve policymaking as opposed to just attempting to explain policymaking. In this sense, then, the policy analyst must think like a practitioner at times and try to see the world from that perspective. Such a different worldview helps the analyst to work to improve policymaking.

Sixth, the policy scientist should **build an appropriate philosophy of knowledge and action.** Dror encourages rejecting positivism as the exclusive methodology recognized as "scientific." Rather, "clinical skills, subjective knowledge based on immersion in applied work and theoretic study, tacit understanding, and similar partly explicated bases of insight are a legitimate source of policy sciences knowledge and a partly acceptable basis for policymaking."[48] For example, the study of classical political thought and philosophy can enhance one's ability to understand and assess the normative choices implied in many policy decisions.

Seventh, the policy scientist should **broaden his or her methodology and experience** by moving to different work locations, by spending some time in another culture, and by studying a major language. Over the course of a lifetime, it is possible to understand and utilize many different techniques, such as those from defense analysis or futures research. Moreover, every striving policy scientist, Dror argues, should spend at least two to three years in each of three types of work locations: a public policy school doing research and teaching, a policy analysis unit within government, and a think tank working on major policy issues. Policy scientists should also try to live in a culture as different as possible from their own country. No substitute exists, he argues, "for working a few years in another culture to broaden one's cognitive maps, to see one's own society in a different and more correct way, and to gain a sense of crucial dimensions of human predicaments and policy issues."[49]

Finally, Dror encourages **multiplying one's disciplinary bases** and **being careful about professional ethics.** Understanding another discipline besides

TABLE 3.4 On Becoming a Better Policy Scientist

1. Gain historical and comparative perspective.
2. Know policymaking realities.
3. Study your own society in depth.
4. Take up grand and diverse policy issues.
5. Move into metapolicymaking.
6. Build up an appropriate philosophy of knowledge and action.
7. Broaden your methodology and experience.
8. Multiply your disciplinary bases.
9. Be careful about professional ethics.

SOURCE: Adapted from Y. Dror, "On Becoming More of a Political Scientist," *Policy Studies Review* 4. Copyright © 1984 by Wiley-Blackwell Publishing Company. Reprinted with permission of Wiley-Blackwell Publishing Company.

political science, such as economics or sociology, is very useful. Ideally, striving policy scientists should study an additional discipline that is contrary in basic assumptions to the discipline that they know best. Last, but not least, personal professional ethics must be a matter of concern for every policy scientist. Each of us must decide for ourselves whether to work for every interesting (or paying) client that comes along, or to work only for clients whose values we respect. In addition, we must balance loyalty to clients with overriding values and the public interest. Finally, when working with elites, we must balance the essential functions of providing emotional support with the task of presenting often unwelcome (or counterintuitive) analyses and findings.[50] Table 3.4 summarizes Dror's main points.

All of these considerations provide useful advice for anyone considering the policy sciences as a profession. In fact, the number of openings for policy analysts within research institutes, universities, and local, state, or national governmental agencies is growing. The 21st century will require many more policy analysts as the number of policy problems proliferates. In deciding to become a policy analyst, one will have chosen an exciting career that will doubtless become even more important in the new century.

DISCUSSION QUESTIONS

1. One of the most important, current debates within the policy studies field is over the relative merits of a positivist approach versus a "naturalistic" approach (see Table 3.2 for a comparison of these two approaches). What are the implications of each approach for the utilization of policy analysis by decision makers?
2. What do you think is (or should be) the purpose of policy analysis?
3. Thinking about the various approaches discussed in this chapter, which one(s) do you find most compelling as your preferred approach to policy analysis?

4. Discuss the relationships between one's approach to policy analysis and one's ideological biases. How does one's ideology influence one's choice of approach?

5. Which of Dror's ways to become a better policy analyst do you find most convincing? Why? Which ones are least convincing?

SUGGESTED READINGS

Gross, Paul R., and Norman Levitt. *Higher Superstition: The Academic Left and Its Quarrels With Science* (Baltimore: Johns Hopkins Press, 1994).

Harding, Sandra. *The Science Question in Feminism* (Ithaca, NY: Cornell University Press, 1986).

Harding, Sandra. *Is Science Multicultural? Postcolonialisms, Feminisms, and Epistemologies* (Bloomington: Indiana University Press, 1998).

Rosenau, Pauline M. *Post-Modernism and the Social Sciences* (Princeton, NJ: Princeton University Press, 1992).

Wilson, Edward O. *Consilience: The Unity of Knowledge* (New York: Alfred A. Knopf, 1998).

NOTES

1. See Philip J. Cook and James W. Vaupel, "What Policy Analysts Do: Three Research Styles," *Journal of Policy Analysis and Management* 4 (Spring 1985), p. 427.

2. See Paul A. Sabatier and Hank Jenkins-Smith, "Policy Change and Policy-Oriented Learning," *Policy Sciences* 21 (1988), pp. 123–277; and Paul A. Sabatier and Hank C. Jenkins-Smith, eds., *Policy Change and Learning: An Advocacy Coalition Approach* (Boulder, CO: Westview Press, 1993).

3. See James P. Lester, ed., *Environmental Politics and Policy: Theories and Evidence,* 2d ed. (Durham, NC: Duke University Press, 1995).

4. See, for example, John E. Chubb and Terry M. Moe, *Politics, Markets, and America's Schools* (Washington, D.C.: The Brookings Institution, 1990); Frances Fox Piven and Richard A. Cloward, *Regulating the Poor* (New York: Pantheon, 1971); James Q. Wilson and Richard J. Herrnstein, *Crime and Human Nature* (New York: Simon and Schuster, 1985); David H. Davis, *Energy Policy* (New York: St. Martin's Press, 1993); Malcolm Goggin, *Policy Design and the Politics of Implementation* (Knoxville: University of Tennessee Press, 1988); or Lawrence M. Meade, *Government Matters: Welfare Reform in Wisconsin* (Princeton University Press, 2004).

5. James M. Rodgers, "Social Science Disciplines and Policy Research," *Policy Studies Review* 9 (Autumn 1989), pp. 13–28.

6. David Hedge and Jin W. Mok, "The Nature of Policy Studies: A Content Analysis of Policy Journal Articles," *Policy Studies Review* 16 (Autumn 1987), pp. 49–61.

7. Charles O. Jones, *Clean Air* (Pittsburgh: University of Pittsburgh Press, 1975).

8. Richard Hofferbert, for example, has often advanced this view in discussions of the role of substance in policy analysis.

9. See Malcolm L. Goggin, Ann O'M. Bowman, James P. Lester, and Laurence J. O'Toole, *Implementation Theory and Practice: Toward a Third Generation* (New York: HarperCollins, 1990), for an example of this approach in implementation research.

10. Deborah A. Stone, *Policy Paradox and Political Reason* (New York: HarperCollins, 1988).

11. Trudi C. Miller, "Normative Political Science," *Policy Studies Review* 9 (Winter 1990), pp. 232–246.

12. Some of the major work in this area includes Terry Moe's classic statement of the principal-agent model in Moe, "The New Economics of Organization," *American Journal of Political Science* 28 (1984), pp. 739–777; as well as B. Dan Wood, "Principals, Bureaucrats, and Responsiveness in Clean Air Enforcements," *American Political Science Review* 82 (1988), pp. 213–234; Matthew D. McCubbins, Roger Noll, and Barry Weingast, "Administrative Procedures as Instruments of Political Control," *Journal of Law, Economics, and Organization* 3 (1989), pp. 243–277; Matthew D. McCubbins and Thomas Schwartz, "Congressional Oversight Overlooked: Police Patrols Versus Fire Alarms," *American Journal of Political Science* 28 (1984), pp. 165–179; and John E. Chubb, "The Political Economy of Federalism," *American Political Science Review* 79 (1985), pp. 994–1015.

13. Miller, "Normative Political Science," pp. 237–238.

14. Ibid., p. 237.

15. Gregory A. Daneke, "On Paradigmatic Progress in Public Policy and Administration," *Policy Studies Journal* 17 (Winter 1988–1989), pp. 277–296; Frank Fischer, "Beyond the Rationality Project: Policy Analysis and the Postpositivist Challenge," *Policy Studies Journal* 17 (Summer 1989), pp. 941–951.

16. In its most extreme forms, it is referred to as the "antipositivist" approach, or the "critical" approach.

17. Charles J. Fox, "Implementation Research: Why and How to Transcend Positivist Methodologies," in *Implementation and the Policy Process,* ed. Dennis J. Palumbo and Donald J. Calista (Westport, CT: Greenwood Press, 1990), pp. 199–212.

18. Daneke, "On Paradigmatic Progress," p. 282.

19. E. G. Guba, "The Context of Emergent Paradigm Research," in *Organizational Theory and Inquiry: The Paradigm Revolution,* ed. Y. S. Lincoln (Beverly Hills, CA: Sage, 1993).

20. Peter DeLeon, *Advice and Consent: The Development of the Policy Sciences* (New York: Russell Sage, 1988); and Peter DeLeon, "Participatory Policy Analysis: Prescriptions and Precautions," *Asian Journal of Public Administration* 12 (June 1990), pp. 29–54; see also Benjamin R. Barber, *Strong Democracy* (Berkeley: University of California Press, 1984); Jayne Mansbridge, *Beyond Adversary Democracy* (Chicago: University of Chicago Press, 1983); and Peter DeLeon, *Democracy and the Policy Sciences* (Albany, NY: State University of New York Press, 1997).

21. See Harold D. Lasswell, *A Pre-View of Policy Sciences* (New York: Elsevier, 1971).

22. See, for example, John S. Dryzek, "Policy Sciences of Democracy," *Polity* 22 (Fall 1989), 97–118; and John S. Dryzek, *Discursive Democracy: Politics, Policy, and Political Science* (New York: Cambridge University Press, 1990).

23. Walter A. Rosenbaum, "The Paradoxes of Participation," *Administration and Society* 8 (1976), pp. 355–383.

24. Dorothy Nelkin, *Technical Decisions and Democracy* (Beverly Hills, CA: Sage, 1977).

25. See, for example, John Dryzek, *Rational Ecology* (New York: Basil Blackwell, 1987).

26. See Laurence H. Tribe, "Policy Science: Analysis or Ideology," *Philosophy and Public Affairs* (Fall 1972), pp. 66–110.

27. Thomas Sowell, *A Conflict of Visions* (New York: William Morrow, 1987).

28. Ibid., pp. 19—23.

29. Ibid., pp. 23—25.

30. Ibid.

31. See, for example, Paul A. Sabatier, "Knowledge, Policy-Oriented Learning, and Policy Change: An Advocacy Coalition Framework," *Knowledge: Creation, Diffusion, Utilization* 8 (June 1987), pp. 649—692; see also Paul A. Sabatier and Hank C. Jenkins Smith, *Policy Change and Learning: An Advocacy Coalition Approach* (Boulder, CO: Westview Press, 1993); T. Alexander Smith, *Time and Public Policy* (Knoxville: University of Tennessee Press, 1988); and Malcolm Goggin, Ann O'M. Bowman, James P. Lester, and Laurence J. O'Toole, *Implementation Theory and Practice: Toward a Third Generation* (New York: HarperCollins, 1990).

32. Arthur Schlesinger, "America's Political Cycle Turns Again," *Wall Street Journal,* 10 December 1987, and "Reaganism Is Dead—Long Live Liberalism," *Manchester Guardian Weekly,* 8 May 1988.

33. See footnote 32 above.

34. See Melvin J. Dubnick and Barbara A. Bardes, *Thinking About Public Policy* (New York: Wiley, 1983).

35. Thomas Dye, *Understanding Public Policy* (Englewood Cliffs, NJ: Prentice Hall, 1987).

36. See Austin Ranney, ed., *Political Science and Public Policy* (Chicago: Markham, 1968).

37. Duncan MacRae, "Policy Analysis: An Applied Social Science Discipline," *Administration and Society* 6 (1975), pp. 376—380. Also cited in Dubnick and Bardes, *Thinking About Public Policy.*

38. Dubnick and Bardes, *Thinking About Public Policy,* p. 259.

39. Ibid., p. 261.

40. Ibid., pp. 261—262. Three other approaches are identified in Donald T. Paris and William Reynolds, *The Logic of Policy Inquiry* (New York: Longman, 1983); they include the behavioral, the economic, and the interpretive approaches.

41. See Janet A. Schneider et al., "Policy Research and Analysis: An Empirical Profile," *Policy Sciences* 15 (1982), pp. 99—114; Susan B. Hansen, "Public Policy Analysis: Some Recent Developments and Current Problems," *Policy Studies Journal* 11 (1983), pp. 14—42; Hedge and Mok, "The Nature of Policy Studies," pp. 49—61; and James M. Rodgers, "Social Science Disciplines and Policy Research: The Case of Political Science," *Policy Studies Review* 9 (1989), pp. 13—28.

42. Hedge and Mok, "The Nature of Policy Studies," pp. 49—61; Schneider et al., "Policy Research and Analysis," pp. 99—114.

43. Yehezkel Dror, "On Becoming More of a Policy Scientist," *Policy Studies Review* 4 (1984), pp. 13—22.

44. Ibid., p. 13.

45. Ibid., p. 14.

46. Ibid.

47. Ibid.

48. Ibid., p. 15.

49. Ibid., p. 19.

50. Ibid., p. 18.

4

Models and Public
Policy Studies

" . . . the major advantage of using formal models is the precision
and clarity of thought which these models require, and the
depth of argument which they allow."

MORRIS FIORINA

Before major development projects are undertaken, builders often construct a scaled-down model of the entire development project so that anyone interested can see beforehand what the project will look like when it is completed. Similarly, to analyze public policy, we often employ certain conceptual tools that help us to visualize reality. Among the conceptual tools that are most common and most useful to the policy analyst are **models** and **typologies.** These mental constructs allow us to better understand the formation or implementation of policies. That is, we need some conception of reality to guide our analysis. According to Thomas Dye, a model is "a simplified representation of some aspect of the real world."[1] Moshe Rubenstein suggests that we frequently use models to "facilitate understanding and enhance prediction."[2] Essentially, a model provides us with a "lay of the land" or a graphical representation of some aspect of the policy process. We are all model builders in the sense that we need to see some sort of pattern in the world around us, and thus we tend to interpret events in terms of a perceived pattern. In this way we *create* reality rather than simply observe it. In this chapter, we discuss various types of models and their usefulness in analyzing public policy.

MODELS

The Uses and Forms of Models

Models help us to "see" an abstraction of reality by indicating relationships among a number of determinants that are thought to cause some phenomenon. Sometimes, models use novel methods of representation, "while at other times models may constrain one's insight on reality."[3] By simplifying policy problems, models help us to better understand reality; on the other hand, they may inherently contribute to a distortion of reality. At any rate, these models may be expressed as concepts, diagrams, graphs, or mathematical equations and may be used to describe, explain, or predict elements of a particular phenomenon. The types of models include descriptive models, normative models, verbal models, symbolic models, procedural models, surrogate models, and perspective models.[4] However, the most common distinctions are between descriptive and normative models, and between "hard" and "soft" models.

Descriptive Models   The purpose of descriptive models is "to explain and/or predict the causes and consequences of policy choices."[5] For example, a model of the determinants of welfare spending in the fifty American states found that economic variables were more important than political variables in explaining variation among the states' spending patterns.[6] Much of the so-called determinants-of-public-policy approach uses descriptive models to explain and predict the causes and consequences of public policy.[7] One of the best-known examples of descriptive models is the Coleman Report, in which various explanations of student performance are assessed against one another.[8] This report found that family background factors, such as the amount of reading material in the home and parents' education, were the most important determinants of student achievement, as opposed to such factors as faculty quality or the amount of resources devoted to the school. In short, descriptive models are very common in public policy literature.

Normative Models   Alternatively, the purpose of normative models is "not only to explain and/or predict but also to provide rules and recommendations for optimizing the attainment of some value."[9] For example, let's say that we are interested in ascertaining the best way to prevent world hunger. We examine several policy options, such as food aid, monetary assistance, birth-control devices, and education, in terms of their contribution to alleviating hunger. We may find that food aid is counterproductive to alleviating hunger; in fact, it may contribute to increased population growth, which in turn increases the amount of hunger. By contrast, birth-control technology and education may be more effective in reducing hunger. Therefore, such a model explains and predicts, as well as suggests, a way to optimize a value—in this case alleviating hunger in the developing world.

Hard and Soft Models   Another useful distinction to be made about models is between those that are "hard," in which "actual phenomena are being symbolized," and those that are "soft," or "representations of purely theoretical or hypothetical conceptual matters of imagined characteristics of some event of our concern."[10] For example, a hard model could be a topographical map that represents the actual geography of the landscape and is accurate (presumably) with respect to reality. On the other hand, a soft model could be a textbook diagram of a political system in which there are inputs, conversion mechanisms, and outputs. The latter is an attempt to take an abstract concept such as a political system and convert it into a series of linkages between these hypothetical elements in the system.

The important thing to remember about models, whether descriptive or normative, hard or soft, is that they are imperfect representations of reality. As such, they may help to guide our thinking and to better understand some phenomenon, but they are still only abstract tools with which to interpret reality.

Criteria for Evaluating Models

How does one know whether models are helping or not? Usefulness, rather than the type of model being used, is the best criterion for evaluating a model. That is, a "good model, like a good map, is rich; it guides us, under suitable interpretation, to many true statements...and facilitates understanding."[11] If we are going to use models when thinking about public policy, then we need to have some criteria for evaluating the usefulness of these models. Thomas Dye has suggested a number of such criteria.[12]

1. Does the model *order* and *simplify* political life so that we can think about it more clearly and understand relationships in the real world? If the model is so simple that it leads to misunderstandings in our thinking about reality, or if it is so complex that it confuses us, then the model may not be of much help in explaining public policy.

2. Does the model *identify* the most important aspects of public policy? The model should focus on the most salient aspects of a political phenomenon, such as the causes or consequences of public policy, and not be concerned with irrelevant variables or conditions. Essentially, the model should direct our attention to what is really significant about public policy.

3. Is the model *congruent with reality?* By this we mean does the model bear a strong relationship to reality, or is it so idealized or abstract that it is unrelated to the real world? A good model should incorporate real-world empirical referents and facilitate a greater understanding of a particular policy situation or process.

4. Does the model *communicate* something meaningful in a way that we all understand? Does the model have the characteristic of intersubjective agreement, in which a concept used in the model is one that we all can understand? If the model communicates a concept for which there is no common understanding, then it is judged to have little intersubjective agreement, and it will not help us better understand a phenomenon.

5. Does the model *direct inquiry and research* into public policy? A good model should suggest a number of testable relationships (hypotheses) that can be observed, measured, and verified. We must be able to apply the model in a way that allows for empirical testing; the model is of little use if there are no testable propositions derived from it or if these relationships cannot be measured and tested with real-world data.

6. Does the model *suggest an explanation* of public policy? A model that merely describes public policy is not as useful as one that explains public policy. Does the model set forth a series of verifiable relationships that add up to a fairly complete explanation of some public policy phenomenon? Two of the best examples of such models are the elitist and pluralist models of community power and public policy.[13]

Some Examples of Models

To better understand the usefulness of models and what constitutes a good model, let's consider two of the best-known models in the public policy literature, the **elitist model** and the **pluralist model.**

The Elitist Model   Elite theory is based on the idea that public policy is the result of the preferences and values of a governing elite.[14] Thomas Dye and Harmon Zeigler summarize the ruling elite model as follows:

1. Society is divided into the few who have power and the many who do not. Only a small number of persons allocate values for society; the masses do not decide public policy.

2. The few who govern are not typical of the masses who are governed. Elites are drawn disproportionately from the upper socioeconomic strata of society.

3. The movement of nonelites to elite positions must be slow and continuous to maintain stability and avoid revolution. Only nonelites who have accepted the basic elite consensus can be admitted to governing circles.

4. Elites share a basic consensus on behalf of the basic values of the social system and the preservation of the system. In America, the bases of elite consensus are the sanctity of private property, limited government, and individual liberty.

5. Public policy does not reflect demands of the masses, but rather the values of the elites. Changes in public policy will be incremental rather than revolutionary.

6. Active elites are subject to relatively little direct influence from apathetic masses. Elites influence masses more than masses influence elites.

7. Thus, public policy is directed from the top to the bottom rather than the reverse. Power flows upward and decisions flow downward.[15] A representation of the elite model is provided in Figure 4.1.

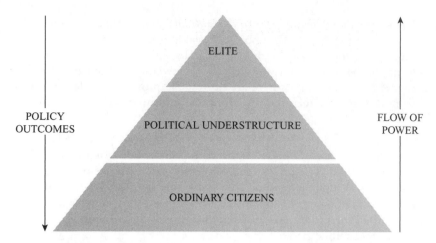

FIGURE 4.1 The Elitist Model.

Some evidence indicates that the elite model is a good characterization of community decision making. Research by Robert and Helen Lynd in the 1920s and the 1930s, as well as Floyd Hunter in the 1960s (and again in the 1980s), found that this model of community power was an accurate representation of reality.[16] Critics of the ruling elite model, however, challenged the empirical findings and put forth their own version of reality in an alternative pluralistic model.[17]

The Pluralist Model   An alternative model of decision making in America is the pluralist model. The proponents of this model of community power and public policy include Robert Dahl and David Truman.[18] It may be briefly summarized as follows:

1. Power is an attribute of individuals in their relationship with other individuals in the process of decision making.

2. Power relationships do not necessarily persist; rather, they are formed for a particular decision. After this decision is made they disappear, to be replaced by a different set of power relationships when the next decision is made.

3. No permanent distinction exists between "elites" and "masses." Individuals who participate in decision making at one time are not necessarily the same individuals who participate at another time. Individuals move in and out of the ranks of decision makers simply by becoming active or inactive in politics.

4. Leadership is fluid and highly mobile. Wealth is an asset in politics, but it is only one of many kinds of assets.

5. There are multiple centers and bases of power within a community. No single group dominates decision making in all issue areas.

6. Considerable competition exists among leaders. Public policy thus reflects bargains or compromises reached between competing leadership groups.

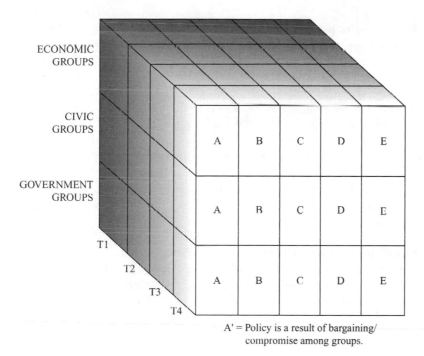

ECONOMIC
GROUPS

CIVIC
GROUPS

GOVERNMENT
GROUPS

T1
T2
T3
T4

A' = Policy is a result of bargaining/
compromise among groups.

FIGURE 4.2 The Pluralist Model.

A representation of the pluralist model is found in Figure 4.2. It is similar to an unsolved Rubik's cube, in which political power is highly fragmented and widely dispersed over different actors, different types of policy, and different points in time.

These are two of the best-known models of public policymaking. They provide us with a mental image of the political processes that characterize public policy. Although both have been criticized for their shortcomings, they remain useful as a means of thinking about how power is distributed in the making of American public policy.[19]

Steps in Building Conceptual Models

How are models developed in the public policy literature? In the following chapters, we present several alternative models of agenda setting, policy formulation, policy implementation, and policy change. It would be useful at this point, however, to begin to understand how these models are derived. We discussed in Chapter 1 the evolutionary process that the public policy literature undergoes over time. A key step in that evolution is model building, in which the builder works with the extant literature, as well as his or her insights, to construct a model of some public policy phenomenon. In constructing a model, one must utilize several distinct steps. According to Dubnick and Bardes, these steps include the following:[20]

Step 1. Examine the problematic phenomenon or situation carefully and proceed to factor (i.e., divide) it into simpler, more manageable problems.[21]   One cannot tackle all public policy problems at once; rather, one must define the dependent variable (what one is seeking to explain) very carefully and precisely. For example, a policy analyst might be interested in explaining what factors influence policy implementation or policy termination. She might want to develop a model that explains the changes in public policy over time, or she might be interested in explaining environmental policy formation. She probably could not, on the other hand, develop a model that at once explains the entire policy process. Some models are more comprehensive than others, but one must be careful to avoid trying to tackle too much with a single model. Parsimony, or the ability to explain the most with the least, is a useful guide in the construction of policy models.

Step 2. Establish the purpose of the model.   What is the model supposed to do? Is it a descriptive or a normative model? That is, does it seek to predict and explain? Does it seek to prescribe policy solutions? No single model is expected to do everything. Rather, one should decide what kind of a model one is seeking to construct and define the model's objectives very carefully. How will the model be used by others?

Step 3. Observe facts relevant to the problematic phenomenon or situation.   The best way to begin at this stage is to read all that has been written about a particular policy phenomenon. Usually, the extant literature is based on case studies about the determinants of some phenomenon. By accumulating these materials, one may be able to begin to piece together multiple explanations about this behavior. As one becomes familiar with the causes and effects of this phenomenon, a pattern will emerge that will lead one to later construct a model.

Step 4. List the elements that may relate to the model's purpose. Select those that are believed to be the most relevant to the problem at hand. Arrange these relevant elements into chunks or clusters that reflect strong structural, functional, or interactive connections.   For example, one may be interested in explaining the utilization of policy analysis by decision makers. The existing literature suggests three broad categories of factors that determine the degree of knowledge utilization: (1) factors related to the environment within which the policy analysis takes place, (2) factors related to the policy analysis itself, and (3) factors related to the potential users of this information.

These three categories of factors may be identified, and together they suggest a testable explanation of this particular phenomenon.

Step 5. Consider these aggregates and the facts they represent relative to the purpose of the proposed model. Try to find patterns or relationships among these factors that will aid in fulfilling that purpose.   This is the most creative part of model building. In this stage, one is looking for the pattern of interrelationships that characterize the model. In the earlier stage, one was simply trying to identify all the kinds of factors that explained the phenomenon, whereas at this stage one is looking for interactions in the categories of factors identified earlier. For example, a well-known model of political development hypothesizes that urbanization leads to industrialization and education, which in turn leads to political development. In this stage causes and effects are very important, in the sense that some of the factors identified earlier will precede others and cause certain effects. Every relationship identified here is a theoretical statement in the policy analyst's model, so he or she should be careful and have strong evidence to support the posited relationships.

Step 6. Elaborate on the constructed model where necessary and simplify where possible.   In working with the constructed model, one will begin to see the need for minor corrections and alterations. These alterations may be based on actual tests of the model, from additional fieldwork that identifies "left-out" variables, or they may be a function of subtleties in the original design that were overlooked in developing the model. At any rate, it is likely (and even desirable) that the policy analyst will make changes in his or her model on the basis of experience with it. These refinements may also come from work by others who use the model in their studies of public policy.

In sum, model construction is crucial to the advancement of public policy studies; indeed, it is a key stage in the evolution of the subfield.

TYPOLOGIES

In addition to models, **typologies** are sometimes used to analyze public policy. A typology is a way of organizing phenomena into discrete categories for systematic analysis. For example, in 1964, Theodore Lowi proposed a typology that he thought would facilitate the understanding of public policymaking.[22] He argued that what was needed was a general framework that could convert discrete facts from case studies into a body of research that could be evaluated, weighed, and cumulated. His main thesis was that a political relationship in policymaking is determined by the type of policy at stake; that is, every type of policy has a distinctive type of political relationship. In developing this typology, he argued that public policy may be categorized into three types: regulatory, distributive, and redistributive.

Regulatory policies attempt to limit the number of specific service providers (e.g., airline regulations) or to protect the public by setting forth conditions under which private activities may occur (e.g., environmental regulation). Essentially, regulatory policy involves a direct choice as to who will be indulged and who will be deprived. Because of this, various groups will engage in conflict, bargaining, and negotiation over who should win and who should lose.

Distributive policies are those policies that are aimed at promoting, usually through subsidies, private activities that are judged to be socially desirable. This type of public policy does not have winners or losers; there is no direct confrontation, and everybody benefits equally (e.g., educational policy).

Finally, redistributive policies are an effort to distribute wealth or other valued goods in society. Essentially, these policies redistribute benefits from one group to another (e.g., welfare policy). Therefore, redistributive policy tends to be characterized by ideological concerns and often involves class conflict.

Lowi argues that these three areas of policy or government activity constitute real "arenas of power." Each arena tends to develop its own characteristic political structure, political process, elites, and group relations (i.e., its own politics). For example, regulatory policy is characterized by coalitions of interest groups that are often in conflict with each other and are very unstable as they seek to bargain and compromise. Thus, pluralism characterizes this arena of power. In the distributive policy arena, decisions are characterized by logrolling rather than conflict; power relations are stable, and there is very little conflict. The elitist model thus characterizes this arena of power. Finally, in redistributive policy there is much conflict, but it is more likely to take place among elite organizations. Lowi's major contribution was to suggest that we cannot generalize across all types of policy with a single model (e.g., elitist or pluralist). Rather, we should focus our investigation within a particular type of policy and develop generalizations by policy type as opposed to broad generalizations that are expected to hold across the entire range of public policy.

The Lowi typology has been criticized on several grounds. Some argue that it is difficult to separate regulatory from distributive and redistributive policy.[23] Moreover, policy is more complex than Lowi's simple typology, as policies often start out as one type of policy and then become another. Recently some defenders of the Lowi typology have asserted, on the other hand, that his typology retains its usefulness if we think of it as a continuum rather than discrete categories. Some policies are more purely regulatory than are others (e.g., crime policy), and some policies are more purely redistributive than are others (e.g., progressive income tax).[24] Nevertheless, today the Lowi typology remains one of the most useful conceptual tools in the study of public policy and has been applied very creatively over the past three decades.[25]

In addition, other scholars have developed typologies that categorize public policies. For example, Mancur Olson distinguishes between public goods and private goods.[26] Public goods are those goods that are available to everyone, and no one may be excluded from their use, whereas private goods are divisible, in the sense that others may be kept from benefiting from their use or be charged for benefiting from their use. Lewis Froman also developed a means for distinguishing policies from one another. He differentiates between policies that are areal and those that are segmental.[27] Areal policies are those that affect the total population of a geographical area by a single policy, whereas segmental policies are those that affect different people at different times in separate areas of a population. Similarly, Eulau and Eyestone distinguish between adaptive and control policies.[28] Adaptive policies are policies that are designed to meet the needs of a group, whereas control policies are those that attempt to direct the environment. In summary, these policy typologies are meant to be helpful as one begins to analyze public policy. Whether they help or not has a lot to do with several evaluative considerations.

Criteria for Evaluating Typologies

How does one know whether a typology is a useful one? How does one evaluate typologies? Although it is difficult to evaluate typologies in any comprehensive way, Lewis Froman has proposed a number of criteria for doing so.[29] Among these criteria are the following:

1. *Inclusiveness.* Does the scheme cover all possible forms of the phenomenon in its categories? In other words, have all dimensions of this phenomenon been included within the typology? Is the typology comprehensive?

2. *Mutual exclusivity.* Are the separate categories within the typology distinct so as to avoid overlap? Are the categories distinct from one another in such a way as to facilitate placement into one category or another?

3. *Validity.* Do the concepts used in the typology measure what they say they measure? For example, what is meant by a federal, state, or local policy? Are not public policies often a mixture of all three levels of government? Is there a close fit between the typology and the empirical world that it purports to measure?

4. *Reliability.* Can the typology be used by others in a consistent manner? Does the typology have the characteristic of "intersubjectiveness," or the trait that implies everyone will use the typology in the same, or nearly the same, way?

5. *Level of measurement.* Does the typology employ an appropriate level of measurement? For example, nominal-level measurement is used to classify cases; ordinal-level measurement is used to order cases; and interval-level data are used for more specific differentiation between items on a scale of measurement.

6. *Operationalization.* Can a phenomenon be measured by a set of attributes? Does the typology lend itself to being measured? Can the concepts used in the typology be measured?

7. *Differentiation.* Are the categories being used in the typology significant and theoretically fruitful?

WHERE DO WE GO FROM HERE?

In the first section of this book, we have introduced students to the context of public policy studies. To gain some perspective on the study of public policy, we examined how the subject has evolved over time, paying particular attention to the evolutionary process by which the literature and subject matter develop. Many approaches may be used to study public policy, and the choice over the single "best" approach must be left to the student's discretion. One of the most useful approaches is the policy process approach, in which we study agenda setting, policy formulation, policy implementation, policy evaluation, policy termination, and policy change. This is the approach that guides the next section of this text.

We will examine the evolution of the public policy literature in each of these areas of the policy process, paying particular attention to how this literature has developed over time.

At the moment, a lively debate characterizes the policy studies field over the most appropriate approach (the positivists versus the post-positivists) to the analysis of public policy. Implicit in this book is a bias toward the positivist approach, though we also recognize that more intuitive and qualitative approaches have merits as well.[30] The policy process is terribly complex, but we will attempt to make some sense of it by working with prevailing models of each aspect of the process. Thus, we introduced the topic of models in order to help us understand the policy process. In the following section, we examine how these models help us to understand agenda setting, policy formulation, policy implementation, and policy change. In some areas of the policy process, the available literature is less developed (e.g., policy evaluation and policy termination) in terms of model building. Nevertheless, the stage has been set for a thorough review of the evolution of thought in several phases of the policy process. By remembering that policy studies are constantly evolving, one begins to appreciate how the knowledge base (both substantive and procedural) expands over time. Based on substantive analyses, one also develops a better understanding of how the process works. In doing so, one also acquires some means of affecting policy outcomes over time.

DISCUSSION QUESTIONS

1. Using your hometown as a case study, what model, elite or pluralist, best describes power in your community? Who are the key "movers and shakers" in the economic, social, and political realms?

2. Many would argue that American politics is best characterized as pluralistic. Do you agree? Assuming that is the case, does pluralism guarantee that democracy in America works as it should?

3. Develop a model of the causes and consequences of poverty in America. What assumptions would that model reflect? What are some of the more important causes and consequences that you would include in your model?

SUGGESTED READINGS

Dahl, Robert A. *Who Governs?* (New Haven, CT: Yale University Press, 1961).

Dye, Thomas R., and Harmon Zeigler. *The Irony of Democracy* (Monterey, CA: Brooks/ Cole, 1981).

Lowi, Theodore. *The End of Liberalism* (New York: W. W. Norton, 1969).

Portney, Kent. *Approaching Public Policy Analysis* (Englewood Cliffs, NJ: Prentice Hall, 1986).

Ripley, Randall, and Grace Franklin. *Congress, the Bureaucracy, and Public Policy* (Homewood, IL: Dorsey Press, 1980).

Sabatier, Paul. *Theories of the Policy Process* (Boulder, CO: Westview Press, 1999).

NOTES

1. Thomas R. Dye, *Understanding Public Policy*, 8th ed. (Englewood Cliffs, NJ: Prentice Hall, 1995), p. 18.

2. Moshe F. Rubenstein, *Patterns of Problem Solving* (Englewood Cliffs, NJ: Prentice Hall, 1975), p. 19.

3. Stephen Toulmin, *The Philosophy of Science: An Introduction* (New York: Harper and Row, 1960), pp. 34–35.

4. William N. Dunn, *Public Policy Analysis: An Introduction* (Englewood Cliffs, NJ: Prentice Hall, 1981), pp. 110–118.

5. Ibid., p. 111.

6. Richard E. Dawson and James A. Robinson, "Inter-Party Competition, Economic Variables, and Welfare Policies in the American States," *Journal of Politics* 25, no. 2 (May 1963), pp. 265–289.

7. See Kent E. Portney, *Approaching Public Policy Analysis* (Englewood Cliffs, NJ: Prentice Hall, 1986).

8. James S. Coleman, *Equality of Educational Opportunity* (Washington, D.C.: U.S. Government Printing Office, 1966).

9. Dunn, *Public Policy Analysis*, p. 111.

10. Marc Belth, *The Process of Thinking* (New York: David McKay, 1977), pp. 15–19.

11. David Hawkins, *The Language of Nature: An Essay in the Philosophy of Science* (Garden City, NY: Doubleday, 1967), pp. 38–39.

12. Dye, *Understanding Public Policy*, pp. 40–41; see also Daniel C. McCool, *Public Policy Theories, Models, and Concepts* (Englewood Cliffs, NJ: Prentice Hall, 1995), pp. 12–18.

13. Thomas R. Dye and Harmon Zeigler, *The Irony of Democracy* (Monterey, CA: Brooks/Cole, 1981).

14. Thomas R. Dye, *Understanding Public Policy*, 6th ed. (Englewood Cliffs, NJ: Prentice Hall, 1987), p. 29.

15. Dye and Zeigler, *The Irony of Democracy*.

16. Robert S. Lynd and Helen M. Lynd, *Middletown* (New York: Harcourt Brace, 1929) and *Middletown in Transition* (New York: Harcourt Brace, 1937). See also Floyd Hunter, *Community Power Structure* (Chapel Hill: University of North Carolina Press, 1969); and Floyd Hunter, *Community Power Succession: Atlanta's Policy-Makers Revisited* (Chapel Hill: University of North Carolina Press, 1980).

17. Robert Dahl, *Who Governs* (New Haven, CT: Yale University Press, 1961).

18. David B. Truman, *The Governmental Process* (New York: Knopf, 1951); and Dahl, *Who Governs*.

19. See Robert A. Dahl, "A Critique of the Ruling Elite Model," *American Political Science Review* 52, no. 2 (June 1958), pp. 463–469; Peter Bachrach and Morton S.

Baratz, "The Two Faces of Power," *American Political Science Review* 66, no. 4 (December 1962), pp. 947–952; Theodore Lowi, *The End of Liberalism* (New York: W. W. Norton, 1969); see also Clarence Stone, "Systemic Power in Community Decision-Making," *American Political Science Review* 74, no. 4 (December 1980), pp. 978–990.

20. Melvin J. Dubnick and Barbara A. Bardes, *Thinking About Public Policy: A Problem-Solving Approach* (New York: Wiley, 1983), pp. 44–48.

21. The following six steps draw heavily from William T. Morris, "On the Art of Modeling," in *The Process of Model-Building in the Behavioral Sciences*, ed. Ralph M. Stogdill (New York: W. W. Norton, 1970), pp. 83–84.

22. Theodore Lowi, "American Business, Public Policy, Case Studies, and Political Theory," *World Politics* 16 (July 1964), pp. 677–715.

23. See G. D. Greenberg et al., "Developing Public Policy Theory: Perspectives from Empirical Research," *American Political Science Review* 71, no. 4 (December 1977), pp. 1532–1543.

24. Robert Spitzer, "Promoting Policy Theory: Revising the Arenas of Power," *Policy Studies Journal* 15, no. 4 (June 1987), pp. 675–689.

25. See Randall Ripley and Grace Franklin, *Congress, the Bureaucracy, and Public Policy* (Homewood, IL: Dorsey Press, 1980).

26. Mancur Olson, *The Logic of Collective Action* (Cambridge, MA: Harvard University Press, 1965).

27. Lewis Froman, "An Analysis of Public Policy in Cities," *Journal of Politics* 29, no. 1 (February 1967), pp. 94–108.

28. Heinz Eulau and Robert Eyestone, "Policy Maps of City Councils and Policy Outcomes," *American Political Science Review* 62, no. 1 (March 1968), pp. 124–143.

29. Lewis Froman, "The Categorization of Policy Contents," in *Political Science and Public Policy,* ed. Austin Ranney (Chicago: Markham, 1968), pp. 46–48.

30. On this point, see Edward O. Wilson, *Consilience: The Unity of Knowledge* (New York: Alfred A. Knopf, 1998), esp. pp. 266–298.

PART II

Analysis in the Policy Process

5

Agenda Setting

"We know more about how issues are disposed of than about how
they came to be issues on the governmental agenda in the first place,
how the alternatives from which decision makers choose were
generated, and why some potential issues and some likely alternatives
never came to be the focus of serious attention."
JOHN W. KINGDON

Where do public policy proposals come from? Why do decision makers pay
more attention to some issues than to others? In this chapter, we begin an
analysis of the policymaking process as a series of developmental stages. Before we
begin this analysis, we need to define a couple of terms. **Policy formation** means
the total process of creating or forming a public policy, whereas **policy formulation** refers to the more discrete stage of adopting a proposed course of action for
dealing with a public problem.[1]

Until the past few decades, most public policy research focused on the policy
adoption aspect of the policy cycle. This phase of the policy cycle was the first to
be explored by researchers. Many models were developed to explain policy adoption. Now, more emphasis has been placed on how issues get onto the agenda in
the first place. Why are some issues more likely to get onto the agenda than
others? This is a key aspect of the policy cycle and an extremely important
one. In answering this question, it seems that several conditions must be met
in order for issues to get onto the agenda. An issue will receive attention if

1. it has reached *crisis proportions* and can no longer be ignored;

2. it has achieved *particularity,* in which the issue exemplifies and dramatizes a larger issue, such as ozone depletion and global warming;

3. it has an *emotive* aspect, or attracts media attention because of a "human interest angle";

4. it has *wide impact;*

5. it raises questions about *power and legitimacy* in society; and

6. it is *fashionable.*[2]

All these factors seem to be necessary conditions for an item to be placed on the agenda. Still, we need to explore these conditions (and others) in greater depth. In this initial chapter on the policy process, we will examine how policies get onto the public, or governmental, agenda. Agenda setting is crucial, because if an issue cannot be placed on the agenda, it cannot be considered for action. Problems must be recognized before a policy choice can be made.

Cobb and Elder define **agenda setting** as "a set of political controversies that will be viewed as falling within the range of legitimate concerns meriting the attention of the polity; a set of items scheduled for active and serious attention by a decision-making body."[3] Others, such as John Kingdon, define agenda setting as "the list of subjects or problems to which government officials...are paying some serious attention at any given time."[4] Still others, such as Baumgartner and Jones, distinguish between "policy images" (how policies are understood and discussed) and "policy venues" (the institutions or groups that have the jurisdictional authority over the issue).[5] The process of agenda setting, according to Barbara Nelson, is that in which "public officials learn about new problems, decide to give them their personal attention, and mobilize their organizations to respond to them."[6] Essentially, agenda setting involves getting an issue to be recognized. Each stage of the policy process is theoretically distinct, but stages nevertheless merge in practice. For example, the nature of the problem affects whether it gets onto the agenda, as well as whether a course of action finally gets enacted into law. Generally speaking, once a proposal is before Congress in the form of a proposed bill, it may be said to be on the agenda. Let us examine agenda setting in a bit more depth.

THE NATURE OF POLICY PROBLEMS

A **policy problem** may be defined as a "condition or situation that produces needs or dissatisfaction on the part of people for which relief or redress is sought."[7] In effect, the tractability of public policy problems varies greatly. Some public policy problems are very easy to define and solve, such as energy conservation; others, such as reducing crime, are more difficult to assess and diagnose. Consider, for example, the following list of public policy problems Kirkpatrick Sale has identified:

> An imperiled ecology, a deepening suspicion of authority and distrust of established institutions, the decline of community, a contempt for law, deteriorating cities, megalopolitan sprawls, ghettoes, overcrowding, traffic congestion, untreated wastes, smog and soot, budgetary insolvency, inadequate schools, mounting illiteracy, declining university standards, dehumanizing welfare systems, police brutality, overcrowded hospitals, clogged court calendars, inhuman prisons, racial injustice, sex discrimination, poverty, crime, alcoholism, divorce, violence, defense overspending, nuclear proliferation, the arms race, unemployment, inflation, the energy crisis, mounting personal debt, mal-distribution of wealth, worldwide inflation, international instability, and the end of the American imperial arrangement, to name a few.[8]

The personal debt problem, for example, may be remedied much more easily than the crime problem or the poverty problem. In many areas of public policy, policy analysts simply do not know how to "solve" the problem with an appropriate policy solution. This is primarily because they often do not understand the cause-and-effect relationship between the problem and its policy solution. Cause and effect are open to interpretation and widely different perceptions. Policy analysts must consider the characteristics and dimensions of the problems if they are to be helpful in designing effective solutions. Yet, many problems are taken as "givens" and little attention is directed toward understanding the problem in the first place. The ongoing debate on welfare policy illustrates this. Michael Harrington's *The Other America* and his more recent book, *Poverty in America,* argue that poverty is "caused" by external or structural factors, such as changes in employment opportunities. Charles Murray, in *Losing Ground,* argues on the other hand that poverty is "caused" by the country's current welfare programs, which offer more incentives to remain on welfare than to get off of it. Others, such as Edward Banfield, argue that individual shortcomings predispose some to a life of poverty, rather than a hostile external environment or structural determinants of poverty.[9]

As the understanding of a problem develops over time, the problem is often defined very differently. For example, until quite recently a reactive policy response to the environmental problem was pursued. Some environmental problem, such as toxic waste, would be identified; and a response to it would be formulated. The passage of the Comprehensive Environmental Response, Compensation, and Liability Act of 1980 (CERCLA), or Superfund, is an example of this kind of strategy. More recently, policymakers are attempting to design environmental policies that are *preventive,* rather than reactive, in nature. They are attempting to anticipate the problem and prevent the buildup of pollutants rather than clean up after the fact. The passage of the Pollution Prevention Act of 1990 is an example of this preventive strategy.

Policy problems are continually being redefined on the basis of new information or a new understanding of the problem. The recent and emerging concern for wetlands is a good example of this phenomenon. In addition, several types of agendas exist to deal with these policy problems.

TYPES OF AGENDAS

Cobb and Elder distinguish several types of agendas, including **systemic agendas** and **institutional agendas.** Systemic agendas consist of all those issues that might be subject to action or that are already being acted on by government. These issues can include pseudo-issues, or issues discussed just to placate clientele groups but without any serious attempt to make policy choices. Systemic agendas include the universe of issues that might be considered for governmental action, whereas institutional agendas are those sets of issues explicitly up for active and serious consideration by decision-making bodies, such as the legislative calendar or the court docket.[10] The institutional agenda is also referred to as the **public agenda**—as opposed to the **popular agenda** (another name for the systemic agenda), which consists of all the issues under consideration by the mass public or professional class.[11] Thus, there are two types of agendas, depending on whether the issues have been formally placed on the public agenda or are merely being discussed in the background and waiting to be placed on the institutional agenda.

TYPES OF ISSUES

Many types of issues are placed on the systemic or institutional agendas. For example, **subject issues** are relatively broad, such as air pollution, water pollution, or health-care issues. Issues surrounding specific legislation, such as the No Child Left Behind Act of 2001 or the Medicare Prescription Drug Act of 2003, are called **policy** issues. **Project issues** relate to a specific project or locality, such as the Denver International Airport issue.[12]

New issues are those that are newly emergent, such as radon and indoor air-pollution issues. **Cyclical issues,** such as the annual budget, occur regularly. Finally, **recurrent issues,** such as health care issues, reemerge because of the seeming failure of previous policy choices.[13]

Now that we have discussed various types of agendas and various types of issues, it is useful to discuss the evolution of the literature on the agenda-setting process. Through this brief review, we may appreciate how our conceptual understanding of this stage of the policy cycle has developed over time.

EVOLUTION OF THE LITERATURE
ON THE AGENDA-SETTING PROCESS

In the early 1970s, the first important work on agenda setting defined the agenda-setting process as a link between mass participation and elite decision making.[14] This research sought to explain the movement of an issue from the systemic agenda to the formal or institutional agenda. The fundamental proposition was that the greater the size of the audience to which an issue may be appealed, the greater the likelihood that the issue will attain status on the systemic agenda and later move to the formal or institutional agenda. Essentially, the process is based on the fundamental assumption that if the issue has several characteristics, such as specificity, social significance, temporal relevance, complexity, or categorical precedence, then it will be more easily expanded to a larger audience and hence have a much better chance of reaching the formal or institutional agenda.[15] Specificity refers to how abstractly or concretely an issue is defined. The more broadly an issue is defined, the greater the likelihood that the issue will remain on the institutional agenda. For example, the issue of toxic waste has been linked broadly with human health as well as environmental issues. Social significance refers to whether an issue is peculiar to the immediate disputants or has more general significance. The battle for school desegregation, for example, was couched in terms of suits between the parents of individual students and local school boards; but these individual suits were part of a larger picture of massive social change. Temporal relevance reflects the extent to which an issue has short-range, circumstantial importance or whether it represents more enduring, fundamental concerns. If an issue contains implications for the management of problems that go beyond the conduct of current program activities, then the issue has a greater likelihood of remaining on the institutional agenda. For problems to be considered temporally relevant, they must have a potential effect on future generations. Complexity refers to how an issue is delineated along a continuum from the highly complex to the simple and easily understood. The less the complexity, the greater the likelihood an issue will remain on the institutional agenda. Finally, categorical precedence refers to the extent to which an issue is a routine matter with clear precedent or whether it is extraordinary, with no clear precedent. The more an issue is defined as lacking a clear precedent, the greater the likelihood that the issue will remain on the institutional agenda. The issue of acid rain, for example, had no clear precedent in the Clean Air Act of 1970 and the amendments of 1977.

Before an issue reaches the institutional agenda, it must reach the systemic agenda. According to Cobb and Elder, three prerequisites were thought to be necessary for an issue to first obtain status on the systemic agenda: (1) widespread attention to, or at least awareness of, the issue; (2) a shared concern of a sizable portion of the public that some type of action is needed to remedy this problem; and (3) a shared perception that the matter is an appropriate concern of some governmental unit and falls within the bounds of its authority.

A second major contribution to the understanding of the agenda-setting process was offered by Davies.[16] He argued that the agenda-setting process consisted of three phases: (1) initiation, (2) diffusion, and (3) processing. In the initiation stage, a public problem creates a demand for action. In the diffusion stage, these demands are transposed into issues for government. In the processing stage, issues are converted into agenda items. A central part of Davies' argument was that the type of issue was an important determinant affecting whether an issue became (or failed to become) an agenda item. Davies also argued that many issues were initiated within government itself, contrary to the common assumption that issues arose within the general public and worked their way onto the governmental agenda.[17]

The next major contribution to this area of research came from Cobb, Ross, and Ross, in which they identified three different models of agenda setting.[18] Their first model was the outside initiative model, which was very similar to the original model proposed by Cobb and Elder. Their second model was the mobilization model, where issues were initiated inside government and eventually achieved agenda status. This second model was similar to the one suggested earlier by Davies. Their third model was called the inside initiative model, which described a process whereby issues arose within government but were not expanded to the general public. The issues' supporters desired to keep the issues within the governmental arena exclusively.[19]

Yet another major contribution to this literature was made by Barbara Nelson. According to Nelson, the process of agenda setting may be divided into four discrete stages:

1. issue recognition,
2. issue adoption,
3. issue prioritization, and
4. issue maintenance.[20]

In the issue recognition phase, a problem is first noticed and then perceived to have potential for governmental action. In this phase, the issue must be important enough for governmental actors to seriously consider. In the issue adoption phase, the decision is made to respond (or not to respond) to the public policy problem. The primary concerns are whether there is a perception that the government has a legitimate responsibility to act on this issue, and whether an appropriate response is available. If the problem is adopted as a potential issue, then the agenda must be reordered to accommodate the new issue, which is the focus of the prioritization phase. Essentially, the new issue must be viewed within the context of other older issues already on the agenda. In the issue maintenance phase, the issue advances to the stage of decision making. Proposals are put forth to be considered by the decision makers. As long as these proposals are being considered, the issue has been maintained on the institutional agenda. If the issue fails to retain interest by the decision makers, then the issue no longer is maintained on the agenda.

Nelson's first stage corresponded to what had been viewed as agenda setting in previous works. Her remaining three stages added new materials to the understanding of the agenda-setting process. She argued that two conditions had to be present for an issue to achieve issue adoption: (1) a shared perception of the legitimacy of government responsibility for action on the issue, and (2) a belief that an appropriate response could be found if the issue were to be adopted for consideration by government actors.[21] She expanded the understanding of the process by making some careful distinctions about the process itself and building on the works of those before her.

Perhaps the most extensive work on the topic of agenda setting is by John Kingdon. His view of the process is by far the most comprehensive to date.

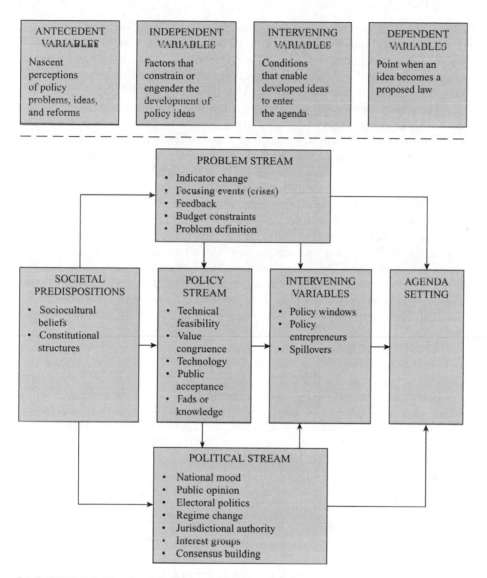

ANTECEDENT VARIABLES	INDEPENDENT VARIABLES	INTERVENING VARIABLES	DEPENDENT VARIABLES
Nascent perceptions of policy problems, ideas, and reforms	Factors that constrain or engender the development of policy ideas	Conditions that enable developed ideas to enter the agenda	Point when an idea becomes a proposed law

FIGURE 5.1 The Agenda-Setting Process: A Model.

SOURCE: John W. Kingdon, *Agendas, Alternatives, and Public Policies.* Copyright © 1984 by John W. Kingdon. Reprinted by permission of Pearson Education, Inc.

Figure 5.1 illustrates his view of the agenda–setting process. His conceptual model is based on the notion of three "streams" of information: (1) the problem stream, (2) the policy stream, and (3) the political stream.[22] The **problem stream** is concerned with the definition of the problem to be addressed. It includes such things as crisis events that focus attention on the problem, budgetary constraints, and how the problem is conceptualized in the first place. For example, the Love Canal crisis in 1978 focused attention on the toxic waste issue. In that case, the discovery that

21,000 tons of hazardous chemicals deposited decades earlier were leaching into the groundwater and into the property and homes around the canal was the crisis. It was officially recognized as such when President Carter declared Love Canal a national emergency, and when a preliminary study of health problems that might have been caused by the chemicals was leaked to the *New York Times*.

The **policy stream** has to do with the technical feasibility of dealing with the problem, the availability of technology to deal with it, and the public degree of acceptance of a solution, among other things. Essentially, the policy stream includes various proposals that are developed to deal with the issue, usually in the form of legislation. Although the study of the Love Canal situation yielded inadequate evidence to conclude that the chemicals had led to health problems among residents, a perception of government insensitivity led to President Carter's decision to relocate 710 persons.

The **political stream** has to do with the politics affecting the solution to the issue. This includes such considerations as the national mood, public opinion, electoral politics, and interest-group activity. When these three streams come together, "policy windows" of opportunity are opened. In addition, policy entrepreneurs "are responsible not only for prompting important people to pay attention, but also for coupling solutions to problems and for coupling both problems and solutions to politics."[23] In the Love Canal case, the ultimate solution was new environmental legislation to clean up abandoned hazardous waste sites.[24]

Prior to these three streams are "societal predispositions" (values, political culture, etc.), which set the context for issues getting on the agenda. Finally, such things as "spillovers" affect agenda status as well. Spillovers are situations in which an issue from one area affects another issue's ability to get onto the agenda.

Simply put, there are times when issues are "ripe" for solutions. And there are individuals, such as a key congressperson or president, who can move an issue to agenda status by virtue of their political clout in the decisional arena. Sometimes, spillovers from other policy areas affect agenda status as well. For example, the issue of dumping wastes at sea affected the status of burning wastes at sea. The former issue affected the latter issue by sensitizing the public to the potential for harm. (Chapter 9 explores this example in greater depth.)

WHO SETS AGENDAS?

Concurrent with these frameworks for understanding agenda setting, various explanations have been advanced about just who sets agendas. These explanations include (1) the elitist argument, (2) the pluralist argument, and (3) the subgovernment argument.

The Elitist Perspective

The elitist argument assumes the existence of a power elite that dominates public decision making. It argues that these elites (including business, military, and political elites) set the agendas. At any one time, one of these elite groups is dominant.

For example, in the period following the Civil War, business-sector elites were dominant in agenda setting; in the New Deal era, politicians were dominant, and in the 1950s, the military elites were dominant.[25] A variant of this perspective—the neo-Marxist view—assumes that the dominant actors placing items on the agenda are the capitalists. These capitalists are believed to be in collusion with big labor against the interests of "the people" and are thus able to control policymaking by government. We have discussed the elitist model in the previous chapter, and Figure 4.1 illustrates this perspective.

The Pluralist Perspective

A second argument is that interest groups dominate the agenda-setting process. It sees the agenda-setting process as reacting to the activity expressed by dominant interest groups. These interest groups identify problems and then apply pressure to have them placed on the public agenda or to oppose their being placed on the agenda. The pluralist perspective was described in Chapter 4 and is illustrated in Figure 4.2.

The Subgovernment Perspective

A third perspective on who sets the public agenda assumes that it is shaped by three sets of actors: (1) key congresspersons on select committees dealing with the issue; (2) agency bureaucrats responsible for the policy in question; and (3) clientele groups with a stake in the issue. The term *subgovernment* was originally coined by Douglas Cater.[26] Other terms for this phenomenon include *subsystem, iron triangle,* and *cozy little triangle.* Cater used *subgovernment* in describing networks of key actors that determined America's policy on sugar import quotas. He discovered that an interlocking network of specialized congressional committees, middle-level executive branch bureaus, and powerful commercial interest groups together hammered out U.S. policy in this area. According to this argument, a subgovernment will likely evolve under these conditions: (1) a relatively narrow policy field; (2) specialized congressional committees responsible for that field and deferred to by the rest of Congress; (3) unequally equipped interest groups in the field, plus general apathy on the subject among the public; and (4) relatively autonomous bureaucratic agencies able to cultivate ties of their own outside the executive branch of government.[27]

The interest groups most capable of cultivating such intimate relationships with Senate and House committees and their bureau counterparts are those possessing at least the following attributes: (1) a clearly defined stake in the field of interest; (2) legitimacy in the eyes of congressional committee members; (3) money enough to afford offices in Washington and staffs able to conduct research of use to the committee's work; (4) additional funds with which to support individual committee members' election (and reelection) campaigns; and (5) organizational bases at the local level and elsewhere from which the committee members are drawn (e.g., clubs, business firms).[28] Essentially, the subgovernment arrangement works by a series of "exchange relationships," whereby favorable

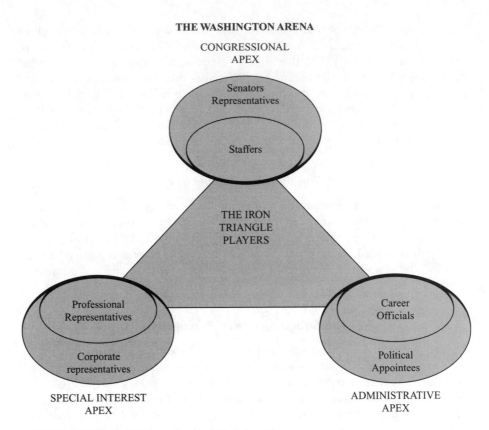

FIGURE 5.2 The Subgovernment Model.

votes for the clientele groups are traded for campaign contributions for congresspersons, information from agency officials to congresspersons is traded for favorable appropriations to the agency from Congress, and personnel exchanges occur between the clientele groups and the agency (i.e., many agency representatives later go to work for the very clientele groups they previously regulated). Figure 5.2 illustrates this perspective. A good example of a subgovernment is the relationships among the Bureau of Land Management (BLM), Western cattlemen's associations, and congressional committees made up of Western representatives who are beholden to the cattle industry. It is argued that these three groups have protected cattle grazing on public lands and kept the grazing fees quite low.[29]

SUMMARY

Who sets agendas can best be explained by examining individual issue areas at specific points in time. For example, energy policy in the 1960s may best be explained by an elitist model; educational policy in the 1970s by a pluralistic model; and environmental policy in the 1980s by a subgovernmental model. Today an interest group model best describes social security reform and educational policy. In addition, as issues evolve over time and expand to include more public awareness and greater public attention, the scope and level of participation in agenda setting may evolve from elite-dominated, to subgovernment, to interest-group models. The key point is that as issues evolve, the participants involved with an issue change over time.

The framework developed by John Kingdon contains all three perspectives. Elite involvement in agenda setting is represented in the concepts of policy stream and policy entrepreneurs. The pluralist perspective is reflected in Kingdon's political stream, and the subgovernmental perspective covers both the political stream and policy entrepreneurs.

CASE STUDIES

The following two case studies of agenda setting illustrate many of the points made in the preceding discussion. Using John Kingdon's model of agenda setting, we first explore the issue of toxic waste cleanup at Love Canal, and the enactment of the Superfund (or the Comprehensive Environmental Response, Compensation, and Liability Act of 1980). Next, we explore the case of acid rain legislation that culminated in the passage of the Clean Air Act Amendments in 1990. These two case studies of agenda setting are useful in illustrating how an issue rises to the top of the policy agenda and becomes the basis for a new law.

Superfund

The Problem Stream   The problem stream, according to Kingdon's model, is concerned with how problems come to be recognized and how conditions come to be defined as problems. "Problems are brought to the attention of people in and around government by systematic indicators, by focusing events like crises and disasters, or by feedback from the operation of current programs."[30] Essentially, the release of hazardous waste from abandoned and inactive sites was brought to the attention of governmental decision makers by the disaster at Love Canal in 1978 and by the feedback from existing legislation. Love Canal was a community of 239 families whose homes were built within the area of a 21,000-ton chemical waste site.[31] As early as 1942, Hooker Chemical Company, the original owner of Love Canal, began disposing of more than eighty compounds of chemicals in the abandoned Love Canal. In 1952, the Niagara Falls Board of Education bought land from Hooker for the sum of $1.00, and in 1954, the 99th Street School was built on the old site.[32] By 1959, there were reports of children being burned while playing near the Canal. In the 1960s, residents reported black sludge appearing on their basement walls, apparently coming from the waste site. The New York State Department of Environmental Conservation and the city of Niagara Falls conducted a number of inspections between 1976 and 1977, and they concluded that "a serious health hazard may exist in the area as a consequence of leaking chemicals."[33] These studies were severely criticized by Lois Gibbs, the president of the Love Canal Homeowners Association, for being done too quickly and for not recognizing what she and others thought was a much more serious problem than what was being reported by the state and local authorities. This crisis escalated during 1979 and 1980 as hearings were held by state, local, and federal authorities. All this focused attention on the need for a law that would provide monies for cleanups like the Love Canal problem. Beyond this crisis at Love Canal, the Environmental Protection Agency (EPA) was estimating that 1,200 to 2,000 hazardous waste sites in the United States might present serious problems for individuals and the environment and that the costs for these cleanups would amount to $26.2 to $44.1 billion. Other states were beginning to report problems similar to Love Canal's in their neighborhoods.

In addition to this reporting of serious hazardous waste problems all across the nation, the existing legislation for hazardous waste regulation—the Federal Water Pollution Control Act of 1972 and the Resource Conservation and Recovery Act of 1976—was inadequate for handling the problem of cleaning up such abandoned waste sites as the Love Canal. For example, sections 311 and 504 of the Federal Water Pollution Control Act of 1972 addressed the cleanup of hazardous waste, but their provisions amounted to only $5 to $10 million. However, the Resource Conservation and Recovery Act had limitations.

It did not empower the Justice Department to subpoena witnesses, nor did it compel the production of documents for conducting investigations of violations of the two statutes. Also, it did not require the existence of a disposal site to be revealed nor allow for monitoring of possible leakage from the inactive sites.[34]

In sum, the Love Canal crisis, together with media attention to similar problems in other jurisdictions and the inadequacies of existing legislation, provided a problem stream that pushed this issue to the top of the governmental agenda in 1979 and 1980.

The Policy Stream   The policy stream, according to Kingdon, is concerned with the generation of policy proposals in the form of bill introductions, speeches, testimony, papers, and conversation. In that process, "proposals are floated, come into contact with one another, are revised and combined with one another, and floated again."[35] The proposals that survive must meet several criteria, such as their technical feasibility, their fit with dominant values and the current national mood, their budgetary workability, and the political support or opposition that they might experience as they are put forth by decision makers.[36]

On March 21, 1979, Representative James Florio (D–New Jersey) introduced a bill for toxic waste cleanup (HR 5790) that failed to gain necessary support by the subcommittee he chaired. In 1980, he introduced HR 7020, a bill that provided $600 million for cleanup of abandoned toxic waste sites. In addition, President Jimmy Carter developed a version of a Superfund bill, which included the cleanup of oil along with hazardous chemicals and proposed a Superfund of $1.6 billion over 4 years. A Senate version (S 1480) was introduced in July 1979, and it provided for a $4.1 billion Superfund program over 6 years. As these three bills moved along in the "policy primeval soup," they were amended in order to gain more votes in the Senate and House of Representatives. One version of a bill compensated victims for medical costs not paid by insurance, liberalized existing rules for evidence so that it would be easier for victims to prove actual injury resulting from the chemical exposure, and made it easier to sue for damages. The chemical industry opposed this stringent version, and eventually the version that passed (HR 7020) was weakened in terms of liability and victim compensation. In sum, the various actors in the policy stream were able to influence the final outcome of the bill that passed the House and Senate in late 1980.

The Political Stream   The political stream is composed of such factors as swings of national mood, administration or legislative turnover, and interest-group pressure. Potential agenda items "that are congruent with the current national mood, that enjoy interest-group support or lack organized opposition, and that fit the orientations of the prevailing legislative coalitions or current administration are more likely to rise to agenda prominence than items that do not meet such conditions."[37]

The 1970s are often referred to as the "environmental decade." Beginning with the National Environmental Policy Act of 1969 (NEPA), environmental issues enjoyed wide support by the American people. Public opinion in support of the environment was at an all-time high in the late 1960s.[38] Although public support for environmental protection declined somewhat in the period of 1973–79, it began to climb again by the early 1980s.[39] In addition, several national environmental organizations—such as the Sierra Club, the National Wildlife Federation, the Audubon Society, and the Environmental Defense Fund—all enjoyed significant increases in membership in the late 1970s and early 1980s.[40] Although the Chemical Manufacturers Association (CMA) led the opposition to the Superfund bill, by September 1980, CMA president Robert Roland indicated that CMA supported the House bill over the Senate bill with a smaller fund and less in the way of liability provisions. Later, CMA sent letters to Congressman Florio stating that it did not support the final bill. This embarrassed many senators and eventually led them to support what many considered to be a dead bill.[41]

At the same time, public support, due to many media reports on the problems at Love Canal in the summer of 1980, continued to focus attention on the problem of toxic waste cleanups. From mid-May to mid-June, problems at Love Canal were reported daily on the major networks. On August 21, 1980, an ABC News feature, "The Killing Ground," focused more attention on the problem. Eventually, this led to the direct involvement of President Carter in the toxic waste issue. His administration strongly supported environmental issues, and he personally called many undecided members of the House and Senate. In summary, all this media attention, the widespread public support for environmental issues in general and toxic waste issues in particular, and the personal involvement of the Carter administration and Congressman James Florio led ultimately to the enactment of HR 7020, in place of S 1480, and it became PL 96-510: The Comprehensive Environmental Response, Compensation, and Liability Act of 1980.

Policy Windows and Policy Entrepreneurs   Kingdon also stresses how separate streams of problems, policies, and politics come together at certain critical times. Policy solutions become joined to problems, and both of them are joined to favorable political forces when **policy windows**—opportunities for pushing pet proposals or conceptions of problems—are open.[42] Windows are opened either by the appearance of compelling problems or by happenings in the political stream. In the case of Superfund, problems at Love Canal and elsewhere presented a compelling case for this legislation to be enacted promptly. Crisis events compel responsive action on the part of key decision makers.

At the same time, Kingdon argues that **policy entrepreneurs,** or people who are willing to invest their resources in pushing pet proposals or problems, are responsible not only for prompting important people to pay attention to the problem but also for coupling solutions to problems and for coupling both problems and solutions to politics.[43] Although governmental agendas are set in the problem or political stream, the chances of items rising on a *decision* agenda are enhanced if all three streams are coupled together by policy entrepreneurs.[44]

In this case, Representative James Florio was an active policy entrepreneur. New Jersey was one of the worst states as far as toxic waste cleanups were concerned, yet Representative Florio solicited support for a Superfund bill from the chemical industry. In addition, he chaired the relevant congressional committee hearings on this issue and carefully guided the eventual bill (HR 7020) around industry adversaries, keeping the bill viable by amending it as necessary. He clearly exhibited the characteristics of a policy entrepreneur as Kingdon defines this role.

This brief case study illustrates Kingdon's model of agenda setting. The next brief case study, of acid rain, also illustrates how an issue rises to agenda status and remains there for some time.

Acid Rain

The problem of acid rain may be one of the most polarizing, yet least understood, environmental issues of the 1980s and 1990s. It has implications for both environmental quality and national energy policy, especially regarding the increased use of coal as a substitute for imported oil. According to one view, acid rain is one of the most serious and deadly environmental problems that humans have ever faced. Others charge that acid rain is a nonissue that is blown out of proportion by antigrowth environmental extremists seeking a rationalization for a continuing attack on emissions. In the end, the former view won the debate, for a new Clean Air Act was passed in 1990 that effectively dealt with the problem of acid rain. The following case vignette uses Kingdon's model of agenda setting to explore how this issue achieved agenda status and remained on the agenda for over 10 years before the Clean Air Act of 1990 was passed.

The Problem Stream   Although a Swedish scientist, Svante Oden, warned in the 1960s that the increasing acidity of Swedish lakes was the result of atmospheric fallout of sulfur dioxides, acid rain first appeared as an American problem when President Carter referred to it in his second annual environmental message in 1979. Before his address, interest in the subject of acid rain had been confined to a small group of American scientists who were worried about the potential problems of this phenomenon for the environment.[45] In his address, President Carter asked for additional research and development funds as well as possible control measures. By 1980, the director of the EPA, Douglas Costle, argued that the time had come to make the transition from further research to action. Initially, the General Accounting Office (GAO) characterized the problem as one that was confined to a small number of lakes and streams in the northeastern United States and southeastern Canada. After the election of President Reagan in 1980, the approach to acid rain was to call for more research. As time wore on, however, the seriousness of the acid rain problem became more apparent.

The Policy Stream   Starting in 1979, various acid rain control bills were introduced in the House and the Senate annually. Before passage of the Clean Air Act Amendments of 1990, at least seventy-four separate bills were introduced in Congress. Table 5.1 indicates how many acid rain bills were before Congress from

TABLE 5.1 Number of Acid Rain Bills Introduced in Congress, 1979 to Mid-1989

	Senate	House	Total
96th Congress			
1979	1	1	2
1980	0	1	1
97th Congress			
1981	2	4	6
1982	3	0	3
98th Congress			
1983	7	8	15
1984	1	9	10
99th Congress			
1985	5	6	11
1986	3	4	7
100th Congress			
1987	4	4	8
1988	2	4	6
101st Congress			
1989	2	3	5
TOTALS	30	44	74

SOURCE: Leslie R. Alm, "Acid Rain and the United States Congress: A Case Study of Issue Maintenance and the Agenda Setting Process" (PhD. diss, Colorado State University, 1990). Reprinted with permission of the publisher.

1979 to 1989. At least twenty-five pieces of legislation concerning acid rain were introduced in the 98th Congress (1983–84) alone.

Support for or against these bills generally reflected the economic interests of the states represented by members of Congress. For example, senators from New England generally supported these bills, whereas those from polluting states generally opposed the bills.[46] Senator Robert Byrd of West Virginia—one of the most polluting states—claimed that "acid rain has been found in ice cores in the Arctic Circle . . . and my state would lose jobs under any scenario."[47]

Broadly speaking, the various pieces of legislation introduced were categorized as either control legislation that mandated reductions in air emissions or research legislation that proposed further study of the acid rain problem. For example, Senate Bill 769, introduced by Senator Robert Stafford (R–Vermont) in 1983, would have reduced emissions by 12 million tons annually within a 31-state region over a 12-year period. From 1979 to 1988, sixty-nine different acid rain bills were introduced in Congress. However, none passed.[48] In June 1989, President Bush sent Congress a new Clean Air Act in which provisions for acid rain were quite strong. His bill called for a 10-million-ton-per-year reduction in sulfur dioxides. On November 15, 1990, President Bush signed the Clean Air Act Amendments of 1990, in which acid rain finally received statutory coverage. The new Clean Air Act of 1990 required coal-burning electric power plants to cut sulfur dioxide emissions by 10 million tons—or roughly in half—by 2000, when emissions were scheduled to be capped at 8.9 million tons a year.

The Political Stream   After the Democratic and Republican National Conventions in the summer of 1988, resistance to acid rain control diminished, especially among the utility companies and the unions. Fearing that both George Bush and Michael Dukakis would favor strong acid rain control laws, opponents of acid rain legislation sought a weaker bill, rather than a strong one. Although the various acid rain bills did not pass in 1988, the opposition softened its stance and focused on who would pay for control of acid rain.[49] The year 1988 represented a turning point in the struggle for acid rain controls. The election of President Bush, who had campaigned as an "environmental president," seemed to send a message to the polluting industries that the time had come for legislation to reduce acid rain.

Policy Windows and Policy Entrepreneurs   The Democrats in Congress dominated the sponsorship of acid rain bills by three to one. Most of the bills introduced in Congress favored control and/or reduction of emissions. Leading actors in the acid rain initiative in Congress included Senator George Mitchell (D–Maine) and Representative Henry Waxman (D–California). These individuals helped to keep the acid rain issue on the public agenda for years. Others, including Senator Robert Stafford of Vermont and Representative Gerry Sikorski of Minnesota, were instrumental as well.[50] Senator George Mitchell was the key spokesman for acid rain control in the Senate. He sponsored more acid rain bills than any other senator in Congress. As the senate majority leader, he was in a good position to play a strong role in this issue. Besides Senator Mitchell,

Representative Waxman in the House also helped to move this issue to the point of policy adoption.[51]

In addition, President H.W. Bush played a major role. As mentioned earlier, he had promised during his 1988 campaign to be the environmental president. Immediately after taking office, he pledged to a joint session of Congress that he would soon introduce legislation to reduce acid rain. The day after that speech, President Bush traveled to Canada, where he repeated his promise to Prime Minister Mulroney and the Canadian people. On June 12, 1989, he proposed acid rain legislation to the Congress. The change in administration from Reagan to Bush provided the "window of opportunity" that was crucial for legislation on this issue. Moreover, with President Bush's support, Senator Mitchell and Representative Waxman were able to keep the issue before Congress, and ultimately a new Clean Air Act was signed into law in November 1990.

These two case studies illustrate how John Kingdon's model of agenda setting can be used to analyze the agenda-setting process. In his model, one sees how the problem stream, the policy stream, and the political stream combine to encourage an issue rising to the agenda-setting stage. In addition, windows of opportunity and policy entrepreneurs enhance the ability of an issue to reach the public agenda and remain on it for some time. To use Kingdon's model of agenda setting, one needs some decision in the form of a policy proposal. Sometimes, however, decisions are never achieved because policy issues are deliberately kept off the governmental agenda. That is the phenomenon called non-decision-making.[52]

THE PROBLEM OF NONDECISIONS

Often items are deliberately kept off the institutional agendas by those who seek to control the decision process for political or economic reasons. Peter Bachrach and Morton S. Baratz identified a phenomenon called **non-decision-making,** which is defined as "a means by which demands for change in the existing allocation of benefits and privileges in the community can be suffocated before they are even voiced; or kept covert; or killed before they gain access to the relevant decision-making arena; or failing all these things, maimed or destroyed in the decision-implementing stage of the policy process."[53]

In one example of a nondecision, the rubber industry and the oil companies have been accused of conspiring to keep the possibility of rapid rail transportation off the institutional agenda; instead, these two industries want to promote highway transportation. It is sometimes argued that these industries forced the shutdown of much of the inner-city rail transportation to promote the use of automobiles. From time to time, there is also discussion of intercity rapid transit using rail transportation, much like the European systems, but it is allegedly kept off the governmental agenda by those who would lose economically from the switch from highway to rail transit— including the bus industry, oil companies, tire manufacturers, and the airlines.[54]

Another example of a nondecision is the case of tobacco. Even though cigarettes and other tobacco products contain a drug (nicotine) and are generally acknowledged to be a leading cause of hundreds of thousands of cancer and heart-related deaths annually, the tobacco industry has kept its product off the regulatory agenda of the Food and Drug Administration (FDA)—despite the efforts of FDA officials and some members of Congress. According to a leading antismoking advocacy group:

> "Today, tobacco products are among the least regulated. They're exempt from basic health protections the U.S. Food and Drug Administration (FDA) applies to other consumer products, such as food, drugs, cosmetics and even dog food. *The FDA can regulate a box of macaroni and cheese but not a pack of cigarettes.*" (Emphasis added)[55]

CONCLUSIONS

The case studies of Superfund and acid rain legislation illustrate how John Kingdon's model may be used to explain agenda setting. Nevertheless, much work remains to be done in the area of agenda setting. What is needed at this point are more applications of existing frameworks on agenda setting, such as the framework developed by John Kingdon. Kingdon's model needs to be applied in many areas of public policy formation, so that the various components of his model may be tested against real-world data. Some of his variables may be less important than others. It would be useful to know, for example, if the problem stream is more important in explaining agenda setting than either the policy stream or the political stream. It may be that a policy entrepreneur is crucial in getting an item on the public agenda.

Getting an item onto the public agenda is only the beginning of the process of developing public policies. Once issues reach the agenda, policy actors still have to consider and choose among policy options. How they do so is the subject of Chapter 6.

DISCUSSION QUESTIONS

1. Using either the case of acid rain legislation (Clean Air Act of 1990) or Superfund legislation (CERCLA), describe what you think helped to get the issue onto the public agenda.
2. What are some examples of issues deliberately kept off the public agenda?
3. What is the relative importance of the three categories of variables (problem stream, policy stream, and political stream) in the Kingdon model of agenda setting?
4. How important are "policy entrepreneurs" in the agenda-setting process?
5. How do changing sociocultural beliefs (such as those discussed in Chapter 2) affect which policy issues get onto the public agenda? Cite some interesting examples that you think illustrate this situation.

SUGGESTED READINGS

Baumgartner, Frank R., and Bryan D. Jones. *Agendas and Instability in American Politics* (Chicago: University of Chicago Press, 1993).

Cobb, Roger W., and March H. Ross, eds.*Cultural Strategies of Agenda Denial* (Lawrence: University of Kansas Press, 1997).

Dearing, James W., and Everett M. Rogers. *Agenda-Setting* (Thousand Oaks, CA: Sage, 1996).

Kingdon, John W. *Agendas, Alternatives, and Public Policies,* Second Edition (New York: HarperCollins, 1995).

Nelson, Barbara J. *Making an Issue of Child Abuse* (Chicago: University of Chicago Press, 1984).

Rochefort, David A., and Roger W. Cobb. *The Politics of Problem Definition: Shaping the Policy Agenda* (Lawrence: University of Kansas Press, 1994).

Schattschneider, E. E. *The Semi-Sovereign People* (Hinsdale, NY: Dryden Press, 1960).

NOTES

1. James E. Anderson, *Public Policymaking: An Introduction* (Boston: Houghton Mifflin, 1990), p. 78.

2. Brian W. Hogwood and Lewis A. Gunn, *Policy Analysis for the Real World* (Oxford: Oxford University Press, 1984), p. 68.

3. Roger W. Cobb and Charles D. Elder, *Participation in American Politics: The Dynamics of Agenda-Building* (Baltimore: Johns Hopkins University Press, 1972).

4. John W. Kingdon, *Agendas, Alternatives, and Public Policies* (Boston: Little, Brown, 1984).

5. See Frank R. Baumgartner and Bryan D. Jones, *Agendas and Instability in American Politics* (Chicago: University of Chicago Press, 1993), pp. 25–31.

6. Barbara J. Nelson, *Making an Issue of Child Abuse* (Chicago: University of Chicago Press, 1984), p. 20.

7. Anderson, *Public Policymaking,* pp. 78–79.

8. Kirkpatrick Sale, *Human Scale* (New York: G. P. Putnam Sons, 1982), pp. 21–22.

9. Michael Harrington, *The Other America* (New York: Viking Penguin, 1971); Charles Murray, *Losing Ground* (New York: Basic Books, 1986); and Edward Banfield, *The Unheavenly City Revisited* (Prospect Heights, IL: Waveland Press, 1990).

10. Cobb and Elder, *Participation in American Politics,* p. 14.

11. See Kingdon, *Agendas,* and Nelson, *Child Abuse.*

12. J. Clarence Davies, "How Does the Agenda Get Set?" in *The Governance of Common Property Resources,* ed. Edwin Haefele (Baltimore: Johns Hopkins University Press, 1974), p. 61. See also Paul S. Dempsey and Joseph Szyliowicz, *The Denver International Airport: Lessons Learned* (New York: McGraw-Hill, 1997).

13. Nelson, *Child Abuse,* p. 22.

14. Roger W. Cobb and Charles D. Elder, "The Politics of Agenda-Building," *Journal of Politics* 33, no. 4 (November 1971), pp. 892–915.

15. Cobb and Elder, *Participation in American Politics,* p. 110.

16. Davies, "How Does the Agenda Get Set?"

17. Ibid., p. 61

18. Roger Cobb, Jennie-Keith Ross, and March Ross, "Agenda Building as a Comparative Political Process," *American Political Science Review* 70 (1976), pp. 126–138.

19. Ibid, p. 127.

20. Nelson, *Child Abuse,* pp. 22–23.

21. Ibid.

22. See Kingdon, *Agendas,* pp. 20–21.

23. Ibid., p. 21.

24. Martin Linsky, *Impact: How the Press Affects Federal Policymaking* (New York: W. W. Norton, 1986), pp. 71–78.

25. See C. Wright Mills, *The Power Elite* (New York: Oxford University Press, 1956).

26. See Douglas Cater, *Power in Washington* (New York: Random House, 1965).

27. Ibid.

28. Ibid.; and Cynthia H. Enloe, *The Politics of Pollution in a Comparative Perspective* (New York: McKay, 1975).

29. See Phillip O. Foss, *The Politics of Grass* (Seattle: University of Washington Press, 1960).

30. Kingdon, *Agendas,* pp. 20–21.

31. John A. Worthley and Richard A. Torkelson, "Managing the Toxic Waste Problem: Lessons from the Love Canal," *Administration and Society* 13 (August 1981), pp. 147–148.

32. For a complete story on the Love Canal situation, see Adeline G. Levine, *Love Canal: Science, Politics, and People* (Lexington, MA: Lexington Books, 1982).

33. Worthley and Torkelson, "Toxic Waste Problem," p. 152.

34. U.S. House of Representatives, Committee on Interstate and Foreign Commerce, Subcommittee on Oversight and Investigations, *Hazardous Waste Disposal* (Washington, D.C.: U.S. Government Printing Office, 1979), p. 721.

35. Kingdon, *Agendas,* p. 21.

36. Ibid.

37. Ibid.

38. See Riley Dunlap, "Public Opinion and the Environment," in *Environmental Politics and Policy: Theories and Evidence,* ed. James P. Lester (Durham, NC: Duke University Press, 1989).

39. Ibid., pp. 86–134.

40. See Helen Ingram and Dean E. Mann, "Interest Groups and Environmental Policy," in Lester, *Environmental Politics,* pp. 139–141.

41. Kathy Koch, "Superfund Cleanup Proposal Apparently Dead This Year," *Congressional Quarterly Weekly Report* (15 November, 1980), p. 3378.

42. Kingdon, *Agendas,* p. 21.

43. Ibid.

44. Ibid.

45. See, for example, Ellis B. Cowling, "Acid Precipitation in Historical Perspective," *Environmental Science and Technology* 16, no. 2 (February 1982), pp. 110–123.

46. James L. Regens, "Congressional Co-sponsorship of Acid Rain Controls," *Social Science Quarterly* 70, no. 2 (June 1989), pp. 505–512.

47. Congressional Record, 98th Congress, 2nd Session, 3 February 1984, p. 1783.

48. Leslie R. Alm, "Acid Rain and the United States Congress: A Case Study of Issue Maintenance and the Agenda-Setting Process" (Ph.D. diss., Colorado State University, 1990), p. 57.

49. Ibid.

50. Ibid.

51. Ibid.

52. See Roger W. Cobb and Marc H. Ross, eds., *Cultural Strategies of Agenda Denial* (Lawrence: University of Kansas Press, 1997).

53. Peter Bachrach and Morton S. Baratz, *Power and Poverty* (New York: Oxford University Press, 1970), p. 44; see also Matthew A. Crenson, *The Unpolitics of Air Pollution* (Baltimore: Johns Hopkins University Press, 1971).

54. Cobb and Ross, op. cit., esp. pp. 49–179.

55. Campaign for Tobacco-Free Kids, "FDA Authority over Tobacco," 2/22/07, www.tobaccofreekids.org/reports/fda/ accessed 3/1/07.

6

Policy Formulation

"All great truths begin as blasphemies."
GEORGE B. SHAW

In this chapter, we examine how policies are formulated. By the term **policy formulation,** we mean the stage of the policy process where pertinent and acceptable courses of action for dealing with some particular public problem are identified and enacted into law.[1] Each of the stages in the policymaking process is theoretically distinct, but they nevertheless merge in practice. For example, the nature of the problem affects whether it gets onto the agenda, as well as whether a course of action is finally enacted into law. Let us examine the policy formulation stage in a bit more depth.

THE NATURE OF POLICY SOLUTIONS

The expected result of policy formulation is some type of solution to a public problem. According to Deborah Stone, there are five types of policy solutions: (1) **inducements,** which can be either positive (e.g., tax credits) or negative (e.g., penalties for pollution); (2) **rules,** or other forms of mandated behavior such as regulations governing pollution; (3) **facts,** or the use of information to persuade target groups to behave in a certain way, such as community right-to-know information; (4) **rights,** which give certain people rights or duties, such as civil rights legislation; and (5) **powers,** whereby a decision-making body is charged with specific powers to improve decision making, such as the budgetary power a legislature has to affect the state budget. These policy solutions can be in the form of congressional legislation, executive orders, judicial decisions, or other forms of policy outputs.[2]

ACTORS IN POLICY FORMULATION

Who is involved in policy formulation? In this discussion of the actors involved in policy formulation, we pay particular attention to the national level of government.

Governmental Agencies

Contrary to conventional logic, most policy proposals are first developed in governmental agencies by career bureaucrats rather than in Congress. These officials have been involved in developing policy for decades, often have more expertise in specific areas of public policy than elected officials do, and are in a particularly good position to engage in the formulation of policy.[3] Sometimes new agency proposals are designed to remedy previous legislation that has loopholes. For example, the Resource Conservation and Recovery Act of 1976 (RCRA) originally regulated businesses that produced 1,000 kilograms or more of hazardous waste per month. This threshold of toxic waste produced by these businesses omitted all those industries that produced less than this amount, such as dry cleaners, paint shops, printing shops, and others. To correct that omission the Environmental Protection Agency developed the Hazardous and Solid Waste Amendments of 1984 (HSWA), which was designed to amend RCRA to bring these smaller businesses within the regulatory regime. Under the provisions of HSWA, all businesses that produce at least 100 kilograms of toxic waste per month are within the purview of the new regulatory regime established by HSWA in 1984.

Government agencies often provide information to Congress and the executive branch that later becomes the basis for legislation. The General Accounting Office (GAO), for example, undertakes research on the effectiveness of previous policies in reaching their goals as defined by Congress. When problems in implementation are detected by the GAO, these shortcomings often become the basis for new legislation. For example, the GAO examined the toxic waste cleanup process under the Comprehensive Environmental Response, Compensation, and Liability Act of 1980 (CERCLA) and made suggestions for improving the process when CERCLA was amended in 1986 under the Superfund Amendments and Reauthorization Act (SARA). In sum, one often thinks that governmental agencies get involved only in policy implementation when, in fact, they usually are involved in the policy formulation process.

The Presidency

The president and/or executive offices are also involved in the policy formulation process. Such involvement includes presidential commissions, task forces, interagency committees, and other arrangements. Quite often, the president is personally involved in policy formulation. For example, President Jimmy Carter was known for his attention to details and for his interest in formulating policy. He preferred to be actively involved in the initiation of legislation and used his staff to help prepare much legislation for congressional review. On the other hand, President Lyndon Johnson used task forces to develop legislative proposals. He appointed over one hundred of these groups during his tenure in office, as he believed that these groups would be more innovative in developing proposals for new policies than would the federal bureaucracy.[4] Throughout history, there has been much variation in the amount of attention given to the policy formulation process by various presidents. Our most recent presidents, Bill Clinton and George W. Bush, provide an interesting contrast in decision styles. Of the two, President Clinton was clearly more comfortable with task forces and working with others outside of the White House. The Welfare Reform Act of 1996 was very much a joint effort between the executive branch, the Congress, the nation's governors, and various interest groups. Probably the most visible task force during the Clinton administration was the task force headed by Hillary Clinton to develop (unsuccessfully) a national health insurance plan. For a variety of reasons, decision making in the Bush White House has been more centralized in the executive office. Policy initiatives typically originate within a relatively small group of advisors including Vice President Cheney, Karl Rove, Karen Hughes, and others close to the president. A good example of that exclusiveness is President Bush's decision in 2007 to increase the number of troops in Iraq by some 20,000—despite opposition from the Congress (including many within his own party), the recommendations of the Iraq Study Group, a bipartisan blue ribbon panel headed by former secretary of state James Baker and former House member Lee Hamilton, and the public's apparent distaste of the war in the 2006 midterm elections for Congress.[5]

Congress

Congress is the institution most commonly associated with policy formulation, either through the development of new legislation or through oversight and legislative review. For example, Congress was actively involved in the revision of the Clean Air Act in 1977 and again in 1990, as discussed in the previous chapter. Congress's primary role in developing legislation is to react to items put forward by the president. In that sense, Congress lets presidents set their agenda but does not hesitate to change, often substantially, the president's proposals. Congressional committees and congressional staff, as well as several relatively new organizations within Congress, also allow substantial involvement. These new organizations, such as the Office of Technology Assessment (OTA), the Congressional Research Service (CRS), and the Congressional Budget Office (CBO), were created to give Congress a greater voice in the design of public policies. For example, during 1985 and 1986, the OTA and its Advisory Group on Waste Minimization helped to formulate legislation that would aid in promoting toxic waste reduction and waste minimization. Ironically, OTA was terminated in 1995 following the Republican takeover of Congress.

Interest Groups

Interest groups are extremely important in policy formulation in the United States. Although there are several alternative explanations of public policy formulation, one of the most frequently mentioned determinants is the role and influence of interest groups. Essentially, **pluralism** means that public policy is shaped by bargaining, negotiation, and compromise among various interest groups in American society. As V. O. Key once said, "group interests are the animating forces in the political process; an understanding of American politics requires a knowledge of the chief interests and their stake in public policy."[6]

The idea that interest groups are a major determinant in public policy may be traced back to the Founding Fathers. For example, James Madison, in *The Federalist,* warned against factions (interest groups) and suggested that a republican form of government with checks and balances would offer the best protection against the domination of public policy by interest groups. Later, Arthur Bentley, in *The Process of Government,* argued that "there are no political phenomena except group phenomena."[7] Most recently, Theodore Lowi has presented the argument that interest groups are strong actors in the American policy process. He argues that "interest group liberalism" has produced a situation in which interest groups have undue power and are able to structure policy outcomes in a way that is characterized by corruption, backroom politics, a lack of long-range planning, and injustice.[8] For example, we discussed the role and influence of the Chemical Manufacturers Association in the development of Superfund legislation in Chapter 5.

In sum, all these actors and institutions are, at one time or another, involved in policy formulation. In the following discussion of models of policy formulation, we describe exactly how these organizations and actors exert their influence on public policy.

EXPLAINING POLICY FORMULATION

The literature on public policy formulation provides several alternative explanations of how policies are formulated in the United States. Because the core activity of policy formulation is choosing between alternatives for dealing with a policy problem, the alternative explanations are, in fact, models of decision making. The use of these explanations is critical to understanding policy formulation and policy analysis. Besides the elitist, pluralist, and subgovernment models (discussed earlier, in Chapters 4 and 5), the rational-comprehensive, the incremental, and the systems models of policy formulation are some of the best-known examples.

The Rational-Comprehensive Model

A well-known model of decision making is the **rational-comprehensive model,** which is primarily based on the assumption that individuals make decisions through a rational calculation of costs and benefits. This model of policy choice usually includes the following components:

1. The decision maker is confronted with a given problem that can be separated from other problems, or at least considered meaningfully in comparison with them.

2. The goals, values, or objectives that guide the decision maker are clarified and ranked according to their importance.

3. A complete set of alternative policies for dealing with the problem are prepared.

4. The consequences (costs and benefits, advantages and disadvantages) that would follow from the selection of each alternative are investigated.

5. Each alternative, and its attendant consequences, can be calculated and compared with the other alternatives.

6. The decision maker chooses the alternative that maximizes the attainment of his or her goals, values, or objectives.

Figure 6.1 illustrates the rational-comprehensive model. The net result of this process is the most rational decision, or one that most efficiently achieves a desired end.

The rational-comprehensive model has been criticized on a number of grounds. First, it is extremely difficult to define the nature of a problem and to identify its various aspects. For example, what is the nature of the crime problem? Are crimes "caused" by the environment, including such things as lack of employment opportunities, poor education, and the like? Or, is crime caused by individual defects, inherent tendencies toward violence, alcoholism, and so forth? Until one knows exactly what causes a problem, it is difficult to set forth alternatives that can be weighted and evaluated.

A second criticism of the rational-comprehensive model is the demands it places on the decision maker. It assumes that complete information exists on various alternatives for dealing with a problem, and that it is possible to predict the consequences with complete accuracy; thus, analysts will be able to make cost-benefit comparisons of each alternative. In reality, this is seldom, if ever, the case. Researchers can never have complete information on any alternative, nor will they be able to predict consequences with the kind of accuracy this model assumes.

Third, even with the most advanced analytical techniques, decision makers do not have the intellectual capacity, or the judgment, to calculate cost-benefit ratios when a large number of diverse political, social, economic, and cultural values are at stake. In addition, decision makers are often motivated not by societal goals, but by self-serving goals; they are interested in an alternative that works for them rather than the one that achieves larger societal goals. Decision makers have personal needs, inhibitions, and inadequacies that prevent them from behaving in a highly rational manner.

Fourth, there is the problem of sunk costs. Previous decisions, commitments, and investments in existing policies and programs prevent decision makers from

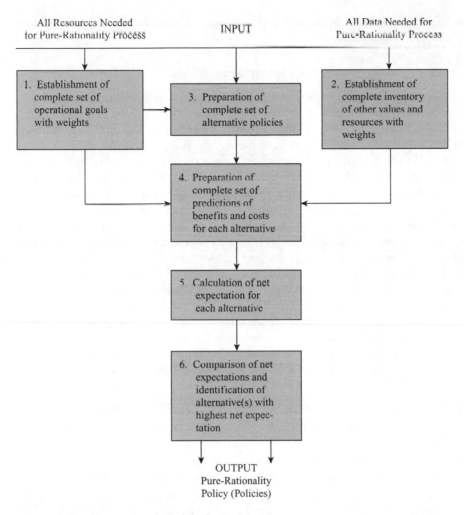

All Resources Needed for Pure-Rationality Process INPUT All Data Needed for Pure-Rationality Process

1. Establishment of complete set of operational goals with weights

3. Preparation of complete set of alternative policies

2. Establishment of complete inventory of other values and resources with weights

4. Preparation of complete set of predictions of benefits and costs for each alternative

5. Calculation of net expectation for each alternative

6. Comparison of net expectations and identification of alternative(s) with highest net expectation

OUTPUT
Pure-Rationality
Policy (Policies)

FIGURE 6.1 A Rational Model of a Decision System.

SOURCE: Thomas R. Dye, *Understanding Public Policy,* 8th ed. Copyright © 1995, p. 29. Reprinted by permission of Pearson Education, Inc., Upper Saddle River, NJ.

reconsidering alternatives that have been foreclosed by previous decisions. Moreover, uncertainty about the policy consequences of new choices compels decision makers to stick closely to previous policies to reduce the possibility of errors in judgment.

Finally, the rational–comprehensive model assumes the existence of a unitary decision maker. This is rarely the case, in that decisions are typically made by groups of policy makers, including legislatures and many courts (the U.S. Supreme Court, for example) each of whom bring their own values and preferences to decisions. Although the rational-comprehensive model has been criticized for its many assumptions, most of which cannot be met, it nevertheless provides a prescription for the making of policy to which one may strive. That is, it provides a guide to follow in the attempt to design more rational public policy, if that is one's objective.

The Incremental Model

The incremental model represents another model of policy formulation. Incrementalism views public policy formulation as continuation of past government activities with only minor modifications. The constraints of time, intelligence, and cost prevent policy makers from identifying the full range of policy alternatives and their consequences. Incrementalism is conservative in that existing programs, policies, and expenditures are considered as a base, and attention is concentrated on new programs and policies and on increases, decreases, or modifications of existing programs or policies. The key assumptions of this model are that (1) decision makers do not have sufficient predictive capabilities to know all the consequences of each alternative; (2) decision makers accept the legitimacy of previous policies; (3) sunk costs prevent serious consideration of all policy alternatives and especially any radical change in policy; (4) incrementalism reduces conflict and is politically expedient; and (5) the characteristics of the decision makers themselves are more suited to the incremental model, in that humans are not value maximizers but are more often "satisficers," acting to merely satisfy particular demands. Thus, in the absence of agreed-upon societal values, a pluralistic government can more easily continue existing policies or programs than it can engage in overall policy planning toward specific policy goals. The key components of the incremental model are listed below:

1. The selection of goals or objectives and the empirical analyses of the action needed to attain them are closely intertwined with, rather than distinct from, one another.

2. The decision maker considers only some of the alternatives for dealing with a problem, which will differ only incrementally from existing policies.

3. For each alternative, only a limited number of important consequences are evaluated.

4. The problem confronting the decision maker is continually redefined. Incrementalism allows for countless ends–means and means–ends adjustments that have the effect of making the problem more manageable.

5. There is no single "best" solution for a problem. The test of a good decision is that various analysts find themselves directly agreeing on it without agreeing that the decision is the most appropriate means to an agreed-upon objective, or for that matter, that there is a single goal.

6. Incremental decision making is essentially remedial and is geared more to the amelioration of present, concrete social imperfections than to the promotion of future social goals.[9]

This model has been criticized on a number of grounds. First, some have argued that this model does not explain dramatic policy change or reversals. Nor does it explain recent governmental efforts at long-range planning, such as

TABLE 6.1 Rational and Incremental Models: A Comparison

Rational Process	Incremental Process
1. The analysis of the situation.	1. The policy maker works directly on agreement on specific projects, policies, or programs, and not toward agreement on abstract goals.
2. End reduction and elaboration.	2. The policy maker is concerned with the comparison and evaluation of increments only.
3. The design of courses of action.	3. The policy maker considers only a restricted number of policy alternatives.
4. The comparative evaluation of consequences in light of ends.	4. Ends are adjusted to means, as well as the other way around. The problem is constantly redefined. Policy objectives are derived largely from an inspection of our means.
5. The selection of the preferable alternative.	5. Many alternatives are attempted in a series of "attacks" on the problem of concern.
6. The assessment of the action taken in light of both ends and means.	6. Assessment relies on experience and feedback because policymaking is remedial. In Lindblom's view: "public problem solving [proceeds] less by aspiration toward a well defined future state than by identified social ills that seem to call for remedy."* In short, ultimate ends are not of great concern.

*Charles Lindblom, quoted in Galloway, p. 170.

SOURCE: Thomas D. Galloway, *The Role of Urban Planning in Public Policy-Making: A Synthesis and Critique of Contemporary Procedural Planning Thought* (Ph.D. diss. [1971], Ann Arbor, Mich.: University Microfilms, 1974). The figure is drawn from material on pp. 71 and 175–180.

the Global 2000 report in 1980, which was produced during the Carter administration and explored the relationships among population, resources, and the environment between 1979 and 2000. Table 6.1 provides a comparison of the incremental and rational-comprehensive models of decision making.

The Systems Model

The **systems model,** originally developed by biologists and then applied to the study of politics by David Easton, suggests that public policy formation is initially affected by demands for new policies or support for the existing policies.[10] These demands and supports are then acted on by a political system, or conversion mechanism, which converts these demands into public policies or decisions, called outputs. Essentially, Easton's model of policy formation proposes that inputs (demands and supports) are converted by the processes of the political system (legislatures, the courts, etc.) into outputs (policies or decisions), and these in turn have consequences both for the system and for the environment in which

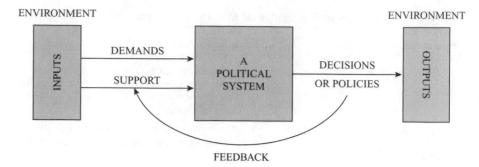

FIGURE 6.2 The Systems Framework.

the system exists. Demands may be internal to the system (e.g., political parties or interest groups) or external to the system (e.g., ecology, the economy, culture, demography). Support, according to Easton, includes actions or orientations that help the system operate and help to sustain it. Support is derived from three directions: (1) the political community; (2) the regime or rules of the game; and (3) the government itself. A political system generates support by meeting demands of the polity and by political socialization. The outputs of the system (political decisions or public policies) create support when they satisfy day-to-day demands, or when system members perceive the government as being generally favorable to their interests. On the other hand, the persistent inability of a government to produce satisfactory outputs for the members of a system may lead to demands for changing the regime or for dissolution of the political community.[11] Figure 6.2 illustrates Easton's systems model.

Other scholars have attempted to modify the systems model for various purposes. Thomas Dye, for example, adapted the systems model for the study of American state politics. His model suggests that socioeconomic variables in the states (e.g., urbanization, industrialization, income, and education) create demands or supports on the political system (e.g., constitutional framework, the electoral system, the party system, interest-group structures, elite or power structures, or political styles), which in turn produce state policy outcomes (e.g., welfare, highway, educational, and tax policies).[12] Since the early 1970s, still others have attempted to elaborate on the systems model developed by Easton, and they have produced several useful additional versions of this model for the comparative analysis of public policy in the American states.[13]

The "mainstream" state politics model has been criticized on several grounds. Specifically, it is argued that the model does not allow for variation in "needs," or the severity of the problem, which in turn produces demands for a solution to some public problem. The model is also somewhat vague about whether political parties are "demands" or an institution. Finally, there is the boundary problem as to what should be included in the "environment" of the political system.[14]

CASE STUDY

At-Sea Incineration of Toxic Waste

The case of designing and finalizing regulations for at-sea burning of toxic wastes provides a useful means for illustrating how the rational, pluralist, and elitist models are sometimes used to account for policy formulation.

Policy as Efficient Goal Achievement   The rational model suggests that policy makers know all of society's preferences, that they know all the policy alternatives available, that they know all the consequences of each policy alternative, that they calculate the ratio of achieved to sacrificed societal values for each policy alternative, and that they ultimately select the most efficient policy alternative.

The Environmental Protection Agency (EPA) has been involved in at-sea incineration of toxic wastes for decades.[15] Beginning in 1974, a series of four research burns were conducted under EPA permits to gather scientific information about incineration of liquid hazardous wastes at sea and to evaluate ocean incineration as an alternative to land-based disposal options. These research burns were conducted under the authority of the Marine Protection, Research, and Sanctuaries Act of 1972, as amended, and the Convention on the Prevention of Marine Pollution by Dumping of Wastes and Other Matter (the London Dumping Convention, as it is commonly called).

Between October 1974 and January 1975, a total of 16,800 metric tons of organochlorine wastes from the Shell Chemical Company's Deer Park manufacturing complex were incinerated in the Gulf of Mexico. In October 1976, Shell was issued a permit to incinerate up to 50,000 metric tons of mixed wastes at the Gulf Incineration Site. Approximately 29,100 metric tons of wastes were actually incinerated. In 1977, the U.S. Air Force incinerated its stock of the herbicide Agent Orange at a site 322 kilometers west of Johnson Atoll in the Pacific Ocean. The last series of burns were performed in 1981 and 1982, when liquid PCB wastes were incinerated at the Gulf Incineration Site under a research permit issued to Chemical Waste Management and Ocean Combustion Services.[16]

Opposition to ocean incineration coalesced on October 21, 1983, when the EPA published a notice in the *Federal Register* announcing that Chemical Waste Management had been granted tentative approval to burn 79.7 million gallons of mixed liquid organic chemicals containing PCBs and DDT at a site 170 miles southeast of Brownsville, Texas. Public hearings were held on November 21, 1983, in Brownsville and November 22 and 23, 1983, in Mobile, Alabama. In what was reputed to be the largest example of citizen participation in EPA history, 6,488 people registered at those two public hearings, and some threatened litigation if any permits were issued.[17]

As a result of these demonstrations, the EPA assistant administrator decided not to grant permits to Chemical Waste Management and Ocean Combustion Services to burn the wastes. Rather, the administrator deferred permit issuance until a more deliberative strategy could be developed for at-sea incineration of toxic wastes. Toward that end, he directed his staff to develop a research strategy that would respond to the need to develop more specific regulations for ocean incineration. The EPA began to develop these regulations between 1985 and 1986. Using its experience with land-based incineration of toxic wastes, the EPA proposed rules that provided a regulatory framework for the ocean incineration program in February 1985. The proposed rules modified provisions in the Ocean Dumping Regulations regarding the issuance of permits and the designation of burn sites. Specifically, the rules required that 99.99 percent of the chemicals burned at sea should be destroyed in the process; and for PCBs and dioxin, burning efficiency should be 99.9999 percent. In addition, each ship would be required to carry a full-time EPA employee to monitor compliance with the conditions of the incineration permits. Thus, these proposed rules imposed stringent licensing and operating restrictions on operators of incinerator ships.

After receiving over 4,500 comments on these proposed rules, in November 1985 the EPA announced a tentative decision to permit the test burning of toxic wastes at sea off the New Jersey coast. However, in February 1986 the National Oceanic and Atmospheric Administration (NOAA) ordered a 6-month delay in plans for burning hazardous wastes aboard *Vulcanus II,* a ship owned by Chemical Waste Management. As a reaction to this concern by NOAA, the EPA released a report on May 1, 1986, that raised more questions about the plan to burn toxic wastes off the mid-Atlantic coast. Finally, in late May 1986, the EPA announced its decision to deny the research permit and to grant no further permits for burning until it finalized its Ocean Incineration Regulations.

Thus, this behavior by the EPA illustrates the rational model of policy formation. The EPA carefully developed its plans for at-sea incineration according to the rational model of policy formation by attempting to develop complete information and carefully considering all policy alternatives in designing its final regulations. In that sense, it attempted to select the most efficient policy solution after receiving public comments and designing (and redesigning) its regime framework for ocean burning of toxic wastes.

Policy as Group Equilibrium   The pluralist model describes all meaningful political activity as competition between interest groups. Policy makers are seen as constantly reacting to group pressures and, because of these competing pressures, reaching policy compromises through bargaining and negotiation. Public policy outcomes reflect a "balancing" of competing group pressures.

The ocean incineration policy subsystem contained a large and diverse set of actors. Essentially, two coalitions developed in the debate over ocean incineration of toxic wastes. These two coalitions included the pro-incineration coalition and the anti-incineration coalition. The pro-incineration coalition was dominated by the waste incineration industry, including Chemical Waste Management (the owners of *Vulcanus I* and *II* incineration vessels), At-Sea Incineration (owners of *Apollo I* and *II* incineration vessels), Precision Conversion and Recovery, Inc., and Sea Burn, Inc. They were joined by the Institute of Chemical Waste Management and Florida's Department of Environmental Regulation (DER), among others. The coalition believed that incineration at sea was the best liquid chemical waste disposal technology available, that it was safe and valuable, and that it added little risk to the already heavy traffic of hazardous waste chemicals through American ports.[18]

The competing anti-incineration coalition was dominated by environmental groups including Greenpeace, the Cousteau Society, Friends of the Earth, and others. It also included several attorneys general of various states, the Texas Shrimp Association, the Texas Rural Legal Aid Association, the Texas Environmental Coalition, some migrant farmworkers, representatives of the land-based incineration industry, resort owners, and some members of the scientific community. This coalition believed that the ocean incineration technology was old and remained unproven; that incinerator stack emissions were toxic and capable of destroying Texas citrus orchards, cattle ranches, and shellfish grounds; and that an accidental or operational spill might devastate the coastal economy, including tourism.[19]

Each coalition attempted to influence the EPA on this issue through grass-roots lobbying efforts, hearings, and demonstrations, especially between 1983 and 1985. The strategy of the pro-incineration coalition was to restore public confidence in the safety of at-sea incineration and to get the EPA to issue permits for incineration ships and for hazardous wastes burn sites. The strategy of the anti-incineration coalition was to get the EPA to undertake additional research before approving procedures and/or to draft broad regulations for ocean incineration before granting permits for burning. At most, this coalition hoped to prevent the EPA from issuing permits for sites and ships for burning toxic wastes, and to bring suit against the EPA challenging the agency's authority to issue final permits if the regulations were perceived as too lax.[20]

Evidence suggests that the EPA was affected by the demands of these two pressure groups. The EPA's decision to require more research before approving permits for burns reflected a "balancing" of the demands by each of these two groups. Thus, the pluralist model helps analysts to understand the formulation of the EPA's policy for burning toxic wastes at sea.

Policy as Elite Preferences   The elitist model suggests that elites (e.g., corporate elites, key politicians, or top military leaders) dominate public policy outcomes. According to elite theorists, the masses are largely passive, apathetic, and ill informed; thus, mass sentiments are more often manipulated by elites, who share a consensus on behalf of the basic values of the social system. Policy questions are seldom influenced by democratic institutions such as elections or political parties; rather, policy outcomes result from the elites redefining their own values.

Some argue that Chemical Waste Management developed a "cozy relationship" with the Environmental Protection Agency during the discussions over burning toxic wastes at sea. Moreover, Chemical Waste Management acknowledges recruiting six former EPA officials to its payroll, and several EPA officials involved in issuing test-burn permits were rebuked in a 1983 inspector general's report for keeping Chemical Waste Management calendars on their office walls, thus creating the appearance of favoritism.[21]

In general, the EPA favored at-sea incineration as a waste disposal option. The agency often said that the at-sea incineration process "will have minimal effects on the marine environment."[22] Moreover, the EPA initially announced a decision to permit the burning of toxic waste at sea at a site off the New Jersey coast; this project alone would have added roughly 8 percent to Chemical Waste Management's earnings, which in 1984 totaled $142.5 million.[23] In addition, some scientists contended that, in its haste to find a solution to the hazardous waste management problem, the EPA itself promoted incineration with "flimsy research." It was argued that EPA staffers deleted sections of an independent scientific advisory's report to make it appear more favorable to the agency's enthusiastic position on at-sea incineration. The EPA, according to many environmental groups, "continues to relentlessly push ocean incineration, with the assumption that siting a hazardous waste disposal facility at sea will avoid the controversy of locating a facility on land in someone's back yard."[24]

Thus, the elitist model of policy formulation finds some support in the preceding description of the EPA's policy for at-sea incineration. The EPA seemed to develop a cozy relationship with the chemical waste industry and favored that industry's desire to burn wastes at sea, at least from 1983 to 1985.

TWO ADDITIONAL MODELS
OF DECISION MAKING

In this and Chapters 4 and 5 we have offered a variety of models to illustrate how agendas are created and policies formulated. As our examples illustrate, each of those models explains much of what happens when governments make decisions. Two other models—*groupthink* and the *garbage can model*—offer additional insights into how policy making proceeds. Each is discussed briefly below.

Groupthink

Social psychologist Irving Janis has argued that decision makers, particularly during times of crisis, are prone to the groupthink syndrome in which the desire for group unanimity overrides reasoned calculations and produces failed policies. The tendency to fall victim to groupthink is most likely to occur when policy makers come from similar backgrounds and share basic beliefs, are insulated from outside information, and lack a tradition of impartial leadership.[25] Based on his analysis of several foreign policy failures, including the Bay of Pigs invasion and the Vietnam War, Janis identified eight symptoms of groupthink: (1) an illusion of invulnerability, excessive optimism, and a willingness to take extreme risks; (2) a belief in the group's morality; (3) a tendency to discount information inconsistent with the group's decision; (4) a propensity to stereotype the enemy as either evil or inept (or both); (5) self-censorship; (6) an overestimation of the group's consensus; (7) pressure on members to conform to the group's pervading beliefs; and (8) the emergence of self-appointed "mindguards" to guard against information that challenges the group's position.[26]

According to Janis, when most of those symptoms are present decision making is likely to be characterized by (1) the incomplete consideration of goals and alternative courses of action; (2) a failure to consider risks; (3) a tendency to filter information that is inconsistent with the preferred policy; and (4) the lack of a contingency plan.[27]

Critics of the war in Iraq maintain that President George Bush and his advisors became "victims of groupthink" as they sought to justify and continue the war. Critics point to a number of examples as evidence of groupthink, including (1) the selective use of intelligence to make the case that Iraq had stockpiles of weapons of mass destruction and long-standing ties to the terrorist group al-Qaeda responsible for the attack on the Pentagon and World Trade Center in 2001; (2) the tendency to underestimate the difficulty and expense of the war; and (3) in an effort to find coalition partners, a tendency to divide the nations of the world into those "who are with us and those who are against us."[28]

Garbage Can Model

An even more radical departure from rational decision making is offered by the garbage can model first outlined by Cohen, March, and Olsen in the early 1970s.[29] A garbage can model begins with the assumption that decision making is inherently irrational, beset by confusion, uncertainty and conflict over goals, options, and worldviews. Where that occurs, policymaking becomes an expressive forum where policy makers "act out" social and political agendas that are largely unrelated to each other or some common problem. At that point, policymaking is characterized by (1) the practice of defining goals and policies only as decisions are made, (2) situations where solutions seek problems (and not vice versa), and (3) the articulation of policy as a rationale for events that have already occurred. Again, the war in Iraq is instructive. Commentaries on the war often contend that the attack on the World Trade Center and the Pentagon in September 2001 was used as a justification for what Paul Wolfowitz, Vice President Cheney, and others had advocated for a number of years—the invasion of Iraq and the removal of Saddam Hussein. In that scenario, invasion was a solution looking for a problem—the attack on 9/11 served as the problem that justified their solution.

THE EVOLUTION OF OUR UNDERSTANDING
OF POLICY FORMULATION

A great deal has been learned over the past several decades about the process of policy formulation. In the 1970s, several scholars attempted to further develop the systems model and to test it within several alternative contexts.[30] These efforts attempted to put "politics" back in the analysis of public policy. By encouraging one to think of politics as being much like a biological system, Easton's systems model provided a new way of thinking about determinants of policy outcomes. Forces both outside the political system as well as within the "black box" affected public policy.

In the 1980s, some causal theories of substantially new portions of the policy process have emerged, including theories and models of agenda setting, policy implementation, policy termination, and policy change.[31] In the 1990s, it was realized that policy formulation is never complete; public policy is constantly being changed through oversight and policy redesign. Thus, policy analysts are beginning to study policy change (the subject of Chapter 9). In this aspect of the policy cycle, analysts are interested in explaining why policies are changed from one type to another. Research from the 1950s until the present time has evolved so that there is a much more complete understanding of each aspect of the policy cycle. What is needed now, however, is a careful application and testing of existing models of the policy process so that they may be validated and accepted or falsified and rejected. Refinement and elaboration of many of these models is also needed, and even the development of new ones, as necessary.[32]

SUMMARY

In conclusion, the policy formulation aspect of the policy cycle is the most "mature" in terms of existing literature. This is the point where scholars began their research on the policy process, although more recently they have turned their attention toward other aspects of the policy cycle, such as policy implementation and policy change. In the next few chapters, we take up the subject of policy implementation, policy evaluation, and policy termination and change. These chapters illustrate the evolution of our understanding in these more "youthful" areas of the policy cycle.

DISCUSSION QUESTIONS

1. Is policymaking in the American system more reflective of the rational-comprehensive model or the incremental model? Illustrate your argument with examples that reflect either model.

2. Why isn't policymaking, in the United States context, more "rational"?

3. "Most problems aren't solved by government, although many are acted on by government." Do you agree or disagree with this statement? Why do you agree or disagree?

4. It is often argued that much policy in the United States is made without the problem ever having been clearly defined. Do you agree? Why or why not?

5. Is policymaking in the American context more reflective of the elitist or the pluralist model? Cite examples to buttress your argument.

6. How might the garbage can and groupthink models account for the renewed interest in formulating (or not) a policy that would address global warming?

SUGGESTED READINGS

Anderson, James E. *Public Policymaking,* Third Edition (Boston: Houghton Mifflin, 1997).

Dye, Thomas R. *Understanding Public Policy,* Ninth Edition (Upper Saddle River, NJ: Prentice Hall, 1998), especially Chapter 2.

Easton, David. *A Framework for Political Analysis* (Chicago: University of Chicago Press, 1979).

Landy, Marc, and Martin A. Levin,eds.*The New Politics of Public Policy* (Baltimore: Johns Hopkins University Press, 1995).

McCool, Daniel. *Public Policy Theories, Models, and Concepts* (Englewood Cliffs, NJ: Prentice Hall, 1995).

NOTES

1. James E. Anderson, *Public Policymaking: An Introduction* (Boston: Houghton Mifflin, 1990), p. 93.

2. See Deborah A. Stone, *Policy Paradox and Political Reason* (Glenview, IL: Scott, Foresman, 1988).

3. Anderson, *Public Policymaking*, p. 94.

4. Ibid., p. 96.

5. Michael Hirsh, "'All the Troops in the World Won't Make Any Difference,'" January 10, 2007. www.msnbc.msn.com/id/16543049/site/newsweek/ accessed 2/22/ 07]. *The Iraq Study Group Report* can be found at the Baker Institute's website at Rice University at www.bakerinstitute.org/Pubs/iraqstudygroup_findings.pdf 2/23/07.

6. V. O. Key, *Politics, Parties, and Pressure Groups,* 5th ed. (New York: T. Y. Crowell, 1964), p. 17.

7. Arthur Bentley, *The Process of Government* (Chicago: University of Chicago Press, 1908), p. 222.

8. Theodore Lowi, *The End of Liberalism* (New York: W. W. Norton, 1979).

9. Charles Lindblom, "The Science of Muddling Through," *Public Administration Review* 19 (Spring 1959), pp. 79–88.

10. David Easton, "An Approach to the Analysis of Political Systems," *World Politics* 9, no. 3 (April 1957), pp. 383–400.

11. Ibid., p. 384.

12. Thomas R. Dye, "A Model for the Analysis of Policy Outcomes," in *Policy Analysis in Political Science,* ed. Ira Sharkansky (Chicago: Markham Publishing, 1970).

13. See, for example, Robert H. Salisbury, "The Analysis of Public Policy: A Search for Theories and Roles," in *Political Science and Public Policy,* ed. Austin Ranney (Chicago: Markham Publishing, 1968), and Richard I. Hofferbert, "Elite Influences in State Policy Formation: A Model for Comparative Inquiry," *Polity* 2, no. 3 (Spring 1970), pp. 316–344.

14. See Joyce Matthews Munns, "The Environment, Politics, and Policy Literature," *Western Political Quarterly* 28, no. 4 (December 1975), pp. 646–667; Charles O. Jones, *Political Science and State and Local Government* (Washington, D.C.: APSA, 1973); James P. Lester and Emmett N. Lombard, "The Comparative Analysis of State Environmental Policy," *Natural Resources Journal* 30, no. 2 (Spring 1990), pp. 301–319; and Stuart H. Rakoff and Guenther F. Schaeffer, "Politics, Policy, and Political Science," *Politics and Society* 1, no. 1 (November 1970), pp. 51–77.

15. This section borrows heavily from an earlier article by James P. Lester and John C. Freemuth entitled "The Formation of Ocean Incineration Policy: Some Predictions from Three Models," *Policy Studies Review* 6, no. 2 (November 1986), pp. 340–347.

16. "Ocean Incineration Regulation," Proposed Rule, *Federal Register* (28 February, 1985), pp. 8222–8280.

17. K. Schneider, "Ocean Incineration: The Public Fumes While EPA Fiddles," *Sierra* 69 (1984), p. 26.

18. R. Reinhold, "States Oppose Burning of Toxic Wastes in Gulf," *New York Times,* 16 June 1985, p. A14.

19. Ibid.

20. Schneider, "Ocean Incineration."

21. Ibid.

22. "E.P.A. to Permit Test of Burning of Toxic Waste off Jersey Coast," *New York Times,* 27 November 1985, p. B2.

23. T. Petzinger and M. Moffett, "Plants That Incinerate Poisonous Waste Run Into a Host of Problems," *Wall Street Journal,* 26 August 1985, p. A1.

24. A. Narvaez, "Decision Due on Burning Toxic Waste off Jersey," *New York Times,* 6 May 1986, p. B2.

25. Irving L. Janis, *Victims of Groupthink: A Psychological Study of Foreign Policy Decisions and Fiascoes* (Boston: Houghton Mifflin Company, 1972).

26. Ibid., pp. 174–175.

27. Ibid., p. 127.

28. A quick search on Google revealed several commentaries that linked Janis' notion of groupthink to the prosecution of the war in Iraq. See, for example, Liza Porteus, "'Group Think' Led to WMD Assessment," Fox News.com, July 11, 2004, at www.foxnews.com/story/0,2933,125123,00.html accessed 3/15/07; Karen Alter "Is 'groupthink' driving us to war?" *Boston Globe,* September 15, 2002, at www.boston.com/news/packages/iraq/globe_stories/091602_alter.htm accessed 3/17/07; and William Branigin and Diana Priest, "Senate Report Blasts Intelligence Agencies Flaws," washingtonpost.com, July 9, 2004, at www.washingtonpost.com/ac2/wp-dyn/A38459-2004Jul9?language=printer accessed 3/17/07.

29. Michael D. Cohen, James G. March, and Johan P. Olsen, "A Garbage Can Model of Organizational Choice," *Administrative Science Quarterly* 17 (1972), pp. 1–25.

30. Richard I. Hofferbert, "Elite Influences in State Policy Formation: A Model for Comparative Inquiry," *Polity* 2, no. 3 (Spring 1970), pp. 316–344; and Mazmanian and Sabatier, "Multivariate Model."

31. See, for example, John Kingdon, *Agendas, Alternatives, and Public Policies* (New York: HarperCollins, 1995); Daniel Mazmanian and Paul A. Sabatier, *Implementation and Public Policy* (Glenview, IL: Scott, Foresman, 1983); and Paul A. Sabatier, "An Advocacy Coalition Framework of Policy Change and the Role of Policy Oriented Learning Therein," *Policy Sciences* 21, nos. 2–3 (1988), pp. 129–168.

32. Paul A. Sabatier, "Toward Better Theories of the Policy Process," *PS: Political Science and Politics* 24, no. 2 (June 1991), p. 153.

7

Policy Implementation

In the early summer or 1952, before the heat of the campaign, President
Truman used to contemplate the problems of the General-become-
President should Eisenhower win the forthcoming election. "He'll
sit there," Truman would remark (tapping his desk for emphasis), "and
he'll say, 'Do this? Do that!' **And nothing will happen.** Poor Ike—it
won't be a bit like the Army. He'll find it very frustrating."
Eisenhower evidently found it so.
RICHARD E. NEUSTADT, **PRESIDENTIAL POWER:**
THE POLITICS OF LEADERSHIP. 1960

This chapter seeks to introduce the reader to the process of implementation and
trace the evolution of implementation research. Our discussion proceeds in
three stages. First, we discuss the concept of implementation, including what we
mean by the term and the various activities and actors it encompasses. Second,
we consider the evolution of public policy implementation research from 1970
to the present. Finally, we review some of the more relevant concerns with this
research and provide some suggestions that will help to achieve further advances
in our understanding of policy implementation over the next few years.

THE CONCEPT OF POLICY IMPLEMENTATION

By implementation, we mean the stage of the policy process immediately after the
passage of a law. Implementation, viewed most broadly, means administration of the
law in which various actors, organizations, procedures, and techniques work

together to put adopted policies into effect in an effort to attain policy or program goals.[1] Previous definitions of implementation have ranged from this broad conceptualization to the more limited or dichotomous view that implementation is either achieved or not achieved. In addition to these two definitions, implementation can be thought of as a process, an output, and an outcome.[2] Consider the decisions and actions that typically must take place when, as is often the case, state governments are called upon to implement federal regulations. In those instances, five recurring activities or functions typically must occur. First, state legislatures pass **enabling laws** and initiate the hearings process associated with such legislation. Next, state agencies undertake **administrative rule making** and establish administrative routines for implementing the laws. Then, states appropriate **resources,** including the money and the human capital needed by the state to carry out the policy as intended. After this activity, federal legislators and regulators **monitor** and, through the application of sanctions and rewards, **enforce** state and in some cases local adherence to the laws and regulations. Finally, after some experience with their operations, lawmakers **redesign policies** in response to design flaws or missed opportunities.[3] The essential characteristic of the implementation process, then, is the timely and satisfactory performance of certain necessary tasks related to carrying out the intent of the law. This is most often termed *compliance.* For example, when implementing the Resource Conservation and Recovery Act of 1976 (RCRA), the process of implementation involved several tasks, such as enacting state enabling legislation that was consistent with the federal law, delegating the authority to run a program to a leading state agency, funding the program, and hiring sufficient staff to provide for adequate implementation.

Implementation can also be defined in terms of **outputs,** or the extent to which programmatic goals are supported, such as the level of expenditures committed to a program or the number of violations issued for failure to comply with the implementation directive. For example, during implementation of the Occupational Safety and Health Act (OSHA), notices of violations were issued to states that were not in compliance with the federal directive.

Finally, at the highest level of abstraction, implementation **outcomes** imply that there has been some measurable change in the larger problem that was addressed by the program, public law, or judicial decision. For example, has poverty been lessened or are citizens safer than at the time before the enactment of social welfare or crime policies?

In summary, implementation as a concept involves all these activities. Although it is a complex phenomenon, it may be understood as a process, an output, and an outcome. It also involves a number of actors, organizations, and techniques of control.

Who Implements Policy?

The Bureaucracy   Generally speaking, public policies in the United States are implemented by administrative agencies. Once Congress or its state and local counterparts has enacted a public law and the president or other chief executives has signed it, the next step is for the various administrative agencies to begin the process of implementation. These agencies have a great deal of discretion in carrying out the public policies under their jurisdiction because they often operate under broad and ambiguous statutory mandates from Congress. This situation exists because those who participate in the legislative process are often unable or unwilling to develop precise guidelines, either due to the complexity of the issue under consideration or because of lack of time, interest, or information.[4] For example, after the Resource Conservation and Recovery Act of 1976 was enacted into law, the Environmental Protection Agency (EPA) was charged with drafting the regulations for putting this law into effect. The EPA had to fill in the details of this legislation and reconcile the various conflicts embodied in the original legislation. The result was legislation that was termed the most complex in the history of environmental protection policy.[5]

Although administrative agencies are the primary actors in public policy implementation, a number of other actors and institutions are also involved in the process. Indeed, many would argue that elected and unelected officials have redoubled their efforts to influence implementation in recent decades.[6] These include legislatures, political executives, the courts, pressure groups, and community organizations.

The Legislature Historically, much of the public administration literature assumed that politics and administration were separate activities. Politics was therefore concerned with the formulation of policy, which should be handled by the "political" branches of government, meaning the legislative and executive branches. Administration of policy, on the other hand, was concerned with implementation of the decisions made by elected officials and was to be handled by the various administrative agencies.[7] Today, this assumption has been called into question because administrative agencies are often involved in formulating, as well as implementing, public policy. For example, when administrative agencies draft regulations in support of existing legislation, they often are formulating policy. We noticed this in the previous chapter on policy formulation in the case of at-sea incineration of toxic waste. Moreover, legislative bodies are often involved in implementing public policy when they draft very specific and detailed legislation. Increasingly, legislative bodies are concerned with implementation and are thus drafting laws that are very specific when it comes to implementation. That is, legislators today are more concerned with details and are attempting to remove much of the bureaucratic discretion previously enjoyed by administrative agencies in the implementation of policy. This practice has become a functional necessity because many implementation failures are due to problems that were not addressed in the original drafting of the law.

Lawmakers use a variety of tools to influence how bureaucrats implement laws. Traditionally, legislatures have relied on their power over an agency's budget, nominations, and oversight review to achieve control over bureaucratic behavior.[8] There is a sense, however, that those traditional mechanisms do not yield the amount of control that legislators desire. Agencies, for example, have learned to get around funding limits; and legislative oversight is time consuming and offers little payoff for individual legislators. Some scholars have argued that lawmakers and others often turn to an alternative set of controls. McCubbins and Schwartz, for instance, argue that lawmakers rely on fire-alarm oversight in which citizens and others are given the legal standing to take action when they feel that implementing agencies are failing to enforce laws as they were intended to be enforced.[9] For instance, under the federal surface mining act, Office of Surface Mining officials in the Department of the Interior are required to conduct an investigation of surface mining sites in response to a citizen's complaint. McCubbins, Noll, and Weingast argue that legislators can "stack the deck" through legislative provisions that either empower certain groups to sit at the regulatory table or mandate administrative procedures that limit the allowable actions agencies can take.[10]

Political Executives   Even though presidents, governors, and other chief executives are legally in charge of the executive branch of government, most learn early in their tenure that just because the "boss" says to do something does not mean it will be done, or done well. In the case of independent regulatory agencies, that is how it is intended to be—legislation creating independent regulatory agencies is written to ensure that the influence of elected officials, including presidents and governors, on the day-to-day operations of administrative agencies will be kept at a minimum. Elsewhere in the administrative sector, the limits on political control reflect the substantial discretion given to public bureaucracies. In that context presidents, governors, and other chief executives often find themselves competing with other political actors to influence administrators who, as it turns out, also bring their own values, beliefs, and resources to their decisions and actions. Like legislatures and the courts, presidents and other chief executives have various tools at their disposal to exert control over their subordinates in the executive branch. Those tools include various mechanisms that centralize agency budget requests and review of agency rulemaking within the chief executive's office, the appointment of most heads of executive departments, and the use of executive orders to set policy. As an example of the latter, in January 2007 President Bush issued an executive order requiring that federal agencies have a regulatory policy office headed by a political appointee who is responsible for supervising the development of regulatory rules and other documents by agency officials. The president's goal ostensibly was to give the White House greater control over regulatory agencies and limit the influence of Congress and agencies themselves on rulemaking.[11] While there are limits on these and other executive efforts at control, the available research indicates that presidents and governors are generally successful in directing the actions of their subordinates.[12]

The Courts   In many instances, public laws are enforced through the judicial branch. For example, in *Roe v. Wade,* the Supreme Court declared a Texas statute prohibiting abortion unconstitutional because it violated the privacy protected by the First and Fourteenth Amendments.[13] In 1989, the Supreme Court undermined *Roe v. Wade* in *Webster v. Reproductive Health Services.* In the latter case, the Court upheld a Missouri law that prohibited abortions in public facilities and the use of state funds for counseling women about abortion.[14] Since that time, the Supreme Court has agreed to hear several other cases on abortion. Thus, the Court will be involved in the implementation of laws governing abortion for some time to come.

Perhaps the courts' most important influence on implementation is through their interpretation of statutes and administrative rules and regulations and their review of administrative decisions in cases brought before them. Affirmative action is a good example of the courts' involvement in implementation. In September 1965, Executive Order 11246 (during the Johnson administration) required "affirmative action" to foster equal opportunity for minorities and women. Specifically, the order required government contractors and others receiving government funds to take concrete measures to promote the hiring of blacks and other minorities. In the late 1960s, the Equal Employment Opportunity Commission (EEOC), acting as **amicus curiae** in civil suits, achieved a number of successes in getting its view of affirmative action accepted by the courts. In 1970, a federal court ruled that "specific hiring goals and timetables" were "no more or less than a means for implementation of the affirmative action obligations of Executive Order 11246." This led to a view that affirmative action should be implemented with a goal of "proportional representation" of minorities in hiring decisions.[15]

Much of the *judicialization* of the administration process reflects the efforts of the U.S. Supreme Court and others to enforce the due process guarantees of the U. S. Constitution. The Fourteenth Amendment to the Constitution dictates that the states cannot "deprive any person of life, liberty, or property without due process of law." That protection has taken a number of forms in recent decades.[16] In some instances the Supreme Court's rulings have drawn upon both the Fourteenth Amendment and the Administrative Procedures Act to require implementing agencies to conduct *hybrid rulemaking* procedures before issuing rules and regulations. In addition, throughout the seventies the Court interpreted property rights to include government jobs and benefits (welfare, an education, a driver's license). Under that interpretation, agencies were obliged to conduct formal hearings before denying anyone welfare, educational, or other government benefits. In a landmark case, *Goldberg v. Kelly* (1970), the Supreme Court ruled that individuals could not be removed from the welfare rolls without going through a formal hearing that provided the individual with "an opportunity to appear in person or through counsel, oral argument and oral testimony, a chance to confront and cross-examine adverse witnesses, a neutral adjudicator, and a written decision based exclusively on the hearing record."[17]

In some instances the courts have gone so far as to effectively take over the management of public programs on behalf of individuals whose substantive and due process rights have been violated. Throughout the seventies, courts in a number of states charged prisons and mental health institutions with violating the rights of their inmates and patients and issued decisions that effectively wrested decision making from the implementing agencies. In a case in Alabama, for example, a federal judge found that living conditions in state prisons during the seventies were, by any standards, deplorable. In one prison, prisoners were fed only one meal a day and two hundred prisoners shared a single toilet. In many of the state's prisons, rapes and stabbings were common and physical facilities were dilapidated. Eventually, the federal judge issued decrees that, among other things, set space requirements for cells, imposed hiring requirements for prison personnel, and required prison officials to conduct regular physical exams of prisoners. In Texas, a federal judge simply ordered two facilities closed (*Morales v. Turman*, 1973).[18]

In recent years the Supreme Court has recognized the need for greater administrative discretion and flexibility in these kinds of due process rulings, but the courts still retain jurisdiction over the actions of federal and state agencies.[19]

Pressure Groups   Because administrative agencies have so much discretion in drafting regulations in support of legislation, they are besieged by various interest groups seeking to influence the guidelines and regulations in a way that will benefit their cause. Sometimes it is argued that various interest groups "capture" administrative agencies.[20] For example, some argue that the U.S. Coast Guard, which is the lead agency responsible for regulating ocean pollution, is involved in a "cozy" relationship with U.S. shipping and oil interests. This close relationship between the U.S. Coast Guard and these business interests may have led to the United States' opposition to "double bottoms" and the retrofitting of U.S. ships with segregated ballast during the 1970s and the 1980s, when the issues of tanker accidents and oil spills were on the agenda.[21]

Community Organizations   Finally, at the local level, community organizations often get involved in the implementation of public programs. An example of this kind of community involvement would include various advisory boards for toxic waste management under the Hazardous and Solid Waste Amendments of 1984, which required small businesses that produced at least 100 kilograms of toxic waste to comply with the federal law. Communities set up various advisory boards in an effort to take stock of the extent of small quantity generators (SQG) of hazardous waste so that they could design procedures for managing this low volume of waste within the community. Other examples include the various farmer committees under the price support and soil conservation programs of the Department of Agriculture, advisory boards for the Bureau of Land Management, and representatives of the poor for community action agencies.[22]

Techniques of Policy Implementation: The Use of Markets

As the scope of the public sector grew dramatically following World War II, scholars and policy makers have continued to debate the merits of using market forces to implement public policies. The move toward finding private sector solutions to public policy problems dates back to the fifties and sixties but found new life during the Reagan presidency. Based on the twin beliefs that governments had grown too large and that we all would be better off if we would just "run governments like we run our businesses," conservatives urged policy makers to take their cues from economics and the economic sector. That discussion typically revolved around two issues: (1) the use of market incentives in government regulation and (2) the use of private sector organizations to implement public programs.

With regard to regulation, much of the discussion about the merits of markets has centered on two approaches: the **command and control** approach and the **economic incentives** (or **market**) approach. The command and control approach involves the use of mechanisms that are somewhat coercive, such as standard setting, inspections, and imposing sanctions on violators who fail to comply with federal or state regulations. The economic incentives approach involves the use of tax credits, subsidies, or other rewards or penalties to encourage private interests to comply. Opponents of the command and control approach argue that it dictates behavior, discourages private initiative and innovation in attaining policy goals, and wastes or misuses societal resources. The incentive system, on the other hand, "lets individuals make their own decisions, thus enhancing freedom and voluntarism, and . . . achieves desired goals at the lowest possible cost to society."[23]

The debate between the two approaches can be illustrated in the area of environmental policy. The incentive or market approach to pollution is to tax companies that discharge pollutants into the air or water according to how much they discharge and how toxic their pollutants are. The standards approach, on the other hand, is to set permissible levels of discharge for various pollutants (called performance standards) and then fine companies that do not comply with these standards.[24] The fundamental difference between these two approaches lies in the use of variable prices (or taxes) in the market approach and relatively fixed prices (or penalties) in the other.

Faith in the wisdom of markets is also found in the move by governments at all levels toward **privatizing** public programs. In recent years there has been a dramatic increase in the range of public services that have been delegated to profit and not-for-profit (including faith-based) organizations. Local governments have always relied on private vendors for municipal services like garbage removal or road repair, but increasingly local authorities and their state counterparts are also turning to the private sector to—among other things—administer welfare programs, child protection services, health-care programs for the poor and elderly, public schools, and even state and local prisons.[25]

The federal government has also discovered the virtues (and problems) of the private sector. Much of the work of federal agencies, including the Department of Defense and various intelligence agencies, is outsourced to private companies. One source, for example, maintains that as much as 50 percent of the nation's intelligence budget goes to private firms.[26] In late 2006 the General Accounting Office (GAO) noted that Department of Defense (DOD) had dramatically increased its reliance on private contractors in recent years, particularly in Iraq and southeast Asia. According to the GAO, estimates provided by the U.S. Army indicated that 60,000 contract employees were serving in Southeast Asia (primarily Iraq) in support of military operations in 2006. That compares with just 9,200 employees during the 1991 Gulf War. Contractors provide a number of recurring services, including equipment repair, minor construction, security, and intelligence. Based on its analysis, the GAO concluded that despite recent efforts to reform the process of oversight of contractors, significant problems still remain, including (1) limited visibility over contractor activities; (2) a low priority given oversight within DOD; (3) no clear focal point for oversight responsibility within the DOD; and (4) a shortage of qualified personnel capable of conducting oversight review.[27]

Privatization is commended as a means of reducing the cost and increasing the quality of government services by drawing upon the forces of competition that operate in the private sector. But the use of private vendors also raises questions of control and accountability. Not surprisingly, the evidence on the relative merits of private versus public provision of services is mixed; and the debate continues both within and outside of government.[28]

THE EVOLUTION OF POLICY
IMPLEMENTATION RESEARCH

The study of policy implementation has grown substantially since Pressman and Wildavsky's case study of the difficulties encountered by the city of Oakland, California, when trying to implement a federal job training program during the late 1960s.[29] There is now an abundance of good theories and analytical frameworks, and there are at least two major approaches—the "top-down" and the "bottom-up" approaches—to understanding how implementation proceeds. This research has resulted in demonstrable progress in at least two respects: first, there is now a better understanding of what implementation is and how it varies across time, policies, and units of government; and second, advances have been made in linking certain characteristics of the policy's design and setting on the one hand with implementation performance on the other. There is no shortage of variables that are believed to explain implementation. Yet despite the progress to date, the "critical" variables have not yet been identified, and the measurement of key variables, as well as the careful testing of hypotheses, has just begun.[30] In this regard, implementation research at the advent of the 21st century is at approximately the same stage of development as was public policy research more generally a decade and a half ago.[31]

For the most part, implementation research has been concerned with acquiring a better understanding of the political, economic, organizational, and attitudinal factors that influence how well (or how poorly) a policy or program has been implemented. Two generations of research have sought to understand the determinants of implementation. First-generation studies of implementation were, for the most part, detailed accounts of how single authoritative decisions were carried out (i.e., case studies). This body of research was primarily directed toward describing the numerous barriers to effective policy implementation.[32] Second-generation studies were concerned with explaining implementation success or failure. A more detailed means of analyzing these two generations of research may be suggested by four distinct stages between 1970 and the present: (1) the generation of case studies; (2) the development of policy implementation frameworks; (3) the application of frameworks; and (4) syntheses and revisions. In the following pages, we briefly discuss these four phases of implementation research, paying careful attention to key contributions during each stage of theoretical development.

Case Studies, 1970–75

In the early 1970s, very little research was available on public policy implementation. This situation existed even though many new public programs were being implemented; moreover, "little knowledge was available to assist in the implementation process, and only a few observers even appreciated the need to understand why implementation failed or succeeded."[33] As one scholar of implementation notes, "initial studies of implementation were, for the most part, detailed accounts of how a single authoritative decision was carried out, either at a single location or at multiple sites."[34] These pioneering studies, such as one by Martha Derthick, came to the pessimistic conclusion that government-sponsored programs seldom achieved their objectives.[35] Little or no attempt was made to develop any dynamic model of the implementation process that could explain such failures, or to provide any real guidance about how to relieve the problems. Moreover, the case study approach, used almost exclusively by the early researchers, made it exceedingly difficult for investigators to either introduce the element of control for multiple explanations or generalize from their findings. Early investigators were plagued by the problem of too many variables and too few cases. Therefore, they could not really extract much from their findings. By the mid-1970s, however, policy implementation scholars had begun to turn their attention toward the next stage of intellectual development— model building.

Policy Implementation Frameworks, 1975–80

Although describing the numerous barriers to effective implementation was extremely useful, it did not result in the development of useful theory about policy implementation. However, the second broad category of implementation literature sought to develop analytical frameworks that identified factors contributing to the realization (or non-realization) of policy objectives. The work conducted in this area can be broadly classified into top-down and bottom-up approaches.[36]

Essentially, the top-down approach starts with a policy decision by central government officials and then asks:

1. To what extent were the actions of implementing officials and target groups consistent with (the objectives and procedures outlined in) that policy decision?

2. To what extent were the objectives attained over time (i.e., to what extent were the impacts consistent with the objectives)?

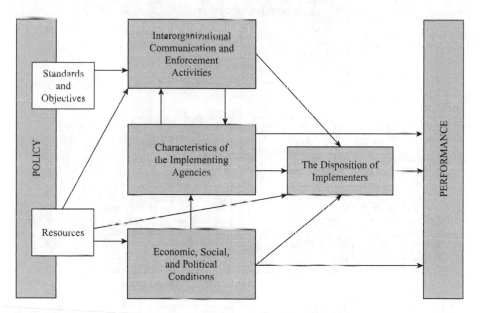

FIGURE 7.1 A Model of the Policy Implementation Process.

SOURCE: Donald Van Meter and Carl Van Horn, "The Policy Implementation Process: A Conceptual Framework," *Administration and Society 6*. Copyright © 1975 by Sage Publications, Inc. Reprinted with permission of Sage Publications, Inc.

3. What were the principal factors affecting policy outputs and impacts, both those relevant to the official policy as well as other politically significant ones?

4. How was the policy reformulated over time on the basis of experience?[37]

The first such top-down effort was undertaken by Donald Van Meter and Carl Van Horn.[38] Their model—as depicted in Figure 7.1—posited six variables that were believed to shape the linkage between policy and performance. Their variables included the following: (1) policy standards and objectives; (2) policy resources (e.g., funds or other incentives); (3) interorganizational communication and enforcement activities; (4) characteristics of implementing agencies (e.g., staff size, degree of hierarchical control, organizational vitality); (5) economic, social, and political conditions (e.g., economic resources within the implementing jurisdiction, public opinion, interest-group support); and (6) the disposition of the implementers.[39]

Other top-down models included those developed by Sabatier and Mazmanian and by Edwards.[40] The most comprehensive list of factors thought to affect the success of implementing a program can be found in the work of Sabatier and Mazmanian, as shown in Figure 7.2. They identified 16 independent variables within 3 major categories: (1) the tractability of the problem; (2) the ability of the statute to structure implementation; and (3) nonstatutory variables affecting implementation. All the variables mentioned in Figure 7.2 were thought to affect implementation.

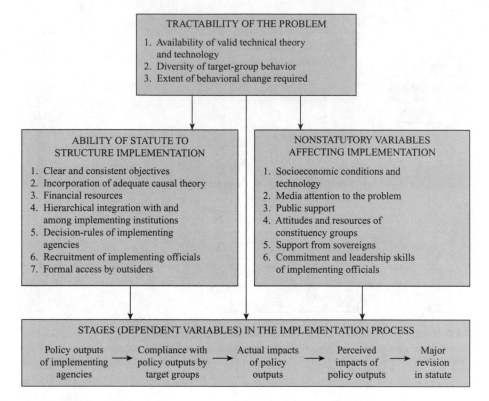

TRACTABILITY OF THE PROBLEM

1. Availability of valid technical theory
   and technology
2. Diversity of target-group behavior
3. Extent of behavioral change required

ABILITY OF STATUTE TO
STRUCTURE IMPLEMENTATION

1. Clear and consistent objectives
2. Incorporation of adequate causal theory
3. Financial resources
4. Hierarchical integration with and
   among implementing institutions
5. Decision-rules of implementing
   agencies
6. Recruitment of implementing officials
7. Formal access by outsiders

NONSTATUTORY VARIABLES
AFFECTING IMPLEMENTATION

1. Socioeconomic conditions and
   technology
2. Media attention to the problem
3. Public support
4. Attitudes and resources of
   constituency groups
5. Support from sovereigns
6. Commitment and leadership skills
   of implementing officials

STAGES (DEPENDENT VARIABLES) IN THE IMPLEMENTATION PROCESS

Policy outputs
of implementing
agencies
→ Compliance with
policy outputs by
target groups
→ Actual impacts
of policy
outputs
→ Perceived
impacts of
policy outputs
→ Major
revision
in statute

FIGURE 7.2 Skeletal Flow Diagram of the Variables Involved in the
Implementation Process.

SOURCE: Daniel H. Mazmanian and Paul Sabatier, *Implementation and Public Policy*. Copyright © 1983
by HarperCollins; Figure 2-1 copyright © 1983 by Scott Foresman & Company. Reprinted with permission of
HarperCollins College Publishers, Inc.

Thus, the number of variables thought to affect implementation ranged from
4 to 16, and although some of these models were able to explain implementation
behavior with very few determinants, all were criticized for failing to identify
which variables were likely to be most important and under what circumstances.[41] In addition to this criticism, others criticized the top-downers for assuming
"that the framers of the policy decision (i.e., the people who drafted the statute)
are the key actors and that others are basically impediments. This, in turn, leads
the top-downers to neglect strategic initiatives coming from the private sector,
from street level bureaucrats or local implementing officials, and from other policy subsystems."[42]

In the light of these criticisms, a competing model of policy implementation,
often termed "backward mapping" or the bottom-up approach, was developed by
several scholars. These individuals included Richard Elmore, Michael Lipsky, and
Benny Hjern and his associates.[43] In contrast to the top-down approach, the bottom-
up approach starts by identifying the network of actors involved in service delivery in
one or more local areas and asks them about their goals, strategies, activities,

and contacts. "It then uses the contacts as a means for developing a network technique to identify the local, regional, and national actors involved in the planning, financing, and execution of the relevant governmental and non-governmental programs."[44] Rather than being controlled by central decision makers, policy is determined by the bargaining (explicit or implicit) between members of the organization and their clients. Therefore, "programs must be compatible with the wishes and desires, or at least the behavioral patterns, of those lower echelon officials."[45]

Similarly, this approach received a great deal of criticism for assuming that policy implementation occurs (or should occur) in a decentralized policymaking environment. Thus, the bottom-up approach was somewhat flawed by a rather limited explanation of implementation behavior as both a desirable form of implementation and the only analytical approach for a complex organizational and political problem. For the next five years, various scholars were involved in testing these top-down or bottom-up models.

Applications of the Frameworks, 1980–85

Most of the major implementation frameworks were tested by their authors or by others during the period of 1980–85. According to Carl Van Horn, four broad lessons could be drawn from these empirical studies. First, the frameworks were quite useful in constructing general explanations for policy implementation success and failure. Second, implementation researchers demonstrated that time periods were important in implementation research (i.e., results varied depending on whether they were limited to only a few years of investigation or longer time frames). Third, some programs were successfully implemented (i.e., the case studies of the late 1960s and early 1970s emphasized failure, whereas later implementation studies suggested a more optimistic outcome). Finally, "scholars found that even simple, modest programs can fail."[46]

Both first- and second-generation implementation research have added much to the knowledge of what implementation is, and how and why it varies as it does. However, the research has been much less helpful in differentiating among types of implementation outcomes or in specifying the explanations associated with these outcomes. Also, the research has not helped explain why these patterns occur so frequently, nor has it identified the relative importance and unique effects of each of the various independent variables that are part of any adequate analysis of implementation performance. Those criticisms have led to recent efforts by various scholars to synthesize what they have learned and to suggest some promising revisions for future research.

Syntheses and Revisions, 1985–Present

Most recently, a number of scholars have provided a synthesis and critique of the implementation literature.[47] These syntheses have produced some criticisms of both the top-down and bottom-up models of policy implementation and have led to at least three attempts to incorporate the best features of each of the two approaches.

The first such attempt (in the United States) was developed by Richard Elmore, who combined his previous work on "backward mapping" with what he termed "forward mapping." In this initial synthesis, Elmore argued that policy makers need to consider both the policy instruments and other resources at their disposal (forward mapping) with the incentive structure of ultimate target groups (backward mapping), because program success is contingent on combining both these considerations. He did not, however, provide a graphic model of the policy implementation process that could be used by scholars to explain this particular phenomenon.[48]

A more ambitious approach was developed by Paul Sabatier, Hank Jenkins-Smith, and their associates.[49] Their synthesis combined the bottom-up influences (e.g., the actions or beliefs of local implementing agents) with top-down forces including relatively stable system parameters like the basic attributes of the programs and constitutional rules and structures. Sabatier and his associates then applied this synthesized perspective to the analysis of policy change over periods of a decade or more in the United States and elsewhere. In contrast to earlier implementation research, their model emphasized developing theory rather than providing policy advice to practitioners. That model also reminds analysts that policy formulation and implementation are not distinct processes, but are bound up in a dynamic fashion. For those who embrace the advocacy coalition framework (ACF), the emphasis should be on how policies (including "policy as implemented") change over time in response to various forces including changes in socioeconomic conditions, public opinion, or governing coalitions. In addition, the appropriate unit of analysis is the policy subsystem that exists within policy areas and subareas. It includes not just implementing administrators, legislators, and interest groups, but political actors at all levels of government—federal, state, and local—as well as journalists and policy analysts. Within policy systems, one or more advocacy coalitions typically emerge. According to Sabatier and Jenkins-Smith, those coalitions are "composed of people from various governmental and private organizations that both 1) share a set of normative and causal beliefs and 2) engage in a nontrivial degree of coordinated activity over time."[50] We look more closely at the ACF model in Chapter 9.

Finally, a third attempt to synthesize elements of both the top-down and bottom-up approaches was developed by Malcolm Goggin and his associates.[51] In their model of intergovernmental policy implementation, they argued that state implementation was in turn a function of inducements and constraints provided to (or imposed on) the states from elsewhere in the federal system—above or below—as well as a function of the states' own propensity to act and their capacity to effectuate their preferences. Moreover, state choices were not those of a single rational actor but may have been the result of bargaining among parties above them (the national level) as well as those below them (the local level) who were involved in state politics. Thus, this approach assumes that state implementation of federal programs ultimately depends on both top-down and bottom-up types of variables. This synthesis yields the conceptual framework displayed in Figure 7.3.

Goggin and his colleagues' approach is predicated on the notion that there is no single explanation for differences in implementation. The national decision

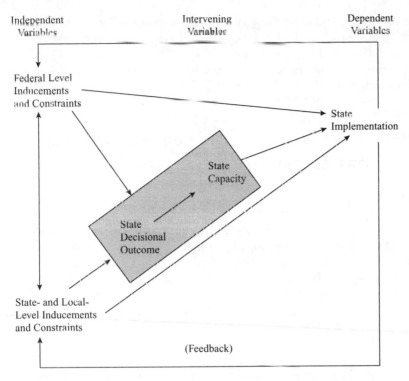

FIGURE 7.3 A Conceptual Model of Intergovernmental Policy Implementation.

SOURCE: Figure 1.1 from Malcolm L. Goggin et al., *Implementation Theory and Practice*. Copyright © 1990 by Malcolm L. Goggin, Ann O'M. Bowman, James P Lester, and Laurence J. O'Toole Jr. Reprinted by permission of Pearson Education, Inc.

that triggers an implementation process constrains by its form and content, to varying degrees, the choices and behaviors of those states and cities that have to execute the legislation. State responses to federal inducements (or local responses to state inducements) and constraints vary, depending on the nature and intensity of the preferences of several key participants (inclusive of the local level) in the state policy process at different points in time. Finally, state responses are also constrained by the state's capacity to act.[52]

In the aftermath of these recent syntheses and revisions, researchers have come to a crossroads in the study of policy implementation. One direction, suggested by Paul Sabatier, takes analysts down the path of studying the "politics of policy change," a topic we discuss in some detail in Chapter 9. This line of research "is primarily concerned with theory construction rather than with providing guidelines for practitioners or detailed portraits of particular situations."[53]

An alternative path is suggested by Elmore and by Goggin and his colleagues. Although both are concerned with policy implementation, Elmore is primarily concerned with aiding policy practitioners, whereas the framework suggested by Goggin and his colleagues is explicitly directed toward *both* theory development and useful advice for policy practitioners.[54] However, a number of conceptual and methodological issues must be addressed before any of these approaches provide either an advance in theory development or useful advice for decision makers.

WHERE ARE WE NOW? THE CURRENT STATUS OF IMPLEMENTATION RESEARCH

Today the study of public policy implementation presents many exciting opportunities for research that could enhance understanding of the concept. In the new century, policy analysts are poised for exciting new breakthroughs in their understanding of the determinants of implementation. Analysts have progressed to the point where they can apply these new frameworks to better understand the key determinants (or critical variables) in the process of implementing public policies. They now know that implementation is affected by top-down as well as bottom-up kinds of variables. Again, the case of state implementation of federal laws is instructive. We know, for example, that state implementation is influenced by federal-level factors, such as the clarity of the message (the law itself or regulations) that the federal government sends to the states. In addition, the amount of resources (money) that the federal government provides to the states is crucial to the successful implementation of public programs. Some states are more dependent on federal intergovernmental aid than others. California, for example, is not very dependent on federal intergovernmental aid for implementation of its environmental programs, whereas Mississippi is very dependent on federal aid for implementing its environmental programs. In this instance, Mississippi's ability to implement federal mandates in the environmental area would be adversely affected by federal cutbacks in the level of intergovernmental aid supporting Mississippi's environmental programs. These kinds of top-down variables are important determinants of the success or failure of state implementation efforts.

At the same time, there are bottom-up conditions that also affect state success or failure in implementation. Such factors include state and local political and economic conditions, state capacities (including resources and personnel) for implementation, and the dispositions of state and local implementers. For example, the "liberalness" or the "conservativeness" of a state's political environment will obviously affect how easily a policy is implemented. Welfare policies might be easier to implement in a more liberal state rather than a more conservative one. In contrast, a "get-tough" crime policy might be more easily implemented in a conservative state. Furthermore, wealthier states are more likely than poorer states are to implement policies that require huge expenditures of state funds.

In addition to these factors, states vary in terms of their institutional and resource capacity to implement federal policies. For example, the availability of staff to implement federal mandates varies greatly among states. In the early nineties, the state of New Jersey had considerably more personnel to implement environmental programs than did states such as Nevada or Wyoming.[55] Similarly, the amount of state resources (funds available) to implement federal programs also varies greatly from state to state. States having more fiscal resources are much more likely to implement public programs than are states with fewer fiscal resources.

Finally, it is also known that the dispositions of state and local implementers are a crucial determinant of implementation. That is, if state and local implementers favor the policy or program, then its implementation will fare much better than that of a policy or program that state and local implementers are hostile to.[56] Similarly, there is evidence that the attitudes toward those being regulated influence the actions of implementing officials.[57] In the opinion of some implementation scholars, the disposition of the implementers is the most important factor influencing implementation of federal or state programs. For almost all implementation scholars, this factor is an important one and is incorporated in many of their frameworks.

In summary, a great deal is known about public policy implementation. Undoubtedly, scholars can learn much more in the future as they turn their attention toward the next generation of implementation research. However, before the next generation is successful in bringing a greater level of understanding, some concerns will need to be addressed.

WHERE ARE WE GOING? TOWARD A THIRD GENERATION OF RESEARCH

Many scholars of policy implementation now agree that the next phase of research must be directed toward theory development. In addition, new questions have to be addressed in order to illuminate what so little is known about (i.e., the full range of outcomes that lie between the extremes of implementation success and failure, the various causal paths leading to each type of outcome, how frequently they occur, and their relative importance in historical analyses of implementation outcomes). This third generation of implementation studies, nonetheless, will first have to overcome some conceptual and methodological difficulties.

First, future research will have to specify the activities that are clearly **implementation** activities, so that policy analysts can say with certainty when implementation has occurred and when it has not. Analysts must agree on what is meant by the term *implementation* (i.e., when it begins and when it ends). Typically, past research has viewed implementation in terms of a success/failure dichotomy, frequently on the basis of a one-time determination during the take-off stage of the implementation period. Yet, as mentioned earlier, implementation can be thought of as a process, an output, and an outcome.

Second, as discussed above, there is no shortage of variables believed to explain implementation, but the crucial variables have not yet been identified. For example, it could be argued that the **policy** itself (i.e., its form and content) is the first critical independent variable, and the **setting** (i.e., the people and organizations involved in implementing a policy) is the second critical independent variable.[58] In any case, researchers need to move beyond their current checklist of presumably important variables that are thought to explain implementation and toward a systematic identification of the fewest number of independent variables that consistently explain implementation behavior across time.

Third, despite an impressive growth in the quantity and quality of implementation research in recent years, such studies are still too often bottom-up investigations of how local communities or school districts (including street-level bureaucrats) negotiate with federal, regional, and state agency personnel and elected representatives and the environment to arrive at a mutually satisfying policy. Or, they are top-down studies of how a federal mandate (e.g., a public law or Supreme Court decision) constrains choices at the state or local government level. Thus, there is still a need to combine elements of both the top-down and bottom-up frameworks into a single model of intergovernmental policy implementation that, in turn, could help to provide a richer and more accurate understanding of the policy implementation process. Recently, scholars have recognized the need to compare and evaluate the relative merits of these two approaches in various settings, and they have proposed combining the variables and insights of both in empirical work.[59]

Finally, many of the insights and conceptual developments resulting from the study of comparative state politics and policy have yet to be applied to the study of policy implementation. Over the past 30 years, the literature of comparative state politics has developed considerable sophistication regarding the relative importance of socioeconomic and political process variables in explaining state policy outputs.[60] There are many reasons to expect state-level factors to be as important in the implementation process as in the process of policy formulation. Yet, very few of these ideas and findings (and their implications) have been introduced into the literature on policy implementation.[61] Thus, future research on policy implementation could benefit from using research designs from the comparative state policy literature, namely, by adopting designs that are genuinely **comparative** (i.e., across the fifty American states), **diachronic** (i.e., across periods of a decade or more), and **across policy types** (i.e., distributive, redistributive, and regulatory).

CASE STUDY

Implementation Failure: The Federal, State, and Local Response to Hurricane Katrina

Perhaps nothing more graphically illustrates the how and why (and with what consequences) of implementation failure than the response of all three levels of government—federal, state, and local—to Hurricane Katrina in August 2005. On Monday, August 29, a category 5 hurricane slammed into the gulf coast states of Louisiana and Mississippi with winds of up to 145 mph. The hurricane caused billions of dollars of property damage, taking the lives of hundreds of gulf coast residents and injuring thousands more. Because of its geography, the devastation was greatest in New Orleans. Although the eye of the storm did not directly hit the city, New Orleans sits below sea level and Lake Pontchartrain. Once the levees protecting the city from the lake were breached on August 30, nearly 80 percent of the city's land area was flooded within a few short hours. Americans watched as families clung to roofs in the baking sun while tens of thousands of the city's residents found shelter in the Superdome and elsewhere waiting for food, water, and medical care. Reports of bodies floating in the storm waters, looting, and violence filled the airwaves as Americans sat transfixed while watching the devastation on the Weather Channel, CNN, Fox News, and other cable stations.

For many, the real tragedy of Katrina was how slowly governments at all levels responded to the plight of those thousands of New Orleans residents who were unable to leave the city. In the weeks and months that followed, federal, state and local officials were criticized for failing to plan for the hurricane, respond to the immediate needs of the city's residents who were unable to evacuate, or adequately aid the city in its attempts to rebuild. New Orleans Mayor Ray Nagin has been criticized, for instance, for ordering the mandatory evacuation just 19 hours ahead of landfall and failing to adequately implement the city's evacuation plan. For her part, Louisiana governor Kathleen Bianco has been faulted for not asking for federal aid soon enough to provide adequate supplies and security. The bulk of the blame for the government's response to Katrina, however, was aimed at the Federal Emergency Management Agency (FEMA) and its then director, Michael Brown. Perhaps the harshest criticism is that Brown and FEMA failed to supply relief in a timely fashion to the thousands who lacked shelter, water, and food. FEMA reportedly had pre-positioned enough water and food to feed just 15,000 of those residents unable to evacuate the city—a number far short of the tens of thousands of New Orleanians who would need immediate relief. In an effort to take control of the situation and coordinate the government's response, Brown also reportedly turned down offers of assistance from police forces, emergency crews, and others.[62] To make matters worse, Brown issued a directive on August 29 that "urged all fire and emergency services departments not to respond to counties and states affected by Hurricane Katrina without being requested and lawfully dispatched by state and local authorities under mutual aid agreements and the Emergency Management Assistance Compact."[63] Not surprisingly, the first large convoy of basic food supplies did not arrive at the Convention Center until midday Friday, September 2—a full four days after the hurricane first hit the city.

A year after Katrina, New Orleans remained much as it was in September 2005. Although things have returned to something like normal in the French Quarter and other tourist areas, much of the city and surrounding parishes remained in ruins, and the city's population had fallen from half a million to less than 200,000. There is also concern that many in the white business community are not committed to rebuilding the city as it was pre-Katrina. And while the levees have been repaired, officials at the Army Corps of Engineers admit that those repairs provide only a temporary fix.[64]

SUMMARY

If policy analysts recognize the limitations of implementation research as it has been practiced in the past and attempt to design research strategies that address some of the weaknesses noted above, they should improve their understanding of the implementation process. The results of these new investigations should also allow analysts to improve implementation outcomes by using the results from these studies to redesign policies so that they "work" better. That is, policy makers and managers should be able to use the knowledge generated from this third generation of implementation research to design or redesign policies so that implementation is facilitated. At the same time the increasing use of the private sector including faith-based organizations to implement public policies raises new challenges for both those who design and those who analyze public policies. Those challenges aside, the future of implementation research is an optimistic one, and one that should greatly improve our understanding of this crucial phase of the policy cycle.

DISCUSSION QUESTIONS

1. What is implementation? How does one distinguish policy implementation from policy formulation?

2. What are the differences between first-generation implementation research and second-generation research? What are the differences between second-generation research and third-generation research?

3. What are the advantages and disadvantages of having not-for-profit organizations administer programs like welfare or child protection services? What policy areas are most susceptible to privatization? Why?

4. The war in Iraq raises a number of questions about the ability of the U.S. Congress to conduct meaningful oversight of the executive branch. What role (if any) should the Congress have played in how the war was conducted?

5. Paul Sabatier advises us to move from the study of policy implementation to the study of policy change. Do you think that policy implementation deserves further study, or is it a concept that has outlived its usefulness?

SUGGESTED READINGS

Bardach, Eugene. *The Implementation Game* (Cambridge, MA: MIT Press, 1977).

Golden, Marissa. *What Motivates Bureaucrats? Politics and Administration During the Reagan Years.* (New York: Columbia University Press, 2000).

Goggin, Malcolm L., Ann O'M. Bowman, James P. Lester, and Laurence J. O'Toole. *Implementation Theory and Practice: Toward a Third Generation* (New York: Harper-Collins, 1990).

Lennon, Mary Clare, and Thomas Corbet, *Policy into Action: Implementation Research and Welfare Reform* (Washington, D.C.: Urban Institute, 2003).

Nakamura, Robert T., and Frank Smallwood. *The Politics of Policy Implementation* (New York: St. Martin's Press, 1980).

Pressman, Jeffrey, and Aaron Wildavsky. *Implementation* (Berkeley: University of California Press, 1973).

Stoker, Robert. *Reluctant Partners: Implementing Federal Policy* (Pittsburgh: University of Pittsburgh Press, 1991).

Werner, Alan. *A Guide to Implementation Research* (Washington, D.C.: Urban Institute, 2004).

NOTES

1. James E. Anderson, *Public Policymaking: An Introduction* (Boston: Houghton Mifflin, 1990), p. 172.

2. Malcolm Goggin, Ann O'M. Bowman, James Lester, and Laurence O'Toole, *Implementation Theory and Practice: Toward a Third Generation* (New York: Harper-Collins, 1990), p. 34.

3. Ibid., pp. 46–47.

4. Anderson, *Public Policymaking*, p. 174.

5. James P. Lester, "Hazardous Waste and Policy Implementation: The Subnational Role," *Hazardous Waste and Hazardous Materials* 2, no. 3 (Fall 1985), pp. 381–397; see also James P. Lester and Ann O'M. Bowman, eds., *The Politics of Hazardous Waste Management* (Durham, NC: Duke University Press, 1983), pp. 9–11.

6. See William Gormley, *Taming the Bureaucracy: Muscles, Prayers, and Other Strategies* (Princeton, NJ: Princeton University Press, 1989); and Kenneth Meier and John Bohte, *Politics and Bureaucracy: Policymaking in the Fourth Branch of Government*, 5th ed. (Belmont, CA: Thomson Wadsworth, 2007).

7. Frank J. Goodnow, *Politics and Administration* (New York: Russell and Russell, 1900).

8. See Meier and Bohte, *Politics and Bureaucracy*.

9. Matthew D. McCubbins and Thomas Schwartz, "Congressional Oversight Overlooked: Police Patrols versus Fire Alarms," *American Journal of Political Science* 28, no. 1 (1984), pp. 165–179.

10. Matthew McCubbins, Roger Noll, and Barry Weingast, "Administrative Procedures as Instruments of Political Control," *Journal of Law, Economics, and Organization* 3, no. 2 (1989), pp. 243–277.

11. Robert Pear, "Bush Signs Order Increasing Sway at U.S. Agencies," *New York Times*, 30 January 2007, pp. A3, A19.

12. See, for example, Gormley, *Taming the Bureaucracy*; B. Dan Wood and Richard W. Waterman, *Bureaucratic Dynamics: The Role of Bureaucracy in a Democracy* (Boulder, CO: Westview Press, 1994); Marissa Golden, *What Motivates Bureaucrats? Politics and Administration During the Reagan Years* (New York: Columbia University Press, 2000); and Meier and Bohte, *Politics and the Bureaucracy*.

13. *Roe v. Wade*, 410 U.S. 113 (1973).

14. See *New York Times*, 4 July 1989, pp. A1, A8–12.

15. Charles Murray, *Losing Ground* (New York: Basic Books, 1984), pp. 93–95; see also Nathan Glazer, *Affirmative Discrimination: Ethnic Inequality and Public Policy* (New York: Basic Books, 1975).

16. Our discussion of the judicialization of the administrative process is drawn from William Gormley's excellent analysis of the courts' role in Gormley, *Taming the Bureaucracy*.

17. Ibid., p. 98.

18. Ibid.

19. Philip J. Cooper, "Conflict or Constructive Tension: The Changing Relationship of Judges and Administrators," *Public Administration Review* (November 1985), pp. 643–652.

20. Marvin H. Bernstein, *Regulating Business by Independent Commission* (Princeton, NJ: Princeton University Press, 1955).

21. James P. Lester, "Domestic Structures and International Technological Collaboration: Ocean Pollution Regulation," *Ocean Development and International Law Journal* 8 (1980), pp. 299–335.

22. Anderson, *Public Policymaking*, p. 178.

23. This discussion draws on Deborah A. Stone, *Policy Paradox and Political Reason* (Glenview, IL: Scott, Foresman, 1988), pp. 224–230.

24. Ibid., p. 225.

25. Demetra Smith Nightingale and Nancy M. Pindus, "Privatization of Public Social Services: A Background Paper" (October 15, 1997), at www.urban.org/url.cfm?OD=407023 accessed September 1, 2006; and David M. Van Slyke, "The Mythology of Privatization in Contracting for Social Services," *Public Administration Review* 63 (2003), pp. 296–315.

26. Tim Shorrock, "The spy who came in from the boardroom," January 8, 2007, at www.salon.com/news/feature/2007/01/08/mcconnell/ accessed February 19, 2007.

27. General Accounting Office, "High Level DOD Action Needed to Address Long-Standing Problems with Management and Oversight of Contractors Supporting Deployed Forces" (Washington, D.C.: GAO, November 2006).

28. See Charles T. Goodsell, *The Case for Bureaucracy*, 4th ed. (Chatham, NJ: Chatham House, 2004); and Nightingale and Pindus, "Privatization of Public Social Services."

29. Jeffrey Pressman and Aaron Wildavsky, *Implementation* (Berkeley: University of California Press, 1973). This discussion draws heavily on James P. Lester et al., "Public Policy Implementation: Evolution of the Field and Agenda for Future Research," *Policy Studies Review* 7, no. 1 (Autumn 1987), pp. 200–216.

30. Laurence O'Toole, "Policy Recommendations for Multi-Actor Implementation: An Assessment of the Field," *Journal of Public Policy* 6 (1986), pp. 181–210; Malcolm Goggin, "The Too Few Cases/Too Many Variables Problem in Implementation Research," *Western Political Quarterly* 38 (1986), pp. 328–347; and James P. Lester and Ann O'M. Bowman, "Implementing Environmental Policy in a Federal System: A Test of the Sabatier-Mazmanian Model," *Polity* 21, no. 4 (Summer 1989), pp. 731–753.

31. George D. Greenberg et al., "Developing Public Policy Theory: Perspectives From Empirical Research," *American Political Science Review* 71 (1977), pp. 1532–1543.

32. Steven H. Linder and B. Guy Peters, "A Design Perspective on Policy Implementation: The Fallacies of Misplaced Prescription," *Policy Studies Review* 6 (1987), pp. 459–475.

33. R. K. Yin, "Studying the Implementation of Public Programs," in *Studying Implementation: Methodological and Administrative Issues*, ed. Walter Williams (Chatham, NJ: Chatham House Publishers, 1982), p. 37.

34. Goggin, "Too Few Cases."

35. Martha Derthick, "Defeat at Ft. Lincoln," *The Public Interest* 20 (1970), pp. 3–39; Pressman and Wildavsky, *Implementation;* and Eugene Bardach, *What Happens After a Bill Becomes a Law* (Cambridge, MA: MIT Press, 1977).

36. Paul A. Sabatier, "Top-Down and Bottom-Up Approaches to Implementation Research: A Critical Analysis and Suggested Synthesis," *Journal of Public Policy* 6, no. 1 (1986), pp. 21–48; and Linder and Peters, "Design Perspective."

37. Sabatier, "Implementation Research."

38. Donald Van Meter and Carl Van Horn, "The Policy Implementation Process: A Conceptual Framework," *Administration and Society* 6 (1975), pp. 445–488.

39. Ibid., pp. 462–464.

40. George Edwards, *Implementing Public Policy* (Washington, D.C.: Congressional Quarterly Press, 1980); and Daniel H. Mazmanian and Paul A. Sabatier, *Implementation and Public Policy* (Glenview, IL: Scott, Foresman, 1983).

41. Helen Ingram, "Implementation: A Review and Suggested Framework," in *Public Administration: The State of the Field*, ed. Aaron Wildavsky and Naomi Lynn (Chatham, NJ: Chatham House, 1987).

42. Sabatier, "Implementation Research," p. 30.

43. Michael Lipsky, "Street Level Bureaucracy and the Analysis of Urban Reform," *Urban Affairs Quarterly* 6 (1971), pp. 391–409; Benny Hjern and David O. Porter, "Implementation Structures: A New Unit of Administrative Analysis," *Organization Studies* 2/3 (1981), pp. 211–227; and Richard Elmore, "Backward Mapping: Implementation Research and Policy Decision," *Political Science Quarterly* 94 (1979), pp. 606–616.

44. Sabatier, "Implementation Research," p. 32.

45. Linder and Peters, "Design Perspective."

46. Carl Van Horn, "Applied Implementation Research" (paper presented at the annual meeting of the American Political Science Association, Chicago, Illinois, 1987).

47. Elmore, "Backward Mapping," Sabatier, "Implementation Research," and Goggin et al., *Implementation Theory;* see also Robert Stoker, *Reluctant Partners: Implementing Federal Policy* (Pittsburgh: University of Pittsburgh Press, 1991); and James P. Lester and Malcolm L. Goggin, "Back to the Future: The Rediscovery of Implementation Studies," a paper prepared for delivery at the annual meeting of the American Political Science Association, Boston, Massachusetts (September 3–6, 1998). Published in *Policy Currents* 8, no. 3 (September 1998) pp. 1–9.

48. Richard Elmore, "Forward and Backward Mapping: Reversible Logic in the Analysis of Public Policy," in *Policy Implementation in Federal and Unitary Systems*, ed. K. Hanf and T. Toonen (Dordrecht, The Netherlands: Martinus Nijhoff, 1985), pp. 33–70.

49. Paul Sabatier, "An Advocacy Coalition Framework of Policy Change and the Role of Policy-Oriented Learning Therein," *Policy Sciences* 21 (1988), pp. 129–168; Paul Sabatier and Hank Jenkins-Smith, *Policy Change and Learning: An Advocacy Coalition Approach* (Boulder, CO: Westview Press, 1993); and Paul Sabatier and Hank

Jenkins-Smith, "The Advocacy Coalition Framework: An Assessment," in Sabatier, ed., *Theories of the Policy Process* (Boulder, CO: Westview Press, 1999).

50. Sabatier and Hank Jenkins-Smith, "The Advocacy Coalition Framework," p. 120.

51. Goggin et al., *Implementation Theory*.

52. Ibid., pp. 31–33.

53. Sabatier, "Implementation Research," p. 39.

54. Elmore, "Forward and Backward Mapping," and Goggin et al., *Implementation Theory*. See also Lester and Goggin, "Back to the Future."

55. On this point see James P. Lester, "A New Federalism? Environmental Policy in the States," in *Environmental Policy in the 1990s*, 2d ed., ed. Norman Vig and Michael E. Kraft (Washington, D.C.: Congressional Quarterly Press, 1994), especially Table 3-1.

56. On this point see Hjern, "Implementation Structures."

57. David M. Hedge, Donald C. Menzel, and George Williams, "Regulatory Attitudes and Behavior: The Case of Surface Mining Regulation," *Western Political Quarterly* 44 (1988), pp. 323–340.

58. Goggin, "Too Few Cases," p. 332.

59. See, for example, Goggin et al., *Implementation Theory*; and Sabatier and Hank Jenkins-Smith's excellent summary of research that applies the advocacy coalition framework over the period 1987–98 in Sabatier and Jenkins-Smith, "The Advocacy Coalition Framework."

60. Jack M. Treadway, *Public Policymaking in the American States* (New York: Praeger, 1985); and James P. Lester and Emmett N. Lombard, "The Comparative Analysis of State Environmental Policy," *Natural Resources Journal* 30, no. 2 (Spring 1990), pp. 301–319.

61. Some notable exceptions include, for example, Patricia M. Crotty, "The New Federalism Game: Primacy Implementation of Environmental Policy," *Publius* 17 (1987), pp. 53–67; Frank Thompson and Michael J. Scicchitano, "State Implementation Effort and Federal Regulatory Policy," *Journal of Politics* 60 (1985), pp. 686–703; Pinky Wassenberg, "Implementation of Intergovernmental Regulatory Programs: A Cost-Benefit Perspective," in *Intergovernmental Relations and Public Policy*, ed. J. Edwin Benton and David Morgan (Westport, CT: Greenwood Press, 1986); David Hedge, Michael Scicchitano and Patricia Metz, "The Principal-Agent Model and Regulatory Federalism," *Western Political Quarterly* 44 (1991); and David Hedge and Michael Scicchitano, "Regulating in Time and Space: The Case of Regulatory Federalism," *Journal of Politics* 56 (February 1994).

62. Online Newshour, "FEMA Faces Intense Scrutiny," September 5, 2005, at http://FEMA/The%20Online%20NewsHour%20After%20Hurricane%20Katrina%20%7C-%20FEMA's%20Role%20%7C%20PBS.webarchive accessed March 12, 2007.

63. FEMA, "First Responders Urged Not to Respond to Hurricane Impact Areas Unless Dispatched by State, Local Authorities," Release Date: August 29, 2005. www.fema.gov/news/newsrelease.fema?id=18470 accessed March 12, 2007.

64. Stephen Sackur, "One Year on: Katrina's Legacy," BBC News online, August 24, 2006 at http://news.bbc.co.uk/1/hi/world/americas/5281396.stm accessed March 12, 2007.

8

Policy Evaluation

"...feeling good is not what science is all about. Getting it right,
and then basing social decisions on tested and carefully weighed
objective knowledge, is what science is all about."
EDWARD O. WILSON

Public policies are intended to have some effect on a particular policy problem.
Moreover, many people often assume that once a law is passed, a bureaucracy
is created to administer it, and if the program is funded, the problem will be remedied. Unfortunately, that is not often the case. If there was a perfect understanding
of what causes a public policy problem and perfect administration of laws intended
to remedy the problem, there would be no need for judging how well a program
has (or has not) worked. However, programs often fail to achieve their intended
effects, even after huge sums of money have been invested in funding them. Experiences with many programs in the 1960s suggested the need for careful appraisal of
the impact of these programs. The federal government often wants to know how
much money was spent for a given program, how many persons were serviced by
the program, how much those services cost, and how effective the programs were
in relation to that cost. On other occasions, the government wants to know
whether a program resulted in positive benefits or, to the contrary, made the problem worse.

The purposes of this chapter are to discuss the evolution of evaluation
research, to identify the types of evaluation that are conducted, to describe the
research designs used in evaluation research, and to discuss the problems in evaluating the impact of public policies.

THE CONCEPT OF POLICY EVALUATION

In its simplest form, **policy evaluation** is concerned with learning about the consequences of public policy. It means evaluating alternative public policies as contrasted with describing them or explaining why they exist. Essentially, there are two distinctive tasks in policy evaluation. One task is to determine what the consequences of a policy are by describing its impact, and the other task is to judge the success or failure of a policy according to a set of standards or value criteria.[1] Robert Haveman claims that the central tenet of policy evaluation research is its focus on the activities of the public sector and its influence on society. As such, it is the "effort to understand the effects of human behavior and, in particular, to evaluate the effects of particular programs (such as the Great Society Programs) on those aspects of behavior indicated as the objectives of this intervention."[2] Put differently "Policy evaluation is the assessment of the overall effectiveness of a national program in meeting its objectives, or an assessment of the relative effectiveness of two or more programs in meeting common objectives."[3] Still another definition is that "the evaluation of agency programs or legislative policy is the use of scientific methods to estimate the successful implementation and resultant outcomes of programs or policies for decision-making purposes."[4] What differentiates policy evaluation from other types of policy analysis (e.g., policy formulation) is the focus on policy results or consequences as opposed to policy characteristics or causes.[5]

The Evolution of Evaluation Research

Early strains of evaluation research were present in the late 1800s. For example, an actual evaluation study was reported by an educator named J. M. Rice in 1897. Rice used a standardized spelling test to relate the length of time spent on drill to spelling achievement.[6] By comparing schools that varied in their emphasis on drill, he generated data that were used to argue that an emphasis on drill did not lead to improved achievement among the students.[7]

Between 1920 and 1940, several attempts were made to use empirical research to determine the effects of social programs in various settings. One of the best-known examples of evaluation research during this period was Stuart Dodd's study of the effects of a health education program on hygiene practices in rural Syria in 1934.[8] He examined the effects of educational clinics on the adequacy of public health practices in experimental and isolated control villages. Other attempts at evaluation research included studies of changes in industrial plant organization and their impact on worker morale.[9] Until World War II, what little evaluation research existed was in the disciplines of sociology, psychology, and public health; economists and education researchers made few contributions.[10]

Between the end of World War II and 1965, a number of evaluation research studies were conducted by social psychologists concerned with social issues. For example, the experimental work of Ronald Lippitt concerning the effects of autocratic and democratic leadership styles on the performance of groups of children is well known.[11] Similarly, work by Kurt Lewin and his associates on the effects of programs designed to change attitudes toward minorities was prominent during this period.[12] This research was not very sophisticated—the use of experimental designs, baseline interviews, and controls for attrition and other forms of selectivity were basically nonexistent.[13]

More sophisticated policy evaluation can find its genesis in the aftermath of the War on Poverty programs of the 1960s. The War on Poverty–Great Society developments initiated in 1965 represented an unprecedented level of social intervention.[14] Although social science scholars did evaluation research prior to the 1960s, as noted above, there was nothing that could be identified as a unique approach or a particular set of questions that evaluation studies should ask.[15] By the late 1960s, however, scholars began to use experimental designs, economics, and statistics in their research. Requirements for program evaluation were written into almost all federal programs in the 1960s and the 1970s. Congress established new organizations for evaluation and steadily increased their personnel and funding during this period. Nevertheless, the support for evaluation research declined as the Nixon administration reduced some budgets for this purpose. The Carter administration attempted to revive some of these functions by instituting a system of zero-based budgeting, but this movement never gained substantial backing. The Reagan administration cuts deeply affected policy evaluation.[16] For example, the Department of Commerce had collected data on state spending for environmental protection from 1969 to 1980, but the Reagan budget cuts in 1981 curtailed this data collection effort. This made it difficult to evaluate the states' efforts to protect the environment. If policy analysts do not have longitudinal data on the levels of state spending, especially after the federal budget cutbacks in the early 1980s, it is difficult to know what effects the cutbacks had on state efforts in this area.

What Does Evaluation Research Study?

Earlier, we stated that evaluation research focuses on the consequences of public policy. Having said that, it is still necessary to know exactly what evaluators study when conducting their evaluations. First, they may examine **policy outputs** such as funds, jobs, material produced, and services delivered.[17] These outputs are the most obvious results of some public policy, but they are by no means all that evaluators study. Another category of results is the impact of the policy on specific target groups, or the state of affairs the policy was intended to produce. For example, a policy may be intended to increase student performance or encourage energy conservation. In this sense, then, there is concern about the policy's **performance.** When analyzing these consequences, one is examining how the policy performed in relation to some stated objective.[18]

In addition, policy evaluators are concerned with the ability of the policy to improve some societal condition, such as by reducing environmental pollution or by reducing crime. These consequences are analyzed as **policy outcomes,** in which the policy is supposed to result in the improvement of a general condition in society.

Finally, evaluators are sometimes concerned with policy consequences in the form of **policy feedback,** which includes the repercussions of a government action or statement on the policymaking system or on some policy makers.[19] For example, if efforts to reduce crime are successful, then the lowered crime rate may increase citizens' satisfaction with government in general and enhance support for the particular officials who are credited with being responsible for the effective policy.

Each of these types of policy consequences provides the policy analyst with a reasonably clear focus for study. Moreover, one can easily see the relationships between these policy consequences: government action programs produce policy outputs, which are then carried out in the form of policy performance, causing policy outcomes, which, in turn, trigger policy feedback.[20]

Types of Policy Evaluation

There are several types of policy evaluation. For example, Bingham and Felbinger identify four types of evaluations. First, there is what is known as **process evaluation.**[21] Process evaluation focuses on the means by which a program or policy is delivered to clients, or the way in which a program is implemented.[22] This type of evaluation focuses on an assessment of program activities and client satisfaction with services. Basically, these evaluations attempt to uncover management problems or assume that none are occurring. Process evaluations ask such questions as "Are the contractual obligations being met?" and "How could this service be done more efficiently?"

The second type of evaluation is **impact evaluation.** This evaluation is concerned with the end results of a particular program. Such evaluations are focused on whether the program's or policy's objectives have been met in terms of outputs. That is, did the program or policy produce the intended result on the target population? For example, how many clients were served by the program? How many workers were trained? This type of evaluation is more straightforward. It is easier to assess outcomes than the process of implementation. In addition, some impact evaluations are concerned with measuring effectiveness, which is concerned with such questions as "Was the program cost-effective?" and "What would have happened to the target population in the absence of the program?"[23] Most evaluations are of this type.

A third type of evaluation is **policy evaluation.** This type of evaluation is concerned with the impact of the policy or program on the original problem to which it was addressed. That is, has the problem (e.g., poverty, illiteracy, pollution) been reduced as a result of the policy or program?[24]

Finally, there are **meta-evaluations.** These evaluations are syntheses of evaluation research findings. They look for commonalities among results, measures, and trends in the literature.[25] Meta-evaluations are very similar to literature reviews in that they are concerned with cumulating the extant findings and looking for patterns in the findings across numerous evaluations. For example, Laurence J. O'Toole conducted a meta-evaluation of implementation studies to see whether he could identify the crucial variables affecting the success or failure of public policy implementation.[26] In his review of over a hundred implementation studies, he concluded that the availability of fiscal resources was a key variable in implementation success or failure.

Who Does Evaluation?

Many institutions and individuals perform policy evaluations. They include **internal evaluators** concerned with congressional oversight, such as the General Accounting Office (GAO), as well as those that provide research support to the Congress, such as the Congressional Research Service (CRS) and the Congressional Budget Office (CBO). Other governmental agencies conduct evaluations as well. For example, executive branch evaluations are conducted by assistant-secretary-level divisions for planning and evaluation, regulatory bodies, inspectors general, boards of inquiry, high-level advisory boards, commissions, panels, and others.[27] Increasingly state and local governments are also conducting "in-house" evaluations as state and local policy makers seek more reliable information on the implementation and impact of existing policies.

A major advantage of internal evaluation is that insiders will have the detailed knowledge of just what is involved in delivering the policy or program.[28] However, there are several major disadvantages as well. First, the insiders may not have the specialized skills necessary to do a good evaluation. Second, because several different organizations may be involved in policy delivery, a complete evaluation cannot be obtained by examining the results of the activity in one organization. Finally, the evaluation may be affected by the insiders' unwillingness to make major changes in the policy or program suggested by the evaluation. Existing personnel have a stake in maintaining the status quo and may be threatened by implied changes suggested by the evaluation.[29]

In addition, **external evaluators,** such as private research organizations, the communications media, pressure groups, and public-interest organizations, conduct evaluation studies of policies that have effects on the public or government officials. For example, the Brookings Institution, the Urban Institute, Resources for the Future, the American Enterprise Institute, the Hoover Institution, and the RAND Corporation have conducted numerous evaluations. In addition, CBS News (e.g., *Sixty Minutes*), Common Cause, and the Citizens Clearinghouse on Hazardous Waste conduct evaluations. Several schools offer programs providing undergraduate—and especially graduate—training in policy analysis, including policy evaluation. Professors from those same schools often conduct policy evaluations. Some of the more prominent programs and schools include

1. The Graduate School of Public Policy, The University of California— Berkeley
2. The Gerald R. Ford School of Public Policy, The University of Michigan
3. The School of Urban and Public Affairs, Carnegie-Mellon University
4. The Woodrow Wilson School of Public and International Affairs, Princeton University
5. The John F. Kennedy School of Government, Harvard University

6. The Maxwell School of Citizenship and Public Affairs, Syracuse University

7. The Lyndon B. Johnson School of Public Affairs, The University of Texas

8. The Hubert H. Humphrey Institute of Public Affairs, The University of Minnesota

9. The Terry Sanford Institute of Public Policy, Duke University

10. The Robert M. LaFollette School of Public Affairs, University of Wisconsin

These and literally dozens of other schools offer training in the methods of policy evaluation, including microeconomics, experimental design, survey research, statistical analysis, causal modeling, decision modeling, benefit-cost analysis, and implementation.[30]

External evaluation has certain advantages. For example, outside evaluation improves the chance of change in the policy or program if the evaluator has involved the internal staff in discussions about objectives and effectiveness of the program or policy. Second, outside evaluators may have the necessary skills that insiders lack. Thus, they may be much better equipped to conduct systematic policy or program evaluation. However, there are disadvantages as well. Outsiders may have an ideological axe to grind; that is, they may be ideologically predisposed one way or another, and their analysis may reflect this bias. In addition, the users of evaluation research often complain that evaluations are neither timely nor relevant to their decision making. At other times, users complain that they do not understand the methods used by policy evaluators in professional organizations or universities.

In an article that critiques evaluation of social policies, James Q. Wilson formulates two general laws about policy evaluation:

> *Wilson's First Law:* All policy interventions in social problems produce the intended effect—if the research is carried out by those implementing the policy or their friends.
>
> *Wilson's Second Law:* No policy intervention in social problems produces the intended effect—if the research is carried out by independent third parties, especially those skeptical of the policy.

He argues,

> Studies that conform to the First Law will accept an agency's own data about what it is doing and with what effect; adopt a time frame that maximizes the probability of observing the desired effect; and minimize the search for other variables that might account for the effect observed. Studies that conform to the Second Law will gather data independently of the agency; adopt a short time frame that either maximizes the chance for the desired effect to appear or, if it does appear, permits one to argue that the results are "temporary" and probably due to the operation of the "Hawthorne Effect"; and maximize the search for other variables that might explain the effects observed.[31]

Despite this rather cynical observation about policy evaluations, it is important to evaluate past policies for their effectiveness. A number of alternative research designs are used in policy evaluations to reduce the kinds of bias Wilson bemoans. These research designs are an attempt to systematically evaluate the effects of various public policies on some societal problem. Let us examine a few of these designs.

Research Designs in Evaluation Research

Systematic evaluation involves **comparisons**—comparisons designed to estimate what changes in society can be attributed to the policy or program that has been implemented. The evaluator simply wants to know whether changes in some identifiable behavior in the individual (e.g., better scholastic performance) or condition in society (e.g., crime rates) actually took place, and whether the program or policy itself produced the change in the behavior or condition net of other circumstances or influences. A number of research designs may be used to answer these questions.

Pre-experimental Designs   These designs include the "one-shot case study" and the "before-and-after study." **One-shot case studies** are intensive analyses of what happened in the course of implementing the policy, and after its implementation, to try to determine whether there was any change in the behavior or condition. This approach is the most common in the political science literature. It examines one group, one event, or one phenomenon at one point in time and has no controls over rival explanations or side effects.

The One-Shot Case Study
X   0

For example, Martha Derthick's study of a housing project in the Washington, D.C., area is an illustration of a case study that sought to determine why the project failed.[32] She identified a host of factors that led to the failure of this proposed remedy for low-cost housing. Her research was valuable for pointing out all the possible things that could go wrong in implementing a low-cost housing program, but there were no controls for rival explanations.

Before-and-after studies are a bit more sophisticated. They compare results at two points in time—one before the program was implemented and the other sometime after implementation. Usually, only the target groups are examined; thus, it is difficult to know whether the observed changes were due to the program or policy itself, or if they were due to some other condition in society that occurred at the same time.[33] For example, one might be interested in knowing whether using seat belts lowered highway fatalities. So, one would measure the highway fatality rate before the introduction of a mandatory seat-belt law and then measure the fatality rate after the law goes into effect. A lowering of the fatality rate could be attributed to the seat-belt law, but those reductions could also be the result of better road conditions or a corresponding reduction in speed limits.

The One-Group Pretest-Posttest Design
0   X   0

True Experiments   The "classic" research design, or **true experiment,** involves the random selection of both control and experimental groups. These two groups are compared in terms of changes within each group before and after the introduction of the policy or program. Careful measurements are taken for each group prior to the introduction of the program, and then post-program differences between the experimental and control groups are carefully measured. Ideally, the experimental group will show marked improvements due to the program that the control group does not experience. With randomization, this design has strong controls for both internal and external validity.

The Pretest-Posttest Control Group Design
R   0   X   0   (Experimental Group)
R   0   0   (Control Group)

Recently, analysts at Mathematica Policy Research used an experimental design to evaluate the Teach for America (TFA) program. TFA was created in 1989 to provide teachers in low-income neighborhoods throughout America. TFA recruits college seniors with outstanding academic and leadership records. Recruits need not, and typically do not, have formal training as teachers. To assess the impact of the program, analysts collected student achievement data for a sample of 1st- through 5th-grade students in six of the program's regions, including Chicago, Los Angeles, and the Mississippi delta. Students were randomly assigned to TFA and non-TFA classrooms, and achievement tests were administered in the fall (pretest) and spring (posttest). A comparison of students in TFA classes with a control group of students in non-TFA classes indicated that TFA teachers had a positive impact on math scores but not on reading achievement.[34]

Quasi-Experimental Designs   The **quasi-experimental design** is similar in every respect to the classic experiment discussed above, except that the cases (individuals, cities, organizations, etc.) in the program being evaluated (the experimental group) and the comparison group are not randomly assigned. Thus, the comparison group (sometimes called the control group) is "nonequivalent" to the experimental (program) group. This potential problem in the research design can be alleviated through a process called *matching*, in which the researcher attempts to identify a group that is comparable in essential respects to those in the treatment (experimental) group. The validity of the quasi-experimental design depends in large part on how closely the comparison group resembles the experimental group in all essential respects.[35]

The Nonequivalent Control Group Design
0   X   0   (Experimental Group)
0   0   (Control Group)

An example of this type of design is a study that attempted to evaluate the effects of energy conservation programs on utility costs.[36] Because the energy conservation program was voluntary, the researcher could not use an experimental design and randomly assign customers into program and control groups. Nevertheless, he found a comparison group that did not participate in the energy conservation program and compared the energy consumption of both groups before and after the introduction of the program. Essentially, the researcher found that there was no significant difference between the energy consumption of the two groups in the pretest period; but after the homes of the experimental group had been weatherized, there was a significant difference in energy consumption. The experimental group used much less energy than the nonexperimental group, which showed that the energy conservation program worked as expected.

Causal Modeling   Another approach often employed in evaluation research is **causal modeling,** which is the use of statistical controls to estimate the effects of policy variables net of the influence of alternative explanations. In this approach, one constructs a mathematical model of the program and its intended effects. This model incorporates the assumptions built into the policy or program and includes program outputs or outcomes as well as the factors presumed to "cause" these outcomes, including the policy that is being evaluated as well as other possible influences on program outcomes. Although this approach is often very appropriate, and at times the only approach available, it carries certain limitations as well. For example, if the original theory behind the program is flawed, then the results may be meaningless as well. A frequent problem is the inability to separate out statistically the relative influence of the program being evaluated and other possible causal influences. Alternately, extraneous variables not included in the model may well be affecting the program outcome. This approach will produce satisfactory results only when the theory behind the model is sound and all of the relevant causal variables are included in the model.

Analysis of the most recent round of welfare reform by economists provides a good example of how multivariate models can be employed to assess the impact of public policies. Following the enactment of the 1996 welfare reforms (discussed in some detail in Chapter 11), some economists sought to determine the relative effects of state welfare programming and economic conditions on caseload reductions. Typically that analysis included measures of state programming (severity of sanctions or work requirements, for example) together with indicators reflecting the states' economy, including levels of employment and median wage rates. Generally those studies concluded that most of the dramatic reductions in the welfare rolls in the late 1990s reflected the states' economies. There is also some evidence (but little consensus) that state policies, most notably time limits and sanction levels, account for at least some of the reductions in caseload levels.[37]

In certain circumstances, such as when only aggregate data are available for evaluation, this approach may be the most appropriate method, but its limitations should be kept in mind when interpreting the results. No matter which research design is used, there are problems affecting evaluation. That is the subject of the following discussion.

Problems in Evaluating the Impact of Public Policy

Evaluating the impacts of programs or policies is difficult even under the best of conditions. Hogwood and Gunn identify several factors that pose severe problems for evaluating public policies or programs.

1. *Objectives.* Nothing illustrates more clearly the problems of doing policy evaluation than the way in which policy objectives shape evaluation. If the policy objectives are unclear, or they are not specified in any measurable form, then the criteria for a policy's success are unclear.[38] However, vagueness in goals can often be a consequence of differences in viewpoints about policy objectives. Even when there is a clear statement of goals, problems remain. For example, how important are goals relative to each other when more than one goal is specified?[39]

2. *Defining the criteria for success.* Even when objectives are clearly stated, there is the question of how the success of the objective will be measured. For example, suppose the objective is to produce an improvement in student performance in math using microcomputers. Even this specific objective is clouded by whether one wants to assess the student's increase in enjoyment of math using computers, or an improvement in understanding math itself, or an ability to apply this improvement to other areas, or a combination of all these.[40]

3. *Side effects.* Sometimes impacts from other policies or programs affect the policy or program under evaluation. Difficulties can be presented when one tries to identify and measure side effects and separate these side effects from the policy or program being evaluated. Thus, there is the problem of how other factors (both adverse and beneficial) should be brought into the evaluation, and how much these factors should be weighted relative to the central objectives.[41] For example, in attempting to evaluate the effects of the 55-mile-per-hour speed limit on reducing traffic fatalities, there is the complicating factor of seat-belt use. To what extent is the reduced speed a factor relative to the use of seat belts?

4. *Data problems.* Quite often the information necessary to assess the impact of a policy or program may not be available or may be available in an unsuitable form.[42] For example, if one were interested in evaluating the impacts of President Reagan's "new federalism" on state environmental protection, he or she would want to have data on the extent to which the individual states replaced the federal budget cuts with their own-source funds. However, not all fifty states (or even very few of them) have kept careful records of the extent to which they replaced federal funds with state funds for environmental protection, nor how much the states provided in this category of expenditure that was unique to the states as opposed to local governments.

5. *Methodological problems.* It is also common for a single problem, or single group of the population, to be the target of several programs with the same or related objectives. For example, several policies are directed to the problem of poverty. In such cases, assessing the impact of a single program is difficult. For example, if crime rates go down, is this due to better policing, better

education, welfare assistance, or employment opportunities? Big problems tend to have a lot of programs directed toward them, which makes it difficult to "sort out" the relative effects of each.[13]

6. *Political problems.* Evaluation is very threatening to some people. The success or failure of a policy or program to which politicians or bureaucrats have committed their personal reputations and careers, and from which clientele groups are receiving benefits, is being evaluated. Evaluation may be seen as a threat to the continuation of a policy or program in which a number of people have an important stake. These considerations will obviously affect both how evaluation results are utilized and how easily the evaluation can be conducted, as the cooperation of public officials and clients is often required in the evaluation.[44]

7. *Cost.* It is not uncommon for a program's evaluation to require as much as 1 percent of the total program cost.[45] This is especially the case when more sophisticated methods are used in evaluation studies, such as experimental designs. Such costs are a diversion from the delivery of the policy or program.

These are just a few of the difficulties posed in the evaluation of public policies and programs. Even though policy analysts have these problems in the process of evaluation, they should not be unduly discouraged from conducting evaluation activities. Rather than seeing these difficulties as insurmountable obstacles, they should see them as challenges for designing effective evaluations. In the following case study, we discuss an example of evaluation research—the impact of school spending on student performance.

CASE STUDY

Compensatory Education

One of the most interesting examples of evaluation research is that of **compensatory education.** In the Elementary and Secondary Education Act of 1965 (ESEA), "poverty-impacted" schools were the beneficiaries of increased federal aid to education programs. ESEA provided for federal financial assistance to "local educational agencies serving areas with concentrations of children from low-income families" for programs that contributed "to meeting the special needs of educationally deprived children."[46] Grants were made to public and private elementary and secondary schools for the acquisition of school library resources, textbooks, and other instructional materials. The logic embodied in ESEA was that an increase in per pupil expenditures (especially to students from poorer school districts) would allow these schools to purchase better educational materials, hire better teachers, and improve the curriculum. As a consequence, student performance would improve, thus allowing the poorer students to be more competitive in the marketplace after graduation. Ultimately, this would help to alleviate the disparities in income and thus reduce poverty in America. Indeed, ESEA was an important component of President Johnson's War on Poverty in the 1960s.

James Coleman, a Harvard sociologist, conducted an evaluation of the logic embodied in ESEA, producing what is popularly known as the Coleman Report.[47] Although his report was strongly criticized,[48] it undermined much of the conventional logic about the impact of increased expenditures on student performance. Prior to his study, legislators, teachers, school administrators, school board members, and the general public assumed that factors such as the number of pupils in the classroom, the amount of money spent on each pupil, library and laboratory facilities, teachers' salaries, the quality of the curriculum, and other characteristics of the school affected student performance (and hence educational opportunity). However, Coleman's analysis revealed that these factors had no significant effect on student learning or achievement. Rather, the only factors that had a significant effect were the family backgrounds of the students themselves and the family backgrounds of their classmates. Family background factors affected the students' verbal abilities and attitudes toward education, which were both strongly related to student performance.[49]

Although the Coleman Report made no policy recommendations, it nevertheless implied that compensatory education had very little educational value. If his report was correct, it seemed pointless to raise per pupil expenditures, increase teachers' salaries, lower the number of pupils per classroom, provide better libraries or laboratories, or adopt any curricular innovations. The reaction of professional educators to the Coleman Report was predictable. Perhaps they hoped that the report would not affect long-standing assumptions about the importance of money, facilities, classroom size, teacher quality, and curricula.[50] The reaction of the educational community points out the difficulties associated with the utilization of public policy analysis, a topic that we will return to in Chapter 13.

SUMMARY

In this chapter, we have discussed policy evaluation, identified some of the ways in which policy evaluation is carried out, and discussed some problems in the evaluation of public policy. Evaluation research can be a valuable tool for policy makers, but evaluators and those who might use evaluations should be forewarned: despite the best efforts of those in and out of government, policies often fall short of their goals. When that occurs, governments have to decide whether those circumstances warrant policy change or, more drastically, policy termination. Those options are discussed in Chapter 9.

DISCUSSION QUESTIONS

1. After evaluating the effects of compensatory educational policies, we continue to associate increased spending for schools with student achievement. Why is this so?

2. What are some of the reasons that evaluation research has had so little effect on policy design or redesign?

3. Discuss some of the problems associated with evaluating the impact of various public policies.

SUGGESTED READINGS

Bickers, Kenneth N., and John T. Williams, *Public Policy Analysis: A Political Economy Approach* (Boston: Houghton Mifflin, 2001).

Bingham, Richard D., and Claire L. Felbinger. *Evaluation in Practice: A Methodological Approach* (Washington, D.C.: CQ Press, 2002).

Fischer, Frank. *Evaluating Public Policy* (Chicago: Nelson Hall, 1995).

Mohr, Lawrence B. *Impact Analysis for Program Evaluation* (Chicago: Dorsey Press, 1988).

Shadish, William R., Thomas D. Cook, and Donald T. Campbell. *Experimental and Quasi-Experimental Designs for Generalized Causal Inference* (Boston: Houghton Mifflin, 2002).

Weiss, Carol. *Evaluation: Methods for Studying Programs and Policies,* Second Edition (Upper Saddle River, NJ: Prentice Hall, 1998).

NOTES

1. Melvin J. Dubnick and Barbara A. Bardes, *Thinking About Public Policy* (New York: Wiley, 1983), p. 203.

2. Robert Haveman, "Policy Evaluation Research After Twenty Years," *Policy Studies Journal* 16, no. 2 (Winter 1987), pp. 191–218.

3. Joseph S. Wholey et al., *Federal Evaluation Policy* (Washington, D.C.: The Urban Institute, 1970), p. 15.

4. Richard D. Bingham and Claire L. Felbinger, *Evaluation in Practice: A Methodological Approach* (New York: Longman, 1989), p. 3.

5. Some useful studies of policy evaluation include Carol Weiss, *Evaluation Research: Methods of Assessing Program Effectiveness* (Englewood Cliffs, NJ: Prentice Hall, 1972); and David Nachmias, *Public Policy Evaluation: Approaches and Methods* (New York: St. Martin's Press, 1979).

6. Francis G. Caro, ed., *Readings in Evaluation Research*, 2d ed. (New York: Russell Sage Foundation, 1977), p. 6.

7. Ibid.

8. Ibid.

9. Haveman, "Policy Evaluation," p. 195.

10. Ibid., p. 196.

11. Ronald Lippitt, *Studies in Experimentally Created Autocratic and Democratic Groups* (Iowa City: University of Iowa, 1940).

12. Kurt Lewin, *Resolving Social Conflicts* (New York: Harper and Brothers, 1948).

13. Haveman, "Policy Evaluation," p. 196.

14. Ibid., p. 191.

15. Ibid.

16. Ibid., p. 200.

17. Dubnick and Bardes, *Public Policy,* p. 207.

18. Ibid.

19. Ibid.

20. Ibid.

21. Richard D. Bingham and Claire L. Felbinger, *Evaluation in Practice: A Methodological Approach* (New York: Longman, 1989), p. 4.

22. Ibid.

23. Ibid., p. 5.

24. Ibid., p. 6.

25. Ibid.

26. Laurence J. O'Toole, Jr., "Policy Recommendations for Multi-Actor Implementation: An Assessment of the Field," *Journal of Public Policy* (1986), pp. 181–210.

27. Garry D. Brewer and Peter DeLeon, *The Foundations of Policy Analysis* (Homewood, IL: Dorsey Press, 1983), pp. 320–321.

28. Brian W. Hogwood and Lewis A. Gunn, *Policy Analysis for the Real World* (New York: Oxford University Press, 1984), p. 234.

29. Ibid., p. 235.

30. Descriptions of programs in public policy and administration can be found on the websites of the Association of Public Policy and Management and the American Society of Public Administration.

31. James Q. Wilson, "On Pettigrew and Armor," *The Public Interest* 30 (Winter 1973), pp. 132–134.

32. Martha Derthick, "Defeat at Ft. Lincoln," *The Public Interest* 20 (Summer 1970), pp. 3–39.

33. Thomas R. Dye, *Understanding Public Policy,* 7th ed. (Englewood Cliffs, NJ: Prentice Hall, 1991), pp. 357–358.

34. Steven Glazerman, Daniel Mayer, and Paul Decker, "Alternative Routes to Teaching: The Impacts of Teach for America on Student Achievement and Other Outcomes," *Journal of Policy Analysis and Management* 25, no. 1 (2006), pp. 75–96.

35. Bingham and Felbinger, *Evaluation in Practice,* p. 97.

36. Tim Newcomb, "Conservation Program Evaluations: The Control of Self-Selection Bias," *Evaluation Review* 8, no. 3 (June 1984), pp. 425–440.

37. See, for example, Stephen Bell, *Why Are Welfare Caseloads Falling?* (Washington, D.C.: Urban Institute, 2001); Rebecca Blank, "What Causes Public Assistance Caseloads to Grow?" *Journal of Human Resources* 36, no. 1 (2001), pp. 85–119; and David N. Figlio and James P. Ziliak, "Welfare Reform, the Business Cycle, and the Decline in AFDC Caseloads," in *Economic Conditions and Welfare Reform,* ed. Sheldon H. Danziger (Kalamazoo, MI: W. E. Upjohn Institute for Employment Research, 1999), pp. 17–48.

38. Hogwood and Gunn, *Policy Analysis,* p. 222.

39. Ibid., p. 223.

40. Ibid., p. 224.

41. Ibid., p. 225.

42. Ibid., p. 226.

43. Ibid.

44. Ibid., p. 227.

45. M. C. Aitken and L. G. Salmon, eds., *The Costs of Evaluation* (Beverly Hills, CA: Sage, 1983).

46. Dye, *Understanding Public Policy*, p. 9.

47. James S. Coleman, *Equality of Educational Opportunity* (Washington, D.C.: U.S. Government Printing Office, 1966).

48. We discuss some of these criticisms in Chapter 10.

49. Coleman, *Equality*.

50. Dye, *Understanding Public Policy*, p. 10.

9

Policy Change and Termination

"Policy entrepreneurs have a responsibility not only to the integrity of
the political process, however, but also to the consequences of their
actions, an obligation to see that ineffective and inefficient
policies are either changed or eliminated."
ROBERT D. BEHN

One might think that once a person reaches policy evaluation, he or she has
reached the end of the policy cycle. However, such a viewpoint would
neglect the **consequences** of policy evaluation as well as how the old policy
often leads into a new policy cycle. After evaluation, the next stages of the policy
cycle are **policy change** and then **policy termination.** In these two stages, policies are reviewed, sometimes terminated, sometimes changed drastically, and then
the entire cycle begins again as policies are reformulated and re-implemented. One
might think of this aspect of the policy cycle as a further extension of thought about
the public policy process (i.e., from the initiation of policy proposals to coming full
circle and beginning the agenda-setting process all over). Political scientists have
traditionally perceived policymaking as primarily the result of a power struggle
among various interest groups, with different resources and interests, operating
within a given institutional structure and a changing socioeconomic environment.[1]
Yet, the implications of policy or program termination and changes in public policy
have only recently begun to be explored.[2]

Sometimes, policies are not completely terminated. Rather, they are changed in some form. In practice, policies are frequently changed as a result of the legislative oversight process, in which policies are reviewed for their effectiveness from time to time. At other times, the desire for change originates within the bureaucracy. Regardless of whether they originate in the legislature or in the bureaucracy, policy changes are much more common than policy terminations.[3]

THE CONCEPT OF POLICY CHANGE

The concept of **policy change** refers to the replacement of one or more existing policies by one or more other policies. This includes both the adoption of new policies and the modification or repeal of existing ones. Essentially, policy change can take any one of three forms: (1) incremental changes in existing policies; (2) enactment of new statutes in particular policy areas; or (3) major shifts in public policy as a consequence of realigning elections.[4] For example, the reauthorization of the Resource Conservation and Recovery Act of 1976 (RCRA) resulted in changing the scope of those affected by this policy. Originally, any company producing at least 1,000 kilograms of toxic waste per month was within the regulatory framework. In the 1984 revision of this act, all companies producing at least 100 kilograms were covered by the new regulations. This change substantially increased the number of firms that the EPA would have to monitor for compliance.

Enactment of the Personal Responsibility and Work Opportunity Reconciliation Act of 1996 (PRWORA) provides a more recent illustration of how long-standing policies, in this case welfare, can change in major ways. The 1996 reforms changed welfare in America in two fundamental ways. First, the reforms "ended welfare as we know it" by eliminating the entitlement program that had essentially guaranteed support to qualifying families for nearly a half a century. In place of the entitlement program, Congress provided block grants to the states and changed the rules for receiving welfare by, among other things, placing a lifetime limit on the receipt of aid and requiring heads of families to engage in some form of work activity. Second, the 1996 legislation shifted what had been primarily a federal program to the American states. Under the new rules, the states were granted considerable discretion within federal guidelines over how welfare would be implemented within their borders. Currently state welfare programs vary substantially in terms of program requirements, the range of services provided recipients, and how the states organize welfare services.[5]

Rarely are policies maintained in the same form as when they were initially adopted; instead, they are constantly evolving. The revision of existing policies depends on such factors as the extent to which the original policy is judged to "solve" the problem at which it is directed, the skill with which such policies are administered, the defects or shortcomings that may be revealed during policy implementation, and the political power and awareness of concerned or affected groups where the policy is delivered.[6] Also, problems themselves will change over time, as will the conventional wisdom about how to address these problems.[7] Thus, public policies evolve after their initial formulation and implementation to begin the policy process all over again. The evolution of public policy is really a cycle in which policies are formulated, implemented, evaluated, and then reformulated and re-implemented based on legislative review of the extent to which these policies achieved their initial objectives. For example, the conventional wisdom about punishment for criminals changed in the 1950s, from a harsh approach to a more lenient and rehabilitative one.[8] Educational policy changed in the 1980s, going from a liberal approach that emphasized innovations in curricula and open classrooms to a back-to-basics approach that stressed reading, writing, and arithmetic. Welfare policy also underwent major changes in the 1980s and 1990s as a conservative approach with its emphasis on work and time limits seemed to replace a more liberal one that was prevalent in the 1960s. Thus, the entire cycle of public policy is really a continuous loop over time.

Some Reasons for Change

Hogwood and Gunn suggest three reasons for expecting policy change to be an increasingly common feature of policy formulation in contemporary Western political systems, and therefore a candidate for greater attention by policy analysts.

1. Governments have, over the years, gradually expanded their activities in particular fields of policy, so that there are relatively few completely new activities in which they could be involved. Proposals for new policies are likely to overlap, at least in part, with existing programs.

2. Existing policies themselves may create conditions requiring changes because of inadequacies or adverse side effects. Legislative oversight may be grounds for changing policies so that they "work better."

3. The relative rates of sustainable economic growth, and the financial implications of existing policy commitments, imply that the latitude for avoiding the problems of policy termination or policy change by instituting a new program without cutting the old one is considerably unlikely.[9]

Although most can identify a number of public policies that they consider unnecessary, wasteful, or inappropriate, there will always be those who consider them to be useful and worth keeping.[10] Changing policies is always easier than terminating them. In any case, policy change takes a variety of forms, as discussed in the following section.

Types of Policy Change

Given the likelihood of more policy change in the future, what forms may policy change take? Policy change, according to Peters, may take several forms:[11]

1. *Linear.* **Linear change** involves the direct replacement of one policy by another, or the simple change of an existing policy. For example, the

replacement of the Comprehensive Employment and Training Act (CETA) by the Job Training and Partnership Act (JTPA) is an example of a linear policy change.

2. *Consolidation.* Some policy changes involve merging previous policies into a new single policy. For example, the rolling together of several health and welfare programs into just a few programs is an example of **consolidation.**

3. *Splitting.* Some agencies (and hence eventual policies from these agencies) are **split** into two or more individual components. For example, the Atomic Energy Commission (AEC) was split into the Nuclear Regulatory Commission (NRC) and the Energy Research and Development Administration (ERDA) in 1974, resolving the conflict between the contradictory programs of regulation and support of nuclear energy that had existed in the earlier organization of the AEC.

4 *Nonlinear.* Some policy changes are complex and involve elements of other kinds of changes. The complex changes involved in creating the Temporary Assistance for Needy Families (TANF) programs from the preexisting Aid for Dependent Children (AFDC) programs are an example of **nonlinear** changes. An entirely new policy, program, or organization is created in the wake of former policies, programs, or organizations.

In addition to various types of policy change, there are several models of policy change. These models help analysts to understand why major changes in policy occur in the United States.

Models of Policy Change

Policy change, although a new and little-researched concept, is nevertheless a crucial aspect of the policy cycle. It is safe to assume that much policy analysis in the future will be directed toward an analysis of policy change over time. To do so, however, requires an understanding of the process of policy change and the development of some theoretical explanations about why policies evolve as they do. To date, several theories have been developed to explain the evolution of public policies. In the following sections, we review four of those theories each of which seeks to describe how and explain why American public policies evolve over several decades or more. Some of these explanations are more developed than others, but all of them are directed toward an explanation of policy change over time.

The Cyclical Thesis   The first explanation is the **cyclical thesis** offered by Arthur Schlesinger, in which he argues that there is a continuing shift in national involvement between public purpose and private interest.[12] More specifically, he argues that American politics follows a fairly regular cyclical alternation between conservatism and liberalism in the national moods. That is, there are swings back and forth between eras when the national commitment is to private interest as the best means of meeting the national problems and eras when the national commitment is to public purpose. At roughly 30-year intervals, Schlesinger argues, the nation turns to reform and affirmative government as the best way of dealing with its troubles. For example, Theodore Roosevelt ushered in the Progressive period in 1901, Franklin Roosevelt brought in the New Deal in the 1930s, and John Kennedy introduced the New Frontier in the 1960s. Alternatively, Ronald Reagan ushered in a conservative era in the 1980s, which was a replay of the conservative 1950s and the Harding-Coolidge era of the 1920s.

Schlesinger claims there is nothing mystical about the 30-year cycle. Thirty years is the span of a generation. People tend to be formed politically by the ideals that are dominant in the years during which they attain political consciousness. When their own generation's turn in power comes 30 years later, they tend to carry forward the ideals they developed when young. Over time, each phase tends to run its natural course. A season of idealism and reform, when strong presidents call for active public interest in national affairs and invoke government as a means of promoting the general welfare, eventually leaves an electorate exhausted by the process and disenchanted by the results. People eventually become attuned to a "new" message telling them that private action and self-interest in an unregulated market will solve their problems. This mood eventually runs its course as problems become acute, threaten to become unmanageable, and demand remedies by governmental actors. This change in the public mood thus ushers in a new era of reform and governmental intervention.

According to Schlesinger, then, a major proposition about the evolution of American public policy over the past hundred years would suggest the following:

Proposition 1:   The evolution of public policy follows a fairly predictable pattern, in which a period of private remedies (and minimal governmental intervention) will be followed by a period of significant governmental intervention and reform. A period of liberalism will be followed by a period of conservatism before the entire cycle repeats itself.

Figure 9.1 illustrates Schlesinger's cyclical thesis by suggesting that a 30-year cycle produces alternate periods of liberalism and conservatism.

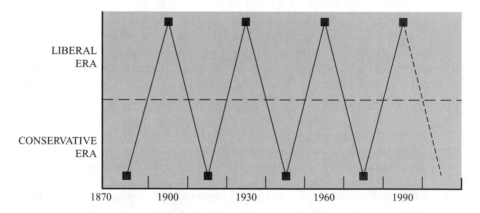

F I G U R E   9.1 An Illustration of Schlesinger's Cyclical Thesis.

SOURCE: Excerpt from *The Cycles of American History*, by Arthur M. Schlesinger Jr. Copyright © 1986 by Arthur M. Schlesinger Jr. Reprinted by permission of Houghton Mifflin. Reuse of material from 2nd edition. All rights reserved.

Samuel Huntington's elaboration of the cyclical model also emphasizes the power of ideas in shaping public policy and institutions. He argues that periods of "creedal passion," or intense and widespread debate over the gap between the ideals and the actual performance of the American government, lead to major bursts of institutional reform. The enactment and implementation of the reforms serve to channel and control the debate over fundamental values and usher in an era of relative calm. In time, the shortcomings of the reforms become increasingly obvious, triggering another period of controversy and another attempt to bring America's political system closer to its mythical ideals. Paradoxically, the reforms of one generation create the vested interests of the next generation.[13]

The Backlash or Zigzag Thesis   Still another explanation of changes in public policy over time is the **zigzag thesis,** which comes from the work of Edwin Amenta and Theda Skocpol.[14] They argue that there is an erratic pattern in the history of American public policies. It is characterized by a "zigzag effect," or a stimulus and response (backlash). It is not so much a shift from liberal to conservative as it is a shift from policy that benefits one group to policy that benefits another group, in backlash. The concept of "class struggle" or competing societal coalitions comes to mind as a useful way to explain these shifts. For example, the late 19th century was characterized by high levels of spending and by the distributive character and patronage for *white men*. Specifically, policy was devised by the "radical Republicans" and included the Civil War pension system, in which benefits were distributed in a partisan way. Benefits went to Northerners who could make a plausible case for their role in preserving the Union. Political affiliation to Republicans was a major criterion for the pension. This led to a backlash against the radical Republicans in the Southern states. There were also federal jobs for those with suitable party connections. The federal bureaucracy could be seen as largely an employment program for the "right people" (i.e., Northern and Midwestern Republicans).

This was followed by the Progressive Era (1900–30), in which there was an attempt to eliminate political machines and patronage from the previous era. Civil service reforms, including the merit hiring system, were instituted. There was a movement away from direct election of administrative officials. There were child labor laws and legislation limiting women's working hours. A variety of public health and safety laws were passed, as was worker's compensation. Gradually, Democrats became more powerful due to their Southern and Western bases of support. Individual and corporate income taxes were established. Democrats became known as the reform party due to their attempt to replace the radical Republicans with their own members. By the end of the 1920s, Democrats allied with the labor movement and threw their support behind social spending. Essentially, the Democrats almost established themselves as a "social democratic" party at this time.

Later, this was followed by the New Deal period (1930–50), in which many of the social insurance programs and welfare programs were enacted. These initiatives were propelled by the Great Depression, and Democrats continued their domination of the public policy debate. Legislation included the 1935 Social Security Act (the centerpiece of the New Deal). According to this model, Keynesian economics was adopted, and the federal government was used as an agency for massive redistribution of wealth through the creation of large social spending programs and direct intervention in the economy. Politically this encouraged deficit spending and did not encourage balanced budgets. As for social spending policy, veterans of World War II and retired veterans of wage-earning employment and their survivors were advantaged relative to other social groups.

Finally, the authors see a postwar period (1950—80s), in which there was a reaction to the free-spending ways of the previous period of Democratic administrations. In particular, the "new federalism" of the 1970s and 1980s represented a backlash against large federal welfare programs. Later cuts deeply reduced the growth in Great Society programs enacted in the late 1960s. Recent economic policies have relied on fiscal stimulation rather than New Deal liberalism, such as tax reduction rather than spending programs to stimulate the economy. There were heavy investments in military spending (jobs in the military have been the counterpart to employment in the civilian bureaucracy in the late 19th century). Patronage today exits in terms of military employment and old-age assistance. This model finds, in effect, policies today are very similar to those in the first period of the late 19th century.

Thus, the arguments of Amenta and Skocpol suggest there is a pattern in the history of American public policies. It is a zigzag effect, or a stimulus and response (backlash), that is not so much a shift from liberal to conservative as from a policy that benefits one group to another policy as a backlash. The following proposition is derived from their argument.

Proposition 2: The evolution of public policy during the period 1890—1990 is best explained by a zigzag pattern, in which the public policies of one era provide the stimulus for a reaction in the next era. Thus, policies undergo drastic changes as a reaction to previous policies. For example, policies that favor one group (e.g., citizen interests) in one era are replaced by policies that favor another group (e.g., the corporate sector) in the next era.

The Advocacy Coalition Framework   A third explanation, the **advocacy coalition framework,** comes from work by Paul Sabatier and his associates.[15] Over the years, those scholars have developed a conceptual framework of the policy process that views policy change as a function of three sets of factors: (1) the interaction of competing "advocacy coalitions" within a policy subsystem/community; (2) changes external to the subsystem including socioeconomic changes, shifts in public opinion, and system-wide changes in governing coalitions; and (3) the effects of stable system parameters. The framework has at least three basic premises. First, understanding the process of policy change—and the role of policy learning therein—requires a time perspective of a decade or more. This is in order to observe a more complete policy cycle (i.e., from policy formation to implementation to evaluation and change). Second, the most useful way to think about policy change over such a time span is through a focus on "policy subsystems," which are composed of "advocacy coalitions" (i.e., the interaction of actors from different institutions interested in a policy area). Third, public policies can be conceptualized in the same manner as "belief systems" (i.e., sets of value priorities and causal assumptions about how to realize them).[16] Basically, policy change is viewed both as the product of changes in system-wide events, such as socioeconomic perturbations or outputs from other subsystems, and the striving of competing advocacy coalitions within the subsystem to realize their core beliefs over time as they seek to increase their resource bases, to respond to opportunities provided by external events, and to learn more about the policy problem(s) of interest to them.[17] Based on perceptions of the adequacy of governmental units and/or the resultant impacts, as well as new information arising from search processes and external dynamics, each advocacy coalition may revise its beliefs and/or alter its strategy. The latter may involve seeking major institutional revisions at the collective-choice level, making minor revisions at the operational level, or even going outside the subsystem—for example, by seeking changes in the dominant electoral coalition at the systemic level.[18]

This framework has special significance for the study of policy-oriented learning (i.e., relatively enduring alterations of behavioral intentions that result from experience and are concerned with the attainment or revision of public policy).[19] Specifically, the framework argues that the core aspects of a governmental action program—and the relative strength of competing advocacy coalitions within a policy subsystem—will typically remain rather stable over periods of a decade or more. Major alterations in the policy core will normally be the product of changes external to the subsystem—particularly large-scale socioeconomic conditions or changes in the system-wide governing coalition. Although changes in the policy core are usually the result of external perturbations, changes in the secondary aspects of a governmental action program are often the result of policy-oriented learning by various coalitions or policy brokers. Moreover, Sabatier and Jenkins-Smith argue that external perturbations will lead to substantial policy changes only if the opportunity they provide "is skillfully exploited by proponents of change, that is, the heretofore minority coalition."[20]

Policy learning involves the feedback loops depicted in Figure 9.2, as well as increased knowledge of the problem and the factors affecting it. Figure 9.2 presents Sabatier and Jenkins-Smith's framework and the factors that condition public policy change over time.

Proposition 3: The evolution of public policy is explained by an extended period of policy change, in which governmental actors repeatedly revise policy on the basis of "policy learning" brought on by events external to subsystem politics. More specifically:

Proposition 3a: Policy-oriented learning across belief systems is most likely when there is an intermediate level of informed conflict between the two. This requires that (1) each have the technical resources to engage in such a debate, and (2) the

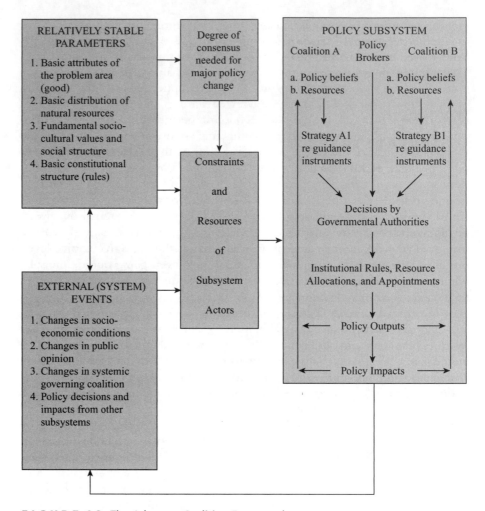

FIGURE 9.2 The Advocacy Coalition Framework.

SOURCE: From *Theories of the Policy Process*, "The Advocacy Coalition Framework: An Assessment," by Paul Sabatier, ed., and Hank Jenkins-Smith. Copyright © 1999 by Westview Press, a member of Perseus Books Group. Reprinted with permission of Westview Press.

conflict is between secondary aspects of one belief system and core elements of the other or, alternatively, between important secondary aspects of the two belief systems.

Proposition 3b: Policy-oriented learning across belief systems is most likely when there exists a forum that is (1) prestigious enough to force professionals from different coalitions to participate, and (2) dominated by professional norms.

The advocacy coalition framework has been tested by Paul Sabatier and others in a number of policy areas, primarily dealing with energy and environmental policy.[21] Thus far, the arguments concerning coalition stability and the prevalence of advocacy analysis have been confirmed, although much work remains for this model to be validated fully as an adequate explanation of policy change over periods of a decade or more.

Punctuated Equilibrium Theory Baumgartner and Jones offer a fourth explanation of policy change that is rooted in the processes of issue definition and agenda setting. That explanation, *punctuated equilibrium theory*, seeks to account for the fact that "Political processes are often driven by a logic of stability and incrementalism, but occasionally they also produce large-scale departures from the past."[22] In analyzing policy change in America, the assumption is that policymaking is characterized by long periods of policy stability but also by periodic spurts of sizable policy change.[23] Those tendencies reflect the fragmented nature of American politics and the ability of policy entrepreneurs to move policy from micro- or subsystem politics to macro- or system-wide politics. As the reader knows, American politics exhibits a great deal of institutional fragmentation due to a separation of powers, federalism, and multiple and overlapping jurisdictions. Given that fragmentation and the inability of key political actors (e.g., the Congress and president) to address every existing policy issue, the tendency is to defer to the decisions and actions of policy subsystems—groups of interest groups, policy makers, and implementing officials that share common interests and beliefs. The result is periods, often long periods, when policies change only incrementally, if at all.

But the fragmentation of American politics can also produce major, if infrequent, policy change as politics move from the micro to macro level of America politics and policy subsystems lose their monopoly over policy making. When will that occur? According to Baumgartner and Jones, "it generally does so in an environment of changing issue definitions and heightened attentiveness by the media and broader publics."[24] During periods of policy stasis, there is typically substantial agreement among policy actors within the policy subsystem on a single policy image—the prevailing mix of empirical "facts" and emotional appeals that buttress the policy. But events often challenge that image, and proponents of a new policy issue are able to move the issue to the national or system-wide agenda. Ironically, those groups are aided by the fragmentation of American politics. While the decentralization of politics and policy frequently acts as a check on change, the opportunity to "shop" among competing policy venues (state governments, the courts, etc.) can also provide a forum for proponents to mobilize support for the new policy image.

Proposition 4: Policy change is likely to occur when events challenge prevailing policy images and political actors are able to mobilize sufficient support for a new image on the national agenda.

The recent movement of global warming on the nation's agenda provides an excellent illustration of how new policy images emerge and proponents are able to use multiple venues to garner support for policies that address the problems and sources of climate change. Just a few years ago, there was substantial disagreement about whether (1) the earth was warming and (2) that warming was the result of

CO_2 emissions and other human actions. Recent events, however—most notably the unusually active hurricane seasons and near unanimous consensus among the scientific community that climate change was occurring because of fossil fuel consumption—have moved the issue to the national and many state policy agendas.

CASE STUDY

Intergovernmental Relations
and Ocean Policy Change: 1971–85

Federal ocean policy underwent considerable change during the 1980s and the administration of Ronald Reagan.[25] The debate over ocean policy pitted those who argued that the oceans are sacrosanct and that any entry of polluting substances is undesirable against those who argued that the oceans have an almost infinite capacity to receive societal wastes. Moreover, it was the position of the Reagan administration that, in general, the nation's environmental laws and regulations needed careful review and modification. More specifically, the Reagan administration was concerned that the benefits to be derived from rigid environmental regulations might not be justified in view of economic costs.[26] These developments led some observers in the 1980s to believe that the United States was undergoing a policy change from an "ocean protection" strategy that was characteristic of the 1970s to an "ocean management" strategy that was characteristic of the 1980s.[27] Those holding to this view maintained that an overarching philosophy for the management of ocean space and resources would evolve resembling the evolution of policies for the management of public lands. Essentially, it was argued that ocean policy had changed from "strict protection" to something akin to "management flexibility."

Changes in Ocean Dumping Policy   The first concerted effort to control ocean dumping began in the early 1970s, when many environmental protection laws were passed. President Nixon, in his address of February 8, 1971, to Congress, announced that the nation's policy should be "to ban unregulated ocean dumping of all material and to place strict limits on ocean disposal of any materials harmful to the environment."[28] Two days later, the EPA transmitted to Congress a bill that eventually became the Marine Protection, Research, and Sanctuaries Act of 1972 (MPRSA). This bill dictated the strictest possible standards in existence at the time for any continued dumping. Indeed, the research program created by this act had the explicit purpose of "determining the means of minimizing or ending all dumping of materials within five years of the effective date of the act."[29] In addition, this act established a permit system under which ocean dumping was regulated jointly by the EPA and the Army Corps of Engineers. The EPA set criteria for evaluation of all permit applications and issued permits for dumping of all materials except dredged spoils; the Army

Corps then issued permits for dumping of dredged spoils using the EPA's criteria.[30]

On October 15, 1973, the EPA promulgated its final regulations and criteria, in which it took a strict, highly restrictive approach toward applying the criteria embodied in the act.[31] In these regulations, the EPA intended to terminate all harmful ocean dumping, regardless of whether the permit applicant could demonstrate that its dumping would not unreasonably degrade the marine environment. In effect, the EPA established a policy of phasing out all ocean dumping of sewage sludge. In doing so, the EPA assumed a highly protective approach to ocean dumping.

In 1980, when the city of New York applied for a permit to continue dumping sewage sludge, the EPA refused to permit this activity after December 31, 1981. The city of New York brought suit in a federal district court in New York. The court endorsed the arguments by the city and limited the EPA's ability to terminate ocean dumping of sewage sludge. By the time this decision was issued on April 14, 1981, a new president who was significantly less enthusiastic about environmental regulations had assumed office. By 1981, a significant change had taken place in ocean dumping policy.

In the aftermath of *City of New York v. EPA*, it became apparent that the EPA was shifting its policy toward ocean dumping. The agency soon stated that in the future it would be more "flexible" about ocean dumping and would now view the oceans as a legitimate disposal option. In sum, the EPA moved from strict, confrontational protection of the oceans toward a more flexible, accommodating posture during the period of 1971–85.

Several factors affected this change in ocean dumping policy:

1. The status of knowledge about the oceans' vulnerability to environmental contamination was changing. During the period of 1971–85, scientific data accumulated that suggested that ocean dumping posed only modest environmental risk as compared to other threats to the oceans' environment.

2. Fundamental sociocultural attitudes during the late 1970s and early 1980s were changing as a result of the oil embargo and the subsequent energy dislocations. Specifically, the "zeal which attended the movement to clean up the environment became tempered by the growing burden of inflation, increased energy consumption, and public discontent with government spending and regulation."[32]

3. The systemic governing coalition changed with the election of Ronald Reagan as president. This administrative change may partially account for the EPA's movement away from confrontational intergovernmental relations to a more accommodating federal stance toward municipal sludge dumping, evident perhaps in the agency's decision not to appeal the lower court decision in *City of New York v. EPA*.

The case of ocean policy in the seventies and eighties illustrates the various explanations of policy change, particularly the advocacy coalition framework and punctuated equilibrium theory. As the events detailed above demonstrate, policy change occurred as new policy images emerged and changes in the economic and political system unfolded. When that occurred, the kinds of policy learning Sabatier and others describe took place; and America took a new approach to ocean dumping.

THE CONCEPT OF POLICY TERMINATION

Sometimes policies or programs are not merely changed, but terminated. Over the next several decades, it is expected that many policies, programs, and organizations will be eliminated. The term **policy termination** refers to agency termination, basic policy redirections, program eliminations, partial terminations, and fiscal retrenchments.[33] As a concept, policy termination became the object of study in the mid-1970s when scholars focused on the termination of organizations as a means of ending outworn or inadequate policies or programs.[34] For several reasons, it is perhaps the most difficult phase of the policy cycle. Once started, policies, programs, and agencies have a life of their own with substantial momentum. In addition, there is no incentive to admit past mistakes. A political reluctance to termination often exists, because vested interests will fight to keep the program due to "sunk costs." Moreover, anti-termination coalitions will mobilize and use all their resources to retain the policy, program, or organization. Finally, the costs of termination activities are high; considerable resources have to be mobilized to counter anti-termination coalitions, and organizations are reluctant to terminate their own programs for this reason.[35]

Interest in termination has grown for a pair of reasons. First, some policies and programs are recognized as simply not effective or no longer needed and should be abolished. Second, a political climate of fiscal retrenchment that began in the late 1970s and early 1980s has led to often substantial cuts in several programs. In recent years, for example, serious efforts have been made to reduce agricultural subsidies, cut NASA's budget, and close dozens of military bases. In any event, termination is an important part of the policy cycle that calls for additional study. Unfortunately, very little policy research on the termination process has been reported since the late 1970s.[36] Despite universal recognition that termination is a vital component of policy studies, it remains the "neglected butt of the policy process."[37]

Types of Termination

There are several types of termination, including functional termination, organizational termination, policy termination, and program termination.

Functional Termination   This type of termination refers to the termination of an entire area (e.g., health care). This type covers many organizations and policies, and it is a rare phenomenon. Privatization of trash collection would be an example of this type of termination.

Organizational Termination   This type of termination refers to the elimination of an entire organization. During the 1980s, the Departments of Energy and Education were unsuccessfully targeted by the Reagan administration for elimination. However, organizations generally will be reorganized, rather than completely eliminated. For example, in 1974, the Atomic Energy Commission (AEC) was split into the Energy Research and Development Administration (ERDA) and the Nuclear Regulatory Commission (NRC). ERDA was responsible for the development of energy sources, and the NRC was primarily responsible for regulating nuclear energy. This reorganization was believed to be necessary to avoid conflicts of interest. The congressional Office of Technology Assessment (OTA), however, was terminated in 1995.

Policy Termination   This type of termination refers to the elimination of a policy when the underlying theory or approach is no longer needed or believed to be correct. For example, the Fair Trade Legislation was terminated in 1975. This legislation was originally adopted in the 1930s to permit manufacturers of trademarked or brand-name products to set mandatory minimum resale prices for their products. Over the years, however, fair trade became a tired, worn-out policy with little congressional support.[38]

Program Termination   This term refers to the elimination of specific measures designed to implement a policy. It is the most common type of termination, because limited constituencies characterize specific programs. Eliminating a specific program with a relatively smaller constituency is always easier than eliminating a policy or organization with a much larger constituency. An example of program termination would be the federal revenue sharing program that was begun in 1972 during the Nixon administration. This program channeled billions of dollars to state and local governments with few strings attached. It was terminated in 1986 due to large federal budget deficits, although there was always considerable congressional opposition to revenue sharing.[39]

Approaches to Termination

Termination can be approached in generally two basic ways. The first approach is called the "**big bang**" termination.[40] This approach usually occurs with a single authoritative decision or one decisive stroke at a single point in time. With this type of termination, the opposition has no time to organize against the termination. Rather, the termination is a swift and closed issue that occurs with a shattering force. Such a termination is usually the product of a long political struggle involving many participants. It is the most common approach to termination. An example of this type of termination was the proposal to terminate the Department of Energy during the Reagan administration in the early 1980s. However, the department was not terminated.

The second type of termination is called the "**long whimper**" approach.[41] This type of termination comes about through a long-term decline in the resources that sustain a policy or organization. It is a moderately paced and deliberate phasing out of a policy, program, or organization. It is sometimes also called *decrementalism,* by which the budget of an organization is slowly reduced or positions are slowly eliminated. Finally, the organization (or program) can no longer function effectively.

The major disadvantage of this type of termination, from the perspective of those trying to terminate the program, is that the opposition can organize to fight the termination. An example of this type of termination is the decision to terminate the Comprehensive Employment and Training Act (CETA) program of the 1970s and replace it with the Job Training and Partnership Act (JTPA) program in 1983.

Reasons for Termination and Types of Terminators

Termination decisions are made for various reasons. Both DeLeon and Cameron hypothesize that political values and ideology play the key role in these decisions.[42] Citing many instances of termination during the Reagan administration, DeLeon argues that "it is ideological stance rather than rigorous analysis or evaluation that (drove) the . . . termination activities."[43] Similarly, Cameron summarizes his points about the role of ideology in terminations:

> Legitimizing the proposal involves a systematic effort to delegitimize the policy it is designed to supplant. This frequently takes the simplistic form of "the right and the good" versus the "wrong and immoral." . . . But the simplistic approach that gives ideology its coalescing force results in ill-considered policy choices: data that are inconsistent with the ideology are ignored or explained away; rigid adherence to credo becomes more important than inquiry into the potential risks attending the prospect of contingencies.[44]

Based on DeLeon's and Cameron's analyses of policy and program termination, political considerations, rather than evaluative elegance, are at the root of most termination decisions. This observation, argues Peter DeLeon, suggests that termination researchers should look beyond the straightforward issues of economics and efficiencies as the basis for termination decisions. "If one wishes to operate effectively in the termination arena, one needs to address the ideological motivations."[45]

Nevertheless, several types of terminators exist. Bardach has identified three types: the *oppositionists,* the *economizers,* and the *reformers.*[46] The oppositionists are those who dislike the policy or program because they feel that it is a bad policy. It is a challenge to their sense of values, or offends their social, economic, or political interests. The economizers are those who see a need to economize. Thus, they favor termination as a means of reducing expenditure outlays; at other times, they are simply more interested in reprogramming expenditures. Finally, the reformers are those who see the termination as essential to the development of a substitute policy, program, or organization that they believe will be more useful.[47] Bardach argues that ideological or political considerations are usually the motives behind the behavior of reformers and oppositionists, whereas programmatic considerations (i.e., economics and efficiency) are usually the motives behind the behavior of the economizers. In any case, sometimes programmatic reasons are used for convenience when in reality they are attempts to mask what are essentially ideological or political motivations.

Some Rules for Would-Be Terminators

Robert Behn suggests the following political strategies that may help policy terminators achieve their objectives.

1. *Don't float trial balloons.* A termination trial balloon will allow the opposition to organize supporters. Therefore, terminators need to prevent information leaks until they have formalized comprehensive justifications for their termination decision.

2. *Enlarge the policy's constituency.* Organized constituencies often determine whether a policy is continued or terminated; consequently, terminators are more successful in eliminating a policy if they can enlarge the termination constituency body beyond the policy's original clientele base.

3. *Focus attention on the policy's harm.* Eliminating policies that can be shown to have a particularly harmful effect is easier than eliminating policies that have general effects, ineffectiveness, or inefficiency.

4. *Take advantage of ideological shifts to demonstrate harm.* Policies are often evaluated on the basis of an ideological framework. Terminators can utilize or create ideological shifts that would create a new perspective that an established policy is actually harmful.

5. *Inhibit compromise.* Political supporters of a policy make compromises to maintain the policy. By making compromises impossible, terminators prevent the possibility that this will be chosen instead of termination.

6. *Recruit an outsider as a terminator.* This facilitates termination because the agency must renounce its programmatic philosophy and disrupt its administrative procedures. The current administration may be reluctant to adopt a negative view of the agency's past behavior and make unpopular statements and directives necessary for termination.

7. *Avoid legislative votes.* Because legislators try to avoid making enemies, they may not be willing to force an unpopular termination. Legislators are interested more in compromise than in asymmetrical decisions.

8. *Don't encroach upon legislative prerogatives.* Executive branch terminators should avoid conflict between constitutional powers of the president and Congress.

9. *Accept short-term cost increases.* Terminating a policy can often cost more in the short term than continuing it due to severance payments and the costs of initiating a replacement policy.

10. *Put off the beneficiaries.* Offer new jobs for the employees of terminated programs and make severance payments to the policy's clientele.

11. *Advocate adoption, not termination.* Make the case that the adoption of policy B necessitates the termination of policy A, rather than simply advocating termination of policy A.

12. *Terminate only what is necessary.* Terminators should be aware of their motivation. Is the target of termination really a harmful or ineffective policy or an expensive agency? Be judicious in deciding what to terminate.[48]

Behn cautions that not all these suggestions will be appropriate for every termination effort. In addition, his suggestions are more relevant to "big bang" terminations than to the "long whimper" variety. Nevertheless, they are useful bits of advice for would-be terminators.

SUMMARY

In the past five past chapters, we have looked at a variety of attempts to describe and account for each "slice" of the policy process. In the next part of this book, we describe the evolution of several domestic policies and examine the extent to which our theories of the policy process explain those phenomena. In Chapters 10 through 12, the evolution of educational policy, welfare policy, and environmental policy during the period from the early 1960s to the present is discussed.

DISCUSSION QUESTIONS

1. Some argue that social security should be drastically changed or even terminated, while others argue that the program just needs to be reformed. What is your position on this question? Defend your position.

2. Based on your understanding of the various theories of change and termination discussed in this chapter, what are the prospects for a major change or termination in social security over the next several years? Who is likely to support and oppose changing or eliminating social security? What events might stimulate change?

3. Why is it so difficult to terminate an organization or a program?

4. If you were hired as an administrator and you were given instructions to terminate a program or policy, how would you proceed? Would you apply the "big bang" or the "long whimper" approach?

SUGGESTED READINGS

Brewer, Garry, and Peter DeLeon. *The Foundations of Policy Analysis* (Homewood, IL: Dorsey Press, 1983).

Daniels, Mark R. *Terminating Public Programs: An American Paradox* (Armonk, NY: M. E. Sharpe, 1997).

Kaufman, Herbert *Are Organizations Immortal?* (Washington, D.C.: Brookings Institution, 1976).

Sabatier, Paul A., and Hank Jenkins-Smith, eds., *Policy Change and Learning: An Advocacy Coalition Approach* (Boulder, CO: Westview Press, 1993).

Schlesinger, Arthur. *The Cycles of American History* (Boston: Houghton Mifflin, 1986).

NOTES

1. See David B. Truman, *The Governmental Process* (New York: Alfred Knopf, 1951); and David B. Easton, *A Systems Analysis of Political Life* (New York: Wiley, 1965).

2. Peter DeLeon, "A Theory of Policy Termination," in *The Policy Cycle,* ed. J. V. May and Aaron Wildavsky (Beverly Hills, CA: Sage, 1978), pp. 279–300; Brian W. Hogwood and B. G. Peters, *Policy Dynamics* (New York: St. Martin's Press, 1983); Brian W. Hogwood and Lewis A. Gunn, *Policy Analysis for the Real World* (Oxford: Oxford University Press, 1984), pp. 241–260; and Paul A. Sabatier, "Top-Down and Bottom-Up Approaches to Implementation Research: A Critical Analysis and Suggested Synthesis," *Journal of Public Policy* 6, no. 1 (1986), pp. 21–47.

3. James E. Anderson, *Public Policymaking: An Introduction* (Boston: Houghton Mifflin, 1990), p. 257.

4. Ibid., p. 402.

5. Renee Johnson, David Hedge, and Marian Currender, "Bootstraps and Benevolence: A Comparative Test of the States' Capacity to Effect Change in Welfare Outcomes," *State and Local Government Review* 36 (2004), pp. 118–129.

6. Anderson, *Public Policymaking: An Introduction,* p. 250.

7. Hogwood and Gunn, *Policy Analysis,* p. 251.

8. Ibid.

9. Ibid., p. 242.

10. Anderson, *Public Policymaking,* p. 255.

11. B. Guy Peters, *American Public Policy: Promise and Performance* (Chatham, NJ: Chatham House, 1986), pp. 143–144.

12. See Arthur Schlesinger, Jr., *The Cycles of American History* (Boston: Houghton Mifflin, 1986); and Arthur Schlesinger, Jr., "America's Political Cycle Turns Again," *Wall Street Journal,* 10 December 1987. See also Walter Dean Burnham, *Critical Elections and the Mainsprings of American Politics* (New York: W. W. Norton, 1970).

13. Samuel P. Huntington, *American Politics: The Promise of Disharmony* (Cambridge, MA: Belknap/Harvard University Press, 1981), p. 284.

14. See Edwin Amenta and Theda Skocpol, "Taking Exception: Explaining the Distinctiveness of American Public Policies in the Last Century," in *The Comparative History of Public Policy,* ed. F. G. Castles (New York: Oxford University Press, 1989).

15. See Paul A. Sabatier, "Knowledge, Policy-Oriented Learning, and Policy Change: An Advocacy Coalition Framework," *Knowledge: Creation, Utilization, Diffusion* 3, no. 4 (June 1987), pp. 649–692; see also Paul A. Sabatier and Hank Jenkins-Smith, eds., *Policy Change and Learning: An Advocacy Coalition Approach* (Boulder, CO: Westview Press, 1993).

16. Paul A. Sabatier, "An Advocacy Coalition Framework of Policy Change and the Role of Policy-Oriented Learning Therein," *Policy Sciences* 21, nos. 2–3 (1988), pp. 129–168.

17. Ibid.

18. Sabatier, "Knowledge, Policy-Oriented Learning, and Policy Change," p. 653.

19. See Hugh Heclo, *Social Policy in Britain and Sweden* (New Haven, CT: Yale University Press, 1974), p. 306.

20. Paul A. Sabatier and Hank C. Jenkins-Smith, "The Advocacy Coalition Framework: An Assessment," in *Theories of the Policy Process,* ed. Paul A. Sabatier (Boulder, CO: Westview Press, 1999), p. 148.

21. Much of that is summarized by Sabatier and Jenkins-Smith in "The Advocacy Coalition Framework: An Assessment."

22. James L. True, Bryan D. Jones, and Frank R. Baumgartner, "Punctuated-Equilibrium Theory: Explaining Stability and Change in American Policymaking," in Sabatier, ed., *Theories of the Policy Process,* pp. 97–116.

23. Bryan D. Jones, *Reconceiving Decision-Making in Democratic Politics: Attention, Choice, and Public Policy* (Chicago: University of Chicago Press, 1994), p. 185.

24. Frank R. Baumgartner and Bryan D. Jones, *Agendas and Instability in American Politics* (Chicago: University of Chicago, 1993).

25. Maynard Silva, ed., *Ocean Resources and U.S. Intergovernmental Relations in the 1980s* (Boulder, CO: Westview Press, 1986).

26. R. L. Swanson and M. Devine, "Ocean Dumping Policy: The Pendulum Swings Again," *Environment* 24, no. 5 (June 1982), pp. 15–20.

27. James W. Curlin, "Ocean Policy Comes of Age: The End of the Beginning or the Beginning of the End," *Sea Technology* 21, no. 1 (1980), pp. 23–28.

28. Alan Bakalian, "Regulation and Control of U.S. Ocean Dumping: A Decade of Progress, an Appraisal for the Future," *Harvard Environmental Law Review* (1984), pp. 193–256.

29. Julian H. Spirer, "The Ocean Dumping Deadline: Easing the Mandate Millstone," *Fordham Urban Law Journal* 11, no. 1 (1982/1983), pp. 1–49.

30. William H. Lahey, "Ocean Dumping of Sewage Sludge: The Tide Turns from Protection to Management," *Harvard Environmental Law Review* (1982), pp. 395–431.

31. Spirer, "Ocean Dumping Deadline."

32. Ibid., p. 36.

33. Peter DeLeon, "Policy Termination as a Political Process," in *The Politics of Program Evaluation,* ed. Dennis Palumbo (Beverly Hills, CA: Sage, 1987), p. 194.

34. Garry D. Brewer, "Termination: Hard Choices, Harder Questions," *Public Administration Review* 38, no. 4 (July/August 1978), pp. 338–344; and Herbert Kaufman, *Are Government Organizations Immortal?* (Washington, D.C.: Brookings Institution, 1976).

35. Hogwood and Gunn, *Policy Analysis,* pp. 247–248.

36. Some notable exceptions are Janet E. Frantz, "Reviving and Revising a Termination Model," *Policy Sciences* 25 (May 1992), pp. 175–189; and Susan E. Kirkpatrick, James P. Lester, and Mark R. Peterson, "The Policy Termination Process: A Conceptual Framework and Application to Revenue-Sharing, "*Policy Studies Review* 16 (Spring 1999), pp. 209–236.

37. Robert Behn, "How to Terminate a Public Policy: A Dozen Hints for the Would-Be Terminator," *Policy Analysis* 4, no. 3 (Summer 1978), pp. 393–413

38. Anderson, *Public Policymaking,* p. 256.

39. Ibid.

40. Eugene Bardach, "Policy Termination as a Political Process," *Policy Sciences* 7, no. 2 (June 1976), pp. 123–132.

41. Ibid.

42. DeLeon, "Theory of Policy Termination," pp. 173–194; James M. Cameron, "Ideology and Policy Termination: Restructuring California's Mental Health Systems," in *The Policy Cycle,* ed. Judith May and Aaron Wildavsky (Newbury Park, CA: Sage, 1978), pp. 301–328.

43. DeLeon, "Theory of Policy Termination," p. 185.

44. Cameron, "Ideology and Policy Termination," p. 306.

45. DeLeon, "Theory of Policy Termination," p. 194.

46. Bardach, "Policy Termination," p. 126.

47. Ibid., p. 127.

48. Behn, "Terminate a Public Policy," pp. 393–413.

Analyzing Public Policy Choices

10

Educational Policy

"The poorest states, if left to their own resources, have no reasonable
prospect of raising the funds to provide adequate education. Some
form of equalization is needed, because it is vital to the nation
that the children in the poorest states also be well educated.
Therefore, Federal participation in the financing of their
schools is essential."

EDUCATIONAL POLICIES COMMISSION (1962)

"Our nation is at risk. Our once unchallenged preeminence in
commerce, industry, science and technological innovation is being
overtaken by competitors throughout the world.... The educational
foundations of our society are presently being eroded by a rising tide of
mediocrity that threatens our very future as a nation and a people....
We have, in effect, been committing an act of un-thinking, unilateral
educational disarmament."

NATIONAL COMMISSION ON EXCELLENCE IN EDUCATION (1983)

"Each student will develop the ability to understand, respect, and accept
people of different races, sex, cultural heritage, national origin, religion,
and political, economic, and social background, and their values,
beliefs, and attitudes."

NEW YORK STATE BOARD OF REGENTS (1990)

"...children must be tested every year in reading and math. Every single
year. Not just in the third grade or the eighth grade, but in the third,
fourth, fifth, sixth and seventh and eighth grade. When schools do not
teach and will not change, parents and students must have other
meaningful options."

PRESIDENT GEORGE W. BUSH (2001)

These quotes from four different decades reflect alternative emphases at various times on issues that have been omnipresent in U.S. educational policy. How public schools should be funded, what should be included in the curriculum, how equal educational opportunities can best be defined, and how educational services are best delivered are issues that have been contested throughout American history and have galvanized both conservative and liberal forces. Today, educational institutions, from elementary schools to universities, are under attack from many directions.[1] In the new century, the conflicts concerning funding redistribution, financial aid to poor children, taxpayer support for all public education, "tracking" of students into different curricula, bilingual education, equal opportunities for racial minorities, testing of students, school choice, community control of schools, and countless other manifestations will continue.

In this chapter we examine some of these concerns. First we provide a brief sketch of the scope of public education in the United States, together with some of the charges that have been leveled against America's schools in the last two decades. Second, we examine where educational policy is made, highlighting the intergovernmental structure inherent in policymaking in America. Third, we look at alternative perspectives on education. Finally, we look at the evolution of education policy over the last fifty or so years.

EDUCATION IN AMERICA

In the fall of 2005, roughly 72 million students were enrolled in educational institutions at all levels.[2] Over the past 20 years, enrollments have experienced a steady incline and are estimated to continue to do so until 2014. According to the U.S. Department of Education, the fastest growth in the public schools in recent years has taken place at the elementary level. Between 1985 and 2005, the number of elementary students increased by 24 percent.[3] In the fall of 2005 there were 3.5 million elementary and secondary teachers serving in America's school, up 18 percent since 1995.[4]

Not surprisingly, spending on America's schools has increased as well. In 2004, governments at all levels spent 536 billion dollars on elementary and secondary schools, or approximately $9,000 for each public school student.[5] Although the federal share of spending on education has increased in recent years to around 9 percent, state and local governments are the principal source of educational spending—accounting for 47 and 44 percent respectively of the totals for K−12 spending (see Figure 10.1).

Given the centrality of education in America, it is not surprising that the nation's schools are much criticized. Beginning in the 1980s a consensus has emerged that America's schools are in "crisis." In 1983 the National Commission

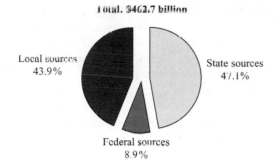

Total. $462.7 billion

Local sources
43.9%

State sources
47.1%

Federal sources
8.9%

FIGURE 10.1 Percent Distribution of Total Public Elementary-Secondary School System Revenue: 2003–04.

SOURCE: U.S. Department of the Census, "Public Education Finances 2004," Figure 1, p. ix, at www2.census.gov/govs/school/04f33pub.pdf, issued March 2006.

on Educational Excellence (NCEE) declared America "A Nation at Risk." According to the authors of the Commission's report, *A Nation at Risk:*

> the educational foundations of our society are presently being eroded by a rising tide of mediocrity that threatens our very future as a Nation and as people.... Our society and educational institutions have lost sight of the basic purposes of schooling, and of the high expectations and disciplined effort needed to attain them.[6]

Among other things, the Commission pointed to a lowering of standards, a corresponding decline in student performance, and both teacher shortages and shortcomings as evidence of educational decline. Equally important, the Commission's report reflected an emerging consensus that the inadequacies of the nations' schools were undermining America's ability to participate effectively in an increasingly competitive international economy.

To their credit, officials at all levels of government have worked hard to find solutions to the problems of education. In the last several decades, policy makers have put into place successive waves of reforms meant to correct the problems the NCEE identified. We will consider those reforms later in this chapter, but first we need to introduce the key players in the educational process as well as the competing ideologies that undergird various proposals to improve America's schools.

THE LOCUS OF EDUCATIONAL POLICYMAKING

Federal Government

Although the federal government has never assumed a large role in funding public elementary and secondary schools—its contribution has never exceeded 10 percent of total expenditures—its interest in education is a long-standing one. Congress offered land for public schools in the new territories with the Northwest Ordinance of 1787 and provided grants of federal land to each state for the establishment of colleges under the Morrill Land Grant Act of 1862. The Smith-Hughes Act of 1917 set up the first program of federal grants-in-aid to promote vocational education, which enabled schools to provide training in agriculture, home economics, trades, and industries.[7] Beginning in 1946, the federal government supported the National School Lunch and Milk programs, in which federal grants and commodity donations were the basis for low-cost lunches and milk served in both public and private schools.

After World War II, the federal government increased its involvement in public education through the Federal Impacted Areas Aid program, in which federal aid was authorized for areas of the country where federal activities (such as a military base) created a substantial increase in school enrollments or a reduction in taxable resources because of a federally owned facility. In the National Defense Education Act of 1958, Congress provided financial aid to the states and public school districts to improve instruction in science, math, and foreign languages. This was largely in response to the Soviet Union's launch of the first satellite in space, and the belief that American education might not be competitive in science and technology with that of other nations.[8]

Beginning with the Elementary and Secondary Education Act (ESEA) of 1965, the federal government began to play an even larger role. This act established the single largest federal aid-to-education program, in which poverty-impacted schools were the beneficiaries of aid for instructional materials and educational research and training. ESEA provided federal financial assistance to local educational agencies that served areas with concentrations of children from low-income families. This aid was used for programs targeted at meeting the needs of educationally deprived children.[9] Federal aid was substantially increased during this period.

A perceived decline in student performance prompted further federal action. In 1983, the National Commission on Excellence in Education recommended a series of reforms in American education. This began the back-to-basics movement that has dominated much of the discussion of educational reform in recent decades. During the presidency of George H. W. Bush (1989–92), the proposed national goals of the White House and the National Governors' Association assumed that schools would improve if standards were set and if incentives were created to force school professionals to pay attention to those standards. This theory of educational policy was the basis for President Bush's "America 2000" plan for national educational reform.

During the Clinton presidency, and particularly because of the budget surplus, there was a renewed effort to pump federal dollars into education. For example, in negotiations with Congress over the 1998–99 budget, President Clinton publicly called on Congress to support his initiatives to spend $1.1 billion dollars to add 100,000 teachers to the educational workforce and to issue billions of dollars worth of bonds to upgrade school facilities nationwide. In April 1993, President Clinton proposed a "national service program" that was designed to make a college education available to all students, regardless of their financial situation. Under this proposal, students could acquire college loans and repay them through automatic deductions from future earnings or by performing community service jobs, such as working as teachers, police officers, or social workers after graduation. In 1993, Congress passed the National Service Bill, which provided up to $9,450 in education grants to volunteers when they completed their community service.[10]

Ironically, the move to a larger federal role in education occurred during the first term of President George W. Bush. Despite his stated position that education is a state and local concern, the president proposed and Congress enacted landmark legislation, the No Child Left Behind Act (NCLB) of 2002, that required states to establish educational standards in reading and math and test all students in grades 3–8 to determine if those standards are being met. Under the federal legislation, actually an amendment to Title I of the Elementary and Secondary Education Act of 1965, schools that fail to make satisfactory progress face cuts in federal funding and are required to give parents the choice of sending their children to another public school, including public charter schools, within the school district. Hailed as a means to ensure greater accountability within the nation's schools, the legislation authorized a sizable increase in federal funding for education and sought to encourage the development of charter schools. Since its enactment federal funding has increased by a third, and some 9,000 schools (roughly 10 percent of all public schools) have been identified as needing improvement.[11]

As this chapter is being written, the new Democratic Congress is considering whether and under what conditions to reauthorize NCLB. Although the NCLB act was passed with broad bipartisan support in 2001, its implementation has engendered a great deal of criticism from both conservatives and liberals. Conservatives contend that the legislation usurps state and local authority and simply adds to federal bureaucratic control of local education. Liberals criticize the administration and earlier Congresses for substantially underfunding the program while imposing substantial costs on state and local governments. And while test scores have increased over the last several years, few families have been able to take advantage of the choice option due to a lack of space in alternative schools.[12]

State Governments

Establishing, supporting, and overseeing public education is a power not granted to the national government, either expressly or by implication. This power is reserved by the states under the Tenth Amendment to the U.S. Constitution. States vary in how much they have centralized and bureaucratized the provision of educational services. Joseph McGivney, building on the earlier work of Lawrence Iannaccone, argues that state educational politics can take one of four forms.[13] In some states, educators, state education agencies, and legislatures try to maintain local control. In a second set of states, the education advocacy coalitions are concerned with issues broader than those defined by local interests, but the relationships between the actors remain cooperative. In yet other states, educational policymaking is more centralized, and different educational interests compete for the establishment or maintenance of a particular set of programs or funds. In a final set of states, educational policymaking is highly centralized, and educational politics may take the form of "iron triangles" of interest groups, state legislators, and agency officials cooperating with each other in competition with other policy subsystems to pursue their goals. McGivney sees a tendency to move toward more centralization over time. Political scientist Fred Wirt agrees that the most important issues in educational policymaking are decided at the state—not local—level, and that even in the most decentralized states, key functions such as teacher certification, accreditation, and minimum attendance policies are performed at the state level.[14]

Beginning in the 1930s, the states have steadily increased their financial involvement in the public schools, as citizens and policy makers have lost confidence in the schools' abilities to provide a quality education.[15] The cornerstone of state educational policymaking is the State Educational Agency (SEA). The SEA is composed of a state board of education, a chief state school official (usually called the commissioner or superintendent of education), and a department of education. The state board of education is ordinarily concerned with the overall educational policies for the state, including minimum high school graduation requirements.[16] The SEA also legitimizes decisions made by the state department of education, and it appoints the chief school officer.

Moreover, the influence of the SEAs has grown over the years as the local school districts look to their SEA to provide educational leadership for the state.[17] The SEA distributes state educational funds to local school districts and provides basic research and information to legislative committees that investigate school problems. Some of the most visible educational reforms in the 1980s, including teacher testing and tighter graduation requirements, were forced on local school districts by governors and state legislatures.[18] The back-to-basics movement of the 1980s was, in large part, spearheaded by the state governments.

The Local Role

Local influence in education has traditionally been thought of as being exercised primarily through financing schools via the property tax. However, the percentage of total school revenues provided by local governments has been declining since the 1930s. Moreover, the taxpayer revolts of the 1970s and 1980s caused a severe erosion of local property tax dollars for public education. For example, in California, the local share of school funding dropped from 70 percent in 1970 to 20 percent in 1982.[19]

What has often been ignored is the local politics of education. The progressive reformers of the early 20th century went to great lengths to remove educational systems from partisan politics and to create the illusion that educational systems were apolitical. All they did, in fact, was change the nature of the politics.

Educational researcher Joel Spring paints a richly textured picture in which the community power structure, the educational needs of the local labor market, the governing style of the local school board, the personal style of the superintendent, and the power of both the educational bureaucracy and the teachers' unions are all factors in local education politics.[20] But even he acknowledges that "local political battles are of little importance when compared to those that occur in state and federal politics."[21]

OTHER ACTORS IN EDUCATIONAL POLICY

Teachers

Aside from parents, teachers are perhaps the most important influence on students' intellectual and emotional development. Yet, many often argue that the quality of individuals who choose to enter the teaching profession has declined over the years.[22] This is true for a number of reasons. First, the decline in quality over the past few decades is due to changes in the workforce. Highly qualified women, who previously found teaching one of the few professions open to them, began to enter traditionally male-dominated jobs after 1965. These new jobs offered better pay and more prestige than the teaching profession. Those who entered the teaching profession in the 1980s had lower average SAT scores than did their predecessors of the 1960s.[23]

In addition, part of the blame for declining quality of teachers rested with the educational programs of colleges and universities, which emphasized "educational methodology" rather than subject matter knowledge.[24] Teachers were given much more training in how to teach than in what to teach.

These problems in teacher quality led Albert Shanker, the president of the American Federation of Teachers, to say: "For the most part you are getting illiterate, incompetent people who cannot go into any other field."[25] Moreover, there is a growing shortage of teachers, especially in math, science, and foreign languages. Between 1989 and 1994, the United States required over 1 million new teachers, while it is estimated that only about 625,000 were available.[26]

These developments have led to the various state efforts to reform education. The movement for "teacher accountability" and "minimum competency testing" for teachers led by many state legislatures and some governors is directly related to the decline in teacher quality. Teachers have become objects of more scrutiny than ever before as state legislatures have become concerned over the decline in teacher quality during the past 30 years.

The Courts

The courts are also important actors in all areas of educational policymaking. Litigation by the disabled, and groups such as language, racial, and religious minorities have sought to affect how schools operate and often have been successful. Examples include cases affecting minority group representation on school boards, cases attempting to ensure equality of educational funding, cases mandating racial and ethnic desegregation, and cases attempting to ban prayers in public schools.

In some instances, these cases have led the courts to fashion remedies affecting school budgets, teacher and pupil assignments, curriculum, transportation, textbooks, and administrative organization.[27] At other times, the courts have refused to get involved. For example, some argue that the vast differences in the amounts of per pupil spending in various school districts violate the equal protection clause of the Fourteenth Amendment to the U.S. Constitution. But, in *Rodriguez v. San Antonio Independent School District,* the U.S. Supreme Court ruled that equalization of school financing was an issue that "must come from the lawmakers and from the democratic pressures of those who elect them."[28] With this decision, the issue of fiscal disparities between school districts was left to the various states to work out. State supreme courts did just that. In *Serrano v. Priest,* California's supreme court in 1971 ordered that action be taken to equalize school expenditures throughout the state. Over the next 30 years, 43 state supreme courts heard cases on educational finance; and in 19 instances, they concluded that state plans were indeed unconstitutional.[29]

In summary, one can see how various actors—including the federal government, state and local governments, teachers, and the courts—have affected the evolution of educational policy. Before discussing this evolution, let us first discuss alternative perspectives on educational policy.

APPROACHES TO EDUCATIONAL POLICY

Why do some students fail? Policy makers have long debated the causes of educational failures in our schools. Basically, there are two major perspectives on the causes of failure, and each view carries with it a set of policies that would remedy the cause of failure. We will briefly explore these two perspectives.

The Liberal (Structural) View

The liberal view begins with an optimistic view of human nature. Much as with Thomas Sowell's "unconstrained vision," liberals believe that everyone can succeed in the educational realm if given the chance and if not shackled by an environment that is not conducive to success. Within this perspective, the failures that do occur are more often the result of the school system itself or the instructional environment, rather than the individual. The liberal believes that, with few exceptions, everyone has the potential to acquire knowledge and develop employable skills.[30] In the 1960s, this perspective saw segregation and the lack of adequate resources as the primary causes of failures in the classroom. Liberals have promoted such policies as mandatory racial desegregation, community control, and the equalization of school funding by school districts. They are committed to the principle of *equity* because they feel that inequities in funding and curriculum offerings produce a hostile learning environment.[31]

The Conservative (Individualist) View

Conservatives begin with a more pessimistic view of human nature, much like Thomas Sowell's "constrained vision" of human nature. They believe that not all persons can succeed in the educational arena, due to constraints within themselves. Perhaps due to a lack of talent, intelligence, motivation, or what it takes to succeed, there will inevitably be a certain percentage of failures in the educational system. For example, Edward Banfield argues that "there will be some number of students who are simply not capable of doing high-school work."[32] The fact that these failures tend to be concentrated in the lower socioeconomic classes and the racial minorities is said to be a function of a "culture of poverty," which inhibits their desire for self-improvement and deferred gratification. Other writers within this perspective attribute poor educational achievement to genetic factors, such as IQ.[33] For example, in their controversial book, *The Bell Curve*, Richard Herrnstein and Charles Murray argue that IQ is more important than socioeconomic status in predicting which white youths will never complete a high school education; moreover, the probability of getting a college degree increases as IQ increases.[34] One of the most controversial scholars, Arthur Jensen, suggests that education for "low-IQ disadvantaged" students should be directed to rote memory learning versus conceptual or cognitive learning.[35] These authors have recently come under much criticism for their views on IQ and scholastic performance.[36]

Conservatives tend to stress *individual* reasons for failure to perform well. This failure is said to be the result of a present-oriented mind-set, genetic imbalances (i.e., IQ deficiencies) within the student population, and/or poor family background. The policies favored by conservatives include a back-to-basics approach; an emphasis on reading, writing, and mathematical skills; rote learning; the voucher system; an opposition to mandatory desegregation; parental choice in schools; and minimum competency testing for students and teachers.

Table 10.1 provides a comparison of the liberal and conservative perspectives on educational policy.[37] In the following discussion, we see how these alternative

T A B L E   10.1   Conflicting Views of Public Education

	Liberals	Conservatives
View of human nature	Optimistic	Pessimistic
Function of education	Promote social and economic mobility	Promote social and economic mobility
View of education curriculum	Advocate reform in education; emphasis on experimentation; "open classroom"	Back to the basics; emphasis on the three Rs; rote learning
View of discipline	Opposed to expelling students; keep disruptive students in the classroom	Emphasis on rigid discipline; favor right to suspend and expel troublesome students
Reasons for failures in education	Stress failure of the school system itself (e.g., segregation and/or a lack of adequate school resources)	Stress individual failure of the student (e.g., culture of poverty, genetic imbalances within student population, poor family background)
Preferred policy solution	Involuntary busing; community control; citizen participation; desegregation; multiculturalism	Educational vouchers; opposed to busing; minimum competency testing for students

SOURCE: John J. Harrigan, Adapted from *Politics and Policy Studies in States and Communities*, 5th ed. Copyright © 1994 by HarperCollins College Publishers. Reprinted with permission of HarperCollins College Publishers.

approaches to educational policy have guided different periods of educational reform from the 1960s to the 1990s. At any given time, one of these approaches seemed to occupy the intellectual high ground and formed a basis for the policies being promoted at that particular time. For example, in the 1960s and the 1970s, the emphasis on compensatory education reflected the liberal view, whereas the back-to-basics movement of the 1980s reflected the conservative view. Currently, one can find each approach being emphasized in different locales.

THE EVOLUTION OF EDUCATIONAL POLICY

The 1960s and 1970s: Inadequate Resources and Compensatory Education

Education is the single biggest expenditure of state and local governments, yet spending for education varies a great deal. Figure 10.2 illustrates the per pupil expenditures among the states for elementary and secondary education in 2003–04. Expenditures range from $12,981 per pupil in New Jersey to $5,008 in the state of Utah. Moreover, the amount of spending per pupil is largely explained by state wealth; the wealthier states spend more than the poorer ones. In the 1960s (and even today) many believed that wealthy states could provide better education for their children with less economic sacrifice than that of poor states. This relationship between state wealth and state spending for education suggested the need for federal aid to education.

In 1965, Congress enacted the Elementary and Secondary Education Act (ESEA) that doubled federal contributions to education and eventually targeted aid to less-affluent school districts. Proponents of the landmark legislation maintained that federal aid could help to equalize educational opportunities throughout the nation and, in doing so, correct some of the worst inequalities in American education. Under subsequent provisions of the ESEA, poverty-impacted schools were the beneficiaries of the increased federal aid-to-education programs. ESEA provided for federal financial assistance to "local educational agencies serving areas with concentrations of children from low-income families" for programs that contributed "to meeting the special needs of educationally deprived children."[38] Grants were made to public and private elementary and secondary schools for the acquisition of school library resources, textbooks, and other instructional materials. The logic embodied in ESEA was that an increase in per pupil expenditures (especially for students from poorer school districts) would allow schools to purchase better educational materials, hire better teachers, and improve the curriculum. As a consequence, student performance would improve, thus allowing the poorer students to be more competitive in the marketplace after graduation. Ultimately, this would help to alleviate the disparities in income and thus reduce poverty in America. Indeed, ESEA was an important component of President Johnson's War on Poverty in the 1960s.

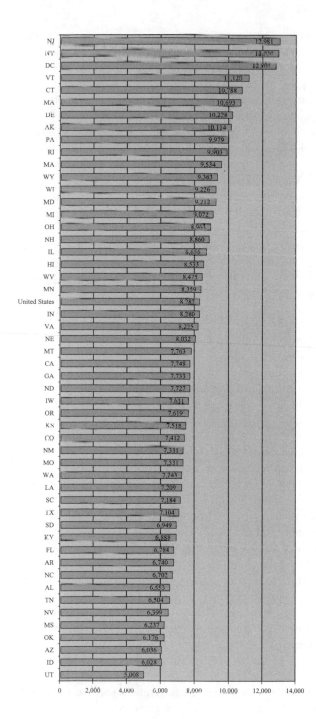

FIGURE 10.2 Elementary-Secondary per Pupil Expenditure Amounts by State: 2003–04.

SOURCE: U.S. Department of the Census, "Public Education Finances 2004," Figure 4, p. xii, at www2.census.gov/govs/school/04f33pub.pdf, issued March 2006.

Subsequent research from a number of quarters challenges the assertion that more resources yield better schools. The classic research on that issue was conducted by James Coleman, a Harvard sociologist, whose study, popularly known as the Coleman Report, tested the logic of compensatory education inherent in the ESEA.[39] Although Coleman's report was much criticized, it undermined much of the conventional logic about the impact of increased expenditures on student performance. Prior to his study, legislators, teachers, school administrators, school board members, and the general public assumed that factors such as the number of pupils in the classroom, the amount of money spent on each pupil, library and laboratory facilities, teachers' salaries, the quality of the curriculum, and other characteristics of the school affected student performance (and hence educational opportunity). However, Coleman's analysis revealed that these factors had no significant effect on student learning or achievement. Rather, the only factors that had a significant effect were the family background of the students themselves and the family background of their classmates. Family background factors affected the students' verbal abilities and attitudes toward education, and both of these were strongly related to student performance.

Although the Coleman Report made no policy recommendations, it nevertheless implied that compensatory education had very little educational value. If the report was correct, one inference that could be—and was—drawn was that it seemed pointless to raise per pupil expenditures, increase teachers' salaries, lower the number of pupils per classroom, provide better libraries or laboratories, or adopt any curricular innovations.[40] Moreover, Coleman's conclusions have been reexamined in more than 150 studies. A review of 120 of these studies showed that only 18 found a statistically significant positive relationship between school expenditures and student performance. Therefore, this review concluded that no strong, systematic relationship existed.[41] Indeed, since the 1960s, there have been approximately 200 studies that examine the relationships among the inputs to schools, the resources spent on schools, and the performance of students. These studies tell a consistent story—"there is no systematic relationship between expenditures on schools and student performance."[42]

In 1972, Christopher Jencks and colleagues sought to examine the relationships between education and mobility or success, as measured by income. Jencks questioned whether schools were performing a redistributive function in society by helping individuals to move from lower-income classes to middle- and upper-income classes on the basis of their education. Essentially, he found that there was little correlation between income and the quality of schooling. Therefore, educational reforms (especially compensatory educational reforms) could no longer be regarded as an effective means of equalizing income.[43] Neither family background, cognitive skills, educational attainment, nor occupational status explained much of the variation in persons' incomes. Income differences seemed to be better explained by the values held by the individuals themselves, their skills, and simply luck.[44]

In his later research, Jencks further examined the relationships among values held by the individual, educational attainment, family background, and economic success.[45] He found that family background (especially the father's education), personality characteristics of the students (e.g., dependability, industriousness, perseverance, and leadership ability), and years of school completed had the strongest effects on men's earnings. However, Jencks said that the "best readily observable predictor of a young man's eventual status or earnings is the amount of schooling he has had."[46] His findings pointed up the need for effective education and the importance of reducing drop out rates. Moreover, his findings, along with *A Nation at Risk,* called into question the adequacy of our public educational system.

The 1980s: Poor Student Performance and Back to Basics

In the 1980s the problems of education were defined not as a lack of resources, as they were in the 1960s and the 1970s, but rather as poor student performance stemming partly from poorly conceived reforms of the earlier era. Specifically, it was argued that educators had allowed schools to drift away from the basics of education, which focused on reading, writing, and mathematical skills. Critics pointed to both educational inputs and outputs as evidence of the schools' failure. During the 1980s there was no shortage of evidence indicating that "Johnny cannot read." A number of studies, for example, pointed to a dramatic decline in student performance and achievement levels. The average Scholastic Aptitude Test (SAT) scores in math and verbal skills declined steadily, beginning in the 1960s and continuing through the early 1980s. The trend alarmed both educators and the public alike and provided part of the catalyst for subsequent commissions and studies. The NCEE found parallel declines in student achievement scores. According to the authors of *A Nation at Risk,* average scores of the nation's high schoolers on most standardized achievement tests were actually lower in the early 1980s than they had been 26 years earlier following the Soviet Union's Sputnik launch.[47]

Along with declines in achievement, a number of studies found what many perceived as dangerously low levels of subject matter competence. *A Nation at Risk* reported that nearly one 17-year-old in six was functionally illiterate.[48] Other studies discovered that many young Americans left school with too little knowledge of math, science, English, and the social sciences. Equally distressing, there was mounting evidence that American education was falling behind that of other countries—countries that America was increasingly finding itself less able to compete with economically. The NCEE, for example, reported that U.S. students ranked last in international comparisons on 7 of 19 tests of achievement taken in the early 1970s.[49]

Over the next two decades, the American states expended considerable time and money in reforming America's schools. In the months and years following the publication of *A Nation at Risk,* dozens of education commissions were formed. State after state enacted legislation aimed at upgrading the nation's schools. Two areas of education—*standards and curriculum* and *teaching*—were the principal foci of educational reform during what has been termed the first wave of reform.

Standards and Curriculum   The belief that students spent too little time learning the basics and that the schools expected too little of them was at the very core of the attack on American education in the early 1980s. Accordingly, much of the early recommendations for reform centered on educational standards and curriculum. State policy makers considered and in many cases enacted a wide range of programs aimed at improving the content of education, including academic enrichment programs, lengthening the time students spent in the classroom, changes in the curriculum, and raising expectations for student performance. Increasing high school graduation requirements and enacting or modifying student competency tests proved to be the most popular reforms during the first wave of educational reform. According to one source, for instance, 42 states had increased graduation requirements by the mid-1980s. Of these, 37 required 4 years of English and over half required at least 3 years of social studies.[50]

Teaching Initiatives   Given their centrality to education, it is not surprising that the states' teachers were a major focus of early state reforms. The picture that emerges from early commission reports and studies is one of a teaching profession that was under siege—underpaid, undertrained, and, in too many cases, underperforming. Worse yet, there was every indication that the nation would very soon face a shortage of teachers. The states responded to these problems by passing a considerable amount of legislation aimed at improving teacher compensation and performance. According to one source, legislators introduced over a thousand pieces of legislation that directly addressed teacher compensation and certification between 1980 and 1986.[51] By the end of the decade, teacher pay had increased nationally by 21 percent even after controlling for inflation.[52]

Most states, however, were reluctant to increase teacher pay without tying increased compensation to performance. Career ladders and merit pay plans were two of the ways that many states sought to make that connection. Career ladders typically establish promotional grades (e.g., master teacher) that link pay increases to movement through these various grades. Teacher competency tests have also proven popular with many state legislators and reflect the sense among many that teachers are poorly trained and underqualified. Throughout the 1980s an overwhelming majority of the states required some form of competency test either for new, incoming teachers or, much less frequently, for teachers already in the profession. Tests vary by state. Some states require knowledge of basic subjects like math and English, while others stress teaching skills.

Within a few short years following the publication of *A Nation at Risk,* the states had spent a lot of money, energy, and political capital on educational reforms intended to refocus American education on the "basics." Yet for all that activity, the conventional wisdom is that the educational reform aimed at moving schools back to the basics simply did not achieve the dramatic results intended for it. Although educators could point to changes in the schools' curriculums, modest gains in test scores, and successful innovations in a number of school districts, and while it is still too early to make any final judgments on the states' efforts, on balance most analysts conclude that the first wave of reform has fallen far short of its goal of ensuring excellence in American education.

Data from a number of quarters support that conclusion. An examination of national test scores in the wake of state reforms, for instance, show at best

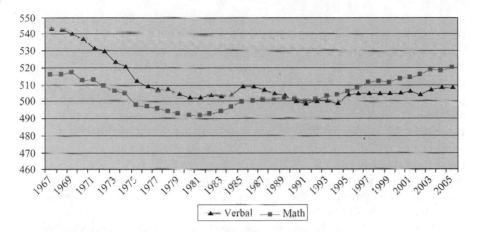

FIGURE 10.3   Mean SAT Scores of College-Bound Seniors: 1967–2005.

SOURCE: College Board, Table 2: Mean SAT Scores of College-Bound Seniors 1967–2005, collegeboard .com, at
www.collegeboard.com/prod_downloads/about/news_info/cbsenior/yr2005/table2-mean-SAT-scores.pdf
accessed March 1, 2007.

only modest improvements in the overall performance of American students.
Figure 10.3 tracks SAT scores, a common if somewhat controversial benchmark,
over the last four decades. As the figure reveals, verbal scores have remained largely
static since the mid-seventies. The news is better in regard to math performance.
Although math scores changed little in the eighties and early nineties, those scores
began to increase in the late nineties and reached a 30-year high in 2005.

Studies that look more closely at the linkage between educational inputs,
including state reforms, and educational outcomes also suggest that the reforms
of the eighties produced only modest gains in school performance. Berger and
Toma, for example, look at the effects of state teacher certification requirements
on state-level SAT performance in 1972, 1978, 1984, and 1990 for each of the 50
states.[53] Their measure of teacher certification is simply whether the state requires
a master's degree for elementary or high school certification. Those authors also
include measures of teacher salaries, pupil teacher ratios, and per pupil expenditures. Berger and Toma's most important finding is that enhanced teacher
certification requirements are *negatively* associated with student performance.
According to their data, average SAT scores were actually lower in those states
that required a master's degree for classroom teachers. Increases in per pupil
spending were also negatively related to student performance. Teacher salaries
proved unrelated to student performance as well. The only educational variable
to be associated (and in the expected direction) with student performance was
pupil-teacher ratios—increases in student-teacher ratios yielded test score
declines.

In contrast, Smith and Meier's analysis of educational reform in the 1980s
provides some evidence that the first wave of reforms had their intended impact,
but even here the findings are mixed. Two sets of findings are generated by those
authors—cross-sectional analyses of educational performance in 48 American

states in 1988 and a pooled-time series analysis that covers all 50 states over the period 1981—90. A number of measures are included to tap the first wave of reforms—whether states required competency tests for high school graduates; whether states had teacher certification requirement; the number of courses required for graduation; the minimal school starting age; educational expenditures; and, to get at mandates for smaller class sizes, teacher-pupil ratios. Smith and Meier's analysis suggests that some reforms worked while others did not. In each model, student SAT/ACT scores were higher in those states that required competency tests for high school graduates. Students also performed better in those states that had teacher certification requirements. In addition, in the pooled time-series analysis, smaller classes yielded higher test scores. And, in the cross-sectional model, students from smaller schools tended to do better on the SAT/ACT exams. Other measures of reform performed less well, however. In the cross-sectional analysis, smaller class sizes were associated with *lower* SAT/ACT scores. In a related fashion, more spending was associated with lower scores in the pooled model.[54]

What has followed is a series of proposals for a second (and some would argue a third and fourth) wave of reform. Unlike the reforms of the eighties, more recent proposals flow from the bottom up and aim at empowering teachers, parents, and local administrators to restructure America's schools through school-based management, school choice, and outcome-based assessment. Currently, the states and local school districts throughout the nation are experimenting with site-based management, charter schools, and, in a handful of cases, vouchers and privatization. We consider the more intriguing but controversial option below—the use of market forces to educate our children.

Why did the reforms of the eighties produce so few gains in educational achievement? Many contended that the states' reforms were largely cosmetic, incremental, and superficial. Teachers complained that state-mandated requirements and curriculum limited their discretion and undercut their ability to exercise their professional judgment in the classroom. For many, however, the problem was more fundamental. Educational reforms failed because they were enacted and implemented within an educational system that was inherently flawed. Schools would get better only if we changed the very nature of education.[55]

What has followed is a series of proposals for a second (and some would argue a third and fourth) wave of reform. Unlike the reforms of the eighties, more recent proposals flow from the bottom up and aim at empowering teachers, parents, and local administrators to restructure America's schools through school-based management, school choice, and outcome-based assessment. Currently, the states and local school districts throughout the nation are experimenting with site-based management, charter schools, and, in a handful of cases, vouchers and privatization. We consider the more intriguing but controversial option below—the use of market forces to educate our children.

The 1990s: Market Reforms

If the first wave of reform was, as critics maintain, about centralized, top-down reform, then it is probably not surprising that the second wave of reform would be about decentralization and a shifting of authority to the local level. In recent years, and even as first-wave reforms were still being put into place, advocates of a second wave of reform have called for a fundamental "restructuring" of America's schools. While the concept is not easily—or for that matter, uniformly—defined, at the heart of most discussions of the concept is the notion that authority over what it is schools do and how they do it should rest primarily at the local level.

Inherent in most discussions of restructuring are two premises. First, as we have seen, many of those critical of the first wave of reform maintain that early reforms failed precisely because they were enacted and implemented within a hierarchal, centralized system of public education that necessarily prevents meaningful reform. Second, advocates of restructuring maintain that only those reforms crafted within the schools themselves and among local stakeholders—parents, school administrators, and teachers—are likely to be implemented in the first instance and truly effective in the second. For many, only those involved in schooling on a daily basis are likely to know what programs are necessary and whether those programs are working—and, equally important, to have the incentive to make those programs work. Support for a decentralized system of education, in turn, flows from a growing consensus, particularly among conservatives, that market mechanisms are far superior to nonmarket (i.e., government) mechanisms for delivering public services. It is no coincidence that calls for decentralization occur at a time when the prevailing political themes center on devolving authority to the state and local governments and privatizing everything from fire protection and prisons to the public schools.

Over the past decade, calls for decentralization and restructuring have taken one of three related forms. Earlier, advocates of restructuring sought greater *school-based management* (SBM) by proposing to shift greater authority over budgets, curriculum, and personnel to the schools themselves and by placing greater authority with teachers and parents. A related form of restructuring, *teacher empowerment,* gives teachers more control over what and how they teach and more of a say in school policy. Teacher empowerment schemes also frequently seek to enhance the professional standing of teaching through teacher-controlled licensing boards or national certification.[56] Increasingly, however, restructuring has become almost synonymous with the notion of *choice* and discussions of the relative merits of vouchers and charter schools. To better illustrate what efforts at restructuring entail, we consider those latter market mechanisms.

Proposals for choice are hardly new. In 1955, the economist Mildred Friedman proposed that parents be given vouchers that could be redeemed at private schools. But it was not until the 1980s and 1990s that choice proposals became a credible part of the states' policy agendas. That growing credibility and legitimacy (but not necessarily acceptance) of choice reflected a number of developments. First, and most broadly, the willingness of key policy actors in the states to even consider various choice mechanisms stems in large part from the increasingly conservative character of American politics. Even before the election of Ronald Reagan, there was a growing sense that governments at all levels had grown too cumbersome and intrusive. Increasingly, Republicans and many Democrats turned to market-based policies, including the privatization of services like garbage collection and fire protection and the use of effluent charges as a means of achieving regulatory compliance, as alternatives to the direct provision of public goods. Because they rely on the market mechanisms of choice and competition to incite preferred behavior, vouchers, charter schools, and other choice options are simply one more set of market alternatives to traditional policy mechanisms. Second, the growing credibility of educational choice reflects a fair amount of consensus that public schools are not doing a very good job of educating our children, but that private schools—in particular Catholic schools—are. As we have seen, there is no shortage of evidence to suggest that students in private schools consistently outperform their public school counterparts. Advocates of choice contend that they do so because they rely on market mechanisms for governing and organizing the schools. Again, Chubb and Moe offer an explanation to account for the relative success of private schools and, in doing so, outline the basic logic of choice.

According to those authors, private schools do so well because they operate within a market system in which they must compete with one another *and* the public schools to attract students. Unlike public education, in a system of private schools, educators must respond not to the preferences of larger political forces but rather to the needs and demands of the primary consumers of education—parents and students. Schools that are responsive to parents-consumers will survive and prosper. Schools that fail to do so will not. The simple facts of competition and choice in turn ensure that private schools eschew the kind of top-down, hierarchal control typical of the public schools in favor of a system of governance in which local schools are granted considerable autonomy and flexibility. As Chubb and Moe note:

> Effective authority within market settings, then, is radically decentralized. In private sector education, the people who run each school decide what they will teach, how they will teach it, who will do the teaching, how much to charge for their services, and virtually everything else about how education will be organized and supplied. Students and parents assess the offerings, reputations, and costs of the various schools and make their own choices about which to attend. No one makes decisions for society. All participants make decisions for themselves.[57]

Efforts to provide parents with some choice over the kinds of schools their children will attend have assumed various forms in recent years. Initially, magnet schools, designed to promote integration, allowed parents, both black and white, to choose among a number of alternative schools. During the 1980s, some states and school districts also expanded the amount of parental choice by adopting open-enrollment plans. In some instances, open-enrollment plans allow parents to choose among public school located within their district; in others, parents can choose to send their children outside their district. Open-enrollment plans are commended on several grounds—they provide parents choice, foster competition between schools, and help reduce social and economic inequalities.

More recent efforts to use markets to educate our children have focused increasingly on two additional mechanisms—charter schools and vouchers. Charter schools have been particularly popular in recent years. Under charter school plans, teachers, parents, and foundations are awarded a charter that allows them to create schools free of most state restrictions and regulations. Those schools receive public funds, usually a proportion of the state per pupil funding. By 2004, three thousand charter schools were in place in 37 states, the District of

Columbia and Puerto Rico.[58] Advocates of charter schools contend that those schools will dramatically improve the quality of education, for a number of reasons. Because charter schools are free of many of the restrictive, top-down regulations that characterize existing public schools, charter schools should prove less costly to operate, will empower teachers and parents, and will allow schools to tailor their curricula to meet the special needs of their students. In addition, the existence of charter schools introduces real competition within school districts, forcing existing schools to improve their programming or run the risk of losing both students and the funding that travels with students. That competition, in turn, also promotes innovation as individual charter schools develop novel approaches to education.

Charter schools are not without their critics, including teacher unions and local school officials, each of whom stand to lose under many charter plans. Critics fear that the creation and funding of charter schools will steer resources away from already fiscally strapped public schools. Many also contend that charter school legislation preempts local school boards in those instances where charter applicants need not seek the approval of the local officials to receive a charter.

How are charter schools doing? The evidence on performance is mixed. While many charter schools, often a majority, are meeting state educational standards, what data exist indicate that charter schools do no better than regular schools in teaching the basics. A study by the U.S. General Accounting Office found that among the 33 states that provided information on the performance of charter schools, 21 of those states reported that at least half of their charter schools met or exceeded state performance standards.[59] A pair of recent large-scale studies use data from the U.S. Department of Education's annual National Assessment of Educational Progress (NAEP) to compare the performance of students in charter and non-charter schools. A 2006 study conducted by the National Center for the study of Privatization in Education at Columbia University, compared the 4th- and 8th-grade math scores of 340,000 students in 13,000 public, charter, and private schools in 2003 to assess the impact of charter schools and privatization. While students in private schools scored higher than their public school counterparts, once analysts controlled for socioeconomic status, race, gender, and disability, the differences between public, charter, and private schools disappeared.[60] A report issued by the DOE in 2006 reached similar conclusions. The study, conducted by the Educational Testing Service, compared reading and math scores for 4th and 8th graders in public and private schools using the 2003 NAEP scores. Among other things, the study found that once student background characteristics were controlled, 4th graders in public schools scored higher in math than their private school counterparts, but that private school 8th graders outperformed public school students in reading. Interestingly, among private religious schools, students in Lutheran schools performed best, while students in conservative Christian schools did worse.[61]

Advocates of choice maintain that to fully realize the advantages of competition and choice, parents should be allowed to choose among a large number of both public and private schools, including religious schools. The mechanism for doing that, of course, is educational vouchers. Although voucher plans vary, a typical plan would provide parents with either a cash voucher or tax credit that could be used toward the payment of tuition in any public or private school.

Milwaukee's pioneering Parental Choice Program, established in 1990, was the first public-private voucher plan established in the United States. In 2005–06, roughly 15,000 students received vouchers of up to $6,400 to attend, in most cases, one of the city's private Catholic schools.[62] Not surprisingly, the Milwaukee plan has met with considerable opposition from the local teachers' union and others who fear, among other things, that the plan siphons resources away from the public schools and violates the First Amendment's prohibition against government establishment of religion. However, Wisconsin's supreme court struck down the constitutional challenge in 1998.

Some states have considered their own voucher plans in recent years. Three states, Oregon, Colorado, and California, placed voucher initiatives on the ballot in the early nineties. In Oregon, for instance, voters were asked in 1990 to approve a plan under which parents would receive a $2,500 tax credit that could be used to offset private school expenses. Colorado and California voters saw similar proposals in 1992 and 1993, respectively. In each case, opposition from teacher unions and others was substantial, and the proposals were defeated by lopsided margins. In 1995, however, voucher supporters won a victory when the Ohio General Assembly appropriated the funds to award nearly 1,500 low-income students in Cleveland scholarships of $2,500 to attend any of the city's public, private, or parochial schools. By the 1999–2000 school year, 3,400 voucher students were enrolled in 52 private schools.[63] As in Wisconsin, opponents challenged the constitutionality of the program but were rebuked by the U.S. Supreme Court's landmark 2002 ruling in *Zelman v. Simmons-Harris et al.* holding that Cleveland's voucher programs *did not* violate the First Amendment of the U.S. Constitution. In 1999, the state of Florida created a voucher program that offered students who attended "failing" schools the opportunity to attend better-performing schools, but the plan was subsequently declared unconstitutional by the state's supreme court in 2006 after serving only 750 students.

Both the Milwaukee and Cleveland programs have been watched closely by advocates as well as opponents of choice, and many evaluations have been conducted on each of the city's programs. The record to date, however, is mixed. For the most part, research for each city has found little evidence that those students who received vouchers achieved more than those who did not.[64] There is, however, some research that challenges those findings. Reanalysis of the Milwaukee data by a team of scholars at Harvard, for example, indicated that voucher students outscored a comparable group of students who had remained in the city's public schools by 11 percentage points in math and 5 percentage points in reading.[65] Reviewing the evidence on vouchers in 2001, analysts at the U.S. General Accounting Office concluded that "None of the findings can be considered definitive because the researchers obtained different results when they used different methods to compensate for weaknesses in the data."[66]

SUMMARY

Few institutions in America are as important as the nation's schools. As political scientist Thomas Dye notes:

> Perhaps the most widely recommended "solution" to the problems that confront American society is more and better schooling. If there ever was a time when schools were expected only to combat ignorance and illiteracy, that time is far behind us. Today, schools are expected to do many things: resolve racial conflict and inspire respect for "diversity"; provide values, aspirations, and a sense of identity to disadvantaged children; offer various forms of recreation and mass entertainment (football games, bands, choruses, cheerleading and the like); reduce conflict in society by teaching children to get along well with others and to adjust to group living; reduce the highway accident toll by teaching students to be good drivers; fight disease and poor health through physical education, health training, and even medical treatment; eliminate unemployment and poverty by teaching job skills; end malnutrition and hunger through school lunch and milk programs; fight drug abuse and educate children about sex; and act as custodians for teenagers who have no interest in education but who we do not permit either to work or roam the streets unsupervised. In other words, nearly all the nation's problems are reflected in demands placed on the nation's schools.[67]

Given those expectations, it should come as no surprise that education in America generates much conflict, criticism, and change.

Table 10.2 summarizes the evolution of educational policy over the last several decades. As the table makes clear, education reform in each decade has been characterized by a unique definition of what is wrong with America's schools, the reasons for that failure, and the remedies for solving the problems of education. In the 1960s and 1970s the problem was unequal resources; and the solution was the kinds of compensatory efforts enacted during that period, including the ESEA.

TABLE 10.2 The Evolution of Educational Policy: 1960–2000

	1960s–1970s	1980s	1990s
Nature of problem	Unequal resources	Poor performance	Poor performance
Reason for failure	Lack of resources	Lack of skills	A failure of institutions
Reform proposed	Compensatory education	Back to basics	Markets
Specifics	ESEA, 1965 School desegregation Head Start Community control	Curriculum reform Improved teacher training, pay, and competency testing	Charter schools Vouchers

In the 1980s Americans became convinced that the schools could no longer provide our children with the basic tools they need to function in a changing society. The solution was efforts to return to the "three Rs" and greater accountability. More recently, parents and policy makers alike argue that the very nature of our educational system needs change. Increasingly, the emphasis is on providing parents choice and looking beyond public schools for educational opportunities. In each decade, hundreds of law and regulations have been passed and millions of dollars spent in an effort to solve the problems of equality and performance.

Yet as we have seen, most of those efforts have fallen short of the aspirations of those who promote change. The Coleman Report demonstrated that more spending will not necessarily produce better schools, assessments of the back-to-basics movement indicate that "Dick and Jane" still can't read, and what little evidence is available cautions against believing that a reliance on market forces will correct the problems of the nation's schools. The challenge for policy makers and policy analysts alike is to redouble their efforts to figure out what is working in American education and what is not. If the record to date is any clue, those efforts will be embedded in larger political scrabbles, suffer faulty implementation, and prove difficult to evaluate. But given the importance of education in America, efforts to find solutions will and should continue to dominate much of the public discussion.

DISCUSSION QUESTIONS

1. Various remedies have been proposed to deal with declining student performance in the schools, including compensatory educational policies, back-to-basics policies, and multiculturalism. Given the results of these policies, how would you propose that we raise student achievement scores?

2. Discuss the relative merits of the following educational policies: vouchers, school choice, neighborhood control of schools, and compensatory education.

3. In the recent past, colleges have been attempting to remedy alleged past discrimination against minorities by instituting preferential treatment policies based on race and gender. Are colleges the proper place to make reparations for past injustices to minorities? Why or why not?

SUGGESTED READINGS

Bloom, Allan. *The Closing of the American Mind* (New York: Simon and Schuster, 1987).

Chubb, John E., and Terry M. Moe. *Politics, Markets, and America's Schools* (Washington, D.C.: Brookings Institution, 1990).

Henig, Jeffrey. *Rethinking School Choice* (Princeton, NJ: Princeton University Press, 1994).

Herrnstein, Richard J., and Charles Murray. *The Bell Curve: Intelligence and Class Structure in American Life* (New York: Free Press, 1994).

Jencks, Christopher. *Who Gets Ahead? The Determinants of Economic Success in America* (New York: Basic Books, 1979).

Smith, Kevin B., and Kenneth J. Meier. *The Case Against School Choice* (Armonk, NY: M. E. Sharpe, 1995).

NOTES

1. See, for example, John E. Chubb and Terry M. Moe, *Politics, Markets, and America's Schools* (Washington, D.C.: Brookings Institution, 1990).

2. U.S. Department of Education, National Center for Education Statistics, *Digest of Education Statistics* (Washington, D.C.: U.S. Government Printing Office, 2005). Available online at http://nces.ed.gov/programs/digest/d05/. Accessed May 19, 2007.

3. Ibid.

4. Ibid.

5. U.S. Department of Education, "10 Facts about K−12 Education Funding," at www.ed.gov/about/overview/fed/10facts/index.html#chart1 accessed March 22, 2007.

6. National Commission on Excellence in Education, *A Nation at Risk: The Imperative for Educational Reform* (Washington, D.C.: U.S. Government Printing Office, 1983), pp. 5−6.

7. Thomas R. Dye, *Politics in States and Communities,* 7th ed. (Englewood Cliffs, NJ: Prentice Hall, 1991), p. 419.

8. Ibid., p. 172.

9. Ibid., p. 173.

10. See Stephen J. Wayne et al., *The Politics of American Government* (New York: St. Martin's Press, 1995), p. 625.

11. Gail Russell Chaddock, "'No Child Left Behind' Losing Steam," *Christian Science Monitor,* csmonitor.com, at www.csmonitor.com/2007/0321/p01s01-legn.html?s=t5 accessed March 21, 2007.

12. Ibid.

13. Joseph H. McGivney, "State Educational Governance Patterns," *Educational Administration Quarterly* 20 (Spring 1984), pp. 43−63; Lawrence Iannaccone, *Politics in Education* (New York: Center for Applied Research in Education, 1967).

14. Frederick Wirt, "School Policy Culture and State Decentralization," in *The Politics of Education,* ed. Jay D. Scribner (Chicago: University of Chicago Press, 1977), pp. 186−187.

15. Ann O'M. Bowman and Richard Kearney, *State and Local Government* (Boston: Houghton Mifflin, 1990), p. 432.

16. John J. Harrigan, *Politics and Policy in States and Communities* (New York: HarperCollins, 1991), p. 391.

17. Ibid.

18. Ibid.

19. Robert B. Hawkins, "Education Reform California Style," *Publius* 14 (Summer 1984), p. 100.

20. Joel Spring, *Conflicts of Interests: The Politics of American Education* (New York: Longman, 1988), pp. 93–124.

21. Ibid., p. 120.

22. Bowman and Kearney, *State and Local Government,* p. 430.

23. Ibid.

24. Ibid.

25. David Savage, "Teaching: The Heart of the Problem," *State Legislatures* 9 (October 1983), pp. 212–224.

26. William E. Blundell, "A Certified Need: Teachers," *Wall Street Journal,* 19 May 1989, p. 1.

27. Michael Rebell and Arthur Block, *Educational Policy Making and the Courts* (Chicago: University of Chicago Press, 1982).

28. *Rodriguez v. San Antonio School District,* 411 U.S. 59 (1973).

29. Bowman and Kearney, *State and Local Government,* p. 426.

30. Harrigan, *Politics and Policy,* p. 396.

31. Ibid., pp. 395–397.

32. Edward Banfield, *The Unheavenly City* (Boston: Little, Brown, 1970), p. 134.

33. See, for example, Arthur Jensen, "How Much Can We Boost IQ and Scholastic Achievement?" *Harvard Educational Review* 39 (Winter 1969), pp. 1–123.

34. See Richard J. Herrnstein and Charles Murray, *The Bell Curve: Intelligence and Class Structure in American Life* (New York: Free Press, 1994), pp. 143–154.

35. Jensen, "How Much Can We Boost IQ?"

36. See, for example, James J. Heckman, "Cracked Bell," *Reason* (March 1995), pp. 49–55; and Arthur S. Goldberger and Charles F. Manski, "Review Article: The Bell Curve by Herrnstein and Murray," *Journal of Economic Literature* 33 (June 1995), pp. 762–776.

37. See Harrigan, *Politics and Policy,* pp. 392–394.

38. Thomas R. Dye, *Understanding Public Policy,* 7th ed. (Englewood Cliffs, NJ: Prentice Hall, 1991), p. 9.

39. James S. Coleman, *Equality of Educational Opportunity* (Washington, D.C.: U.S. Government Printing Office, 1966).

40. Dye, *Understanding Public Policy,* p. 10.

41. Eric Hanushek, "Throwing Money at Schools," *Journal of Policy Analysis and Management* 1, no. 1 (Fall 1981), pp. 19–41; and "The Economics of Schooling: Production and Efficiency in Public Schools," *Journal of Economic Literature* 24 (September 1986), 1141–1177.

42. See Eric Hanushek, "How Business Can Save Education: A State Agenda for Reform" (paper presented at the Heritage Foundation Conference, April 24, 1991).

43. Christopher Jencks and Marshall Smith, Henry Acland, Mary Jo Bane, David Cohen, Herbert Gintis, Barbara Heyns, and Stephan Michelson, *Inequality: A Reassessment of the Effect of Family and Schooling in America* (New York: Basic Books, 1972).

44. Ibid., p. 219.

45. Christopher Jencks, *Who Gets Ahead? The Determinants of Economic Success in America* (New York: Basic Books, 1979).

46. Ibid., p. 230.

47. National Commission on Excellence in Education, *A Nation at Risk.*

48. Ibid.

49. Ibid., p. 8.

50. Richard Coley and Margaret Goertz, "Educational Standards in the 50 States: 1990," Educational Testing Service, Report Number: RR-90-15, 1990.

51. William Firestone, Susan H. Fuhrman, and Michael W. Kirst, "Implementation Effects of State Education Reform in the 1980s," *NASSP Bulletin* 74 (February 1990), pp. 75–84.

52. Bowman and Kearney, *State and Local Government.*

53. Mark C. Berger and Eugenia F. Toma, "Variation in State Education Policies and Effects of Student Performance," *Journal of Policy Analysis and Management* 13 (1994), pp. 447–491.

54. Kevin B. Smith and Kenneth J. Meier, *The Case Against School Choice: Politics, Markets, and Fools* (Armonk, NY: M. E. Sharpe, 1995).

55. Chubb and Moe, *Politics, Markets, and America's Schools.*

56. Ibid.

57. Ibid., p. 29.

58. National Education Association, "Charter Schools," at www.nea.org/charter/index.html accessed May 15, 2007.

59. U.S. General Accounting Office, "Charter Schools: To Enhance Education's Monitoring and Research, More Charter School-Level Data Are Needed," January 2005, at www.gao.gov/new.items/d055.pdf accessed May 15, 2007.

60. Christopher Lubienski and Sarah Theule Lubienski, "Charter, Private, Public Schools and Academic Achievement: New Evidence from NAEP Mathematics Data," National Center for the Study of Privatization in Education, p. 3, at www.ncspe.org/publications_files/OP111.pdf accessed March 12, 2007.

61. Educational Testing Service, "Comparing Private Schools and Public Schools Using Hierarchical Linear Modeling," National Center for Educational Statistics, July 2006, at www.nytimes.com/packages/pdf/national/20060715report.pdf accessed May 15, 2007.

62. National School Boards Association, "Milwaukee Voucher Program," at www.nsba.org/site/page.asp?TRACKID=&DID=32345&CID=1316 accessed March 25, 2007.

63. The U.S. General Accounting Office, "School Vouchers: Publicly Funded Programs in Cleveland and Milwaukee," August 2001, at www.gao.gov/new.items/d01914.pdf accessed May 14, 2007.

64. See, most notably, Kim Metcalf et al., *A Comparative Evaluation of the Cleveland Scholarship Program and Tutoring Program and Evaluation of the Cleveland Scholarship Program Second Year Report, 1997–98* (Bloomington, Indiana: Indiana University, Indiana Center for Evaluation, 1998); and John Witte, *The Market Approach to Education* (Princeton: Princeton University Press, 2000).

65. Jay Greene, Paul Peterson, and Jiangtao Du, *Effectiveness of School Choice: The Milwaukee Experiment* (Cambridge, MA: Harvard University, 1997); and Jay Greene and Paul Peterson, *Methodological Issues in Evaluation Research: The Milwaukee School Choice Plan* (Cambridge, MA: Harvard University, 1996).

66. U.S. General Accounting Office, "School Vouchers: Publicly Funded Programs in Cleveland and Milwaukee," p. 30.

67. Thomas R. Dye, *Understanding Public Policy,* 12th ed. (Upper Saddle River: NJ: Prentice Hall, 2007), p. 125.

11

Welfare Policy

"The poor are still there. Two decades after the President of the United States declared an 'unconditional' war on poverty, poverty does not simply continue to exist; worse, we must deal with structures of misery, with a new poverty much more tenacious than the old."
MICHAEL HARRINGTON

"What emerged in the 1960s was an almost unbroken intellectual consensus that the individualist explanation of poverty was altogether outmoded and reactionary."
CHARLES MURRAY

"The best hope is to understand the real causes of poverty and to address them directly."
DAVID T. ELLWOOD

"The poverty of today's underclass differs appreciably from poverty in the past: underclass poverty stems less from the absence of opportunity than from the inability or reluctance to take advantage of opportunity."
LAWRENCE M. MEAD

The problem of poverty is a highly charged issue today, as it has been for the past 400 years. Even after centuries of public and private attention to this problem, the real causes of poverty are still not fully understood. The four quotations on this page illustrate various perspectives about the most appropriate welfare policy for the 21st century. In the 1930s, and again in the 1960s, social welfare programs were expanded to provide for the poor in America. However, these efforts were judged by many to be a failure in the 1980s. Some argued that the programs actually did harm, developing a **welfare dependency** among the poor.[1] In the 1980s and 1990s the newest round of welfare reform occurred as decision makers tried to develop a better social welfare system. Beginning in 1981, individual states (such as Wisconsin) tried to develop innovative ways to combine work with welfare. By 1987, twenty-six states had implemented some degree of workfare programs, though many of the "statewide" programs were tested or implemented in only a few counties.[2] In 1996, those efforts came together when the U.S. Congress enacted the Personal Responsibility and Work Opportunity Reconciliation Act (PRWORA). As we shall see, that legislation fundamentally altered the nature of welfare in America by replacing the entitlement program that had been in place for over 50 years with a block grant to the states.

In the pages that follow we look at the evolution of welfare policy in America over the last 200 years, paying particular attention to developments since the 1930s. We conclude by assessing the impact of welfare policy. We begin by examining how poverty is defined and identifying those in America who are poor.

POVERTY IN AMERICA

Defining Poverty

The first step in constructing appropriate policy solutions is to try to understand the scope and nature of the public policy problem. Thus, the extent of poverty in the United States needs to be measured, which can be done in several ways. These alternative measures of poverty include both *quantitative* and *qualitative* indices. For example, the official definition of poverty developed by the U.S. Social Security Administration is a quantitative index. An individual or family is defined as "poor" if their income is below a certain level. This level is adjusted for the size of the family, for urban or rural residence, and for changes in prices each year. It is usually defined as three times the amount of income needed to feed one's familiy according to a modest food plan. In 2005, the poverty line for a nonfarm family of four was $22,000. By this definition, about 37 million Americans, or 12.6 percent of the U.S. population, were classified as poor.

This official definition of poverty has been criticized on many grounds. For example, liberal critics argue that this definition of poverty does not take into account regional differences in the costs of living, climate, or accepted styles of living.[3] Moreover, the "thrifty" food budget on which the poverty level is based is too low for good nutrition and health. Also, this definition of poverty does not consider what poor people actually think they need to live. Conservative critics also challenge this definition of poverty on the grounds that it does not consider the value of family assets, such as homes owned, furniture, and automobiles. Moreover, this index contains many individuals who do not consider themselves poor, such as students and the elderly. Finally, this index excludes in-kind

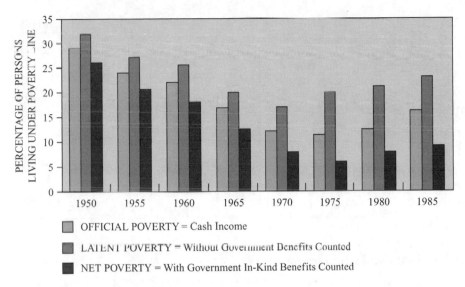

FIGURE 11.1 Three Definitions of Poverty.

SOURCE: Charles Murray, *Losing Ground: American Social Policy 1950–1980,* © 1984 by Basic Books. Reprinted with permission of Basic Books, a division of HarperCollins Publishers, Inc.

benefits given to the poor by governments—such as food stamps, free medical care, public housing, and school lunches.[4]

Another definition of poverty is that reported by Charles Murray in his book, *Losing Ground.*[5] He distinguishes among *official poverty,* which is based on cash income only, *latent poverty,* which is based on the number of people who would be considered poor without the assistance they receive from federal programs, and *net poverty,* which refers to people who remain poor even after counting their in-kind government benefits. Murray considers the latent poverty figure as the most damning statistic because it counts the number of people in our society who are economically dependent and could not exist on their own.[6] Figure 11.1 illustrates the three types of poverty defined by Murray.

Another definition of poverty is based on the distribution of wealth in America. This definition of poverty is based on the concept of relative deprivation, or the amount of income inequality in America. Figure 11.2 divides all American families into three groups—the poorest two-fifths, the middle fifth, and the wealthiest two-fifths of the population—from 1929 to 1990. From this figure one can see that income distribution has changed relatively little over the past 70 years. However, the gap between the richest two-fifths and the poorest two-fifths has widened. Liberal critics of our welfare system point to these data in defining the scope of the poverty problem.

Finally, Edward Banfield in *Unheavenly City Revisited* used a qualitative index whereby poverty was described in four stages or levels. The most severe stage was described as *destitution,* in which there was a lack of sufficient income to prevent

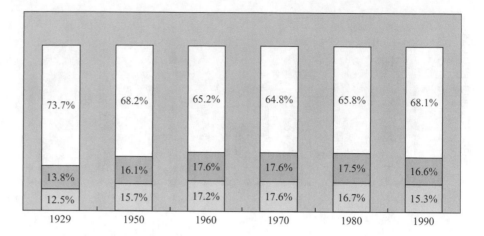

RICHEST TWO-FIFTHS of the population

MIDDLE FIFTH of the population

POOREST TWO-FIFTHS of the population

FIGURE 11.2 Trends in Income Inequality, 1929–90: Percentage of the National Income Earned by Each of Three Income Groups.

SOURCES: For 1970 through 1988, Bureau of the Census, *Current Population Reports: Trends in Income by Selected Characteristics: 1947 to 1988* (Washington, D.C.: U.S. Government Printing Office, 1990), p. 9. For earlier data, *Statistical Abstract of the United States*, various years. For 1990, *Statistical Abstract: 1992*, p. 450.

starvation. The second level of poverty was described as *want,* or lack of enough income to support essential welfare, including food, clothing, and shelter. The third level of poverty was described as *hardship,* or a lack of sufficient income to prevent acute discomfort, including food, clothing, shelter, health, and transportation needs. The least severe level of poverty was called *relative deprivation,* or a lack of enough income to prevent one from feeling poor. He argued that poverty in America was typified by the third and fourth levels, rather than the first two. Moreover, he argued that poverty by this definition was in decline.[7]

In sum, the extent of poverty in America can be measured in numerous ways. Quite often, the measure of poverty used is related to the orientation of the analyst. That is, liberals like to use the distribution of wealth as their measure, whereas conservatives like to use the official index or qualitative indices such as Edward Banfield's levels of poverty. Using their respective measures of poverty, liberals conclude that the extent of poverty in America has remained pretty much the same for the past 70 years, whereas conservatives argue that poverty in America has significantly declined over this same period.

Who Are the Poor?

Table 11.1 presents a comparative profile of those considered poor by the U.S. government's definition. Poverty occurs most commonly among female-headed

TABLE 11.1 America's Poor: 2005

Number of Poor	37 million
% of Population Poor	12.6
By Race/Ethnicity	
White	8.7%
Black	24.9
Hispanic	21.8
By Age	
Under 18	17.6
Over 65	10.1
By Family Status	
Married couple	5.1
Female head of household, no husband	28.7

SOURCE: U.S. Bureau of the Census, Current Population Survey, Annual Social and Economic Supplements. Poverty and Health Statistics Branch, Poverty: 2005 Highlights, at www.census.gov/hhes/www/poverty/poverty05/pov05hi.html; Table 2. Poverty Status of People by Family Relationship, Race, and Hispanic Origin: 1959 to 2005, at www.census.gov/hhes/www/poverty/histpov/hstpov2.html; Table 4. Poverty Status of Families, by Type of Family, Presence of Related Children, Race, and Hispanic Origin: 1959 to 2005, at www.census.gov/hhes/www/poverty/histpov/hstpov4.html accessed March 14, 2007.

families, blacks, Hispanics, and children. Poverty is also more likely in large families and in families headed by a high school dropout or an unemployed person. The aged in America, on the other hand, experience less poverty than the non-aged do. The elderly are generally *not poor,* because they typically own their homes and have paid-up mortgages, receive Medicare and Social Security, and have fewer living expenses. Thus, even with reduced incomes, the aged are much less likely to be poor than younger, female-headed families are.

An Illustration in Welfare Assistance An illustration of the dilemma of poverty and the need for welfare assistance is provided by the case of Josie Hill of Larimer County, Colorado. Ms. Hill was married for 10 years to her former husband, Tom, a construction worker. Tom lost his job and began to drink heavily. Shortly thereafter, Ms. Hill decided to divorce her husband. At the time of the divorce trial her husband was unemployed; consequently, the judge in the trial awarded no alimony and only minimal child support payments to Ms. Hill. Although she was employed as a hairdresser, she earned only about $400 a month even though she worked full-time. In short, she was a member of the "working poor." To meet living expenses for herself and two young daughters, she decided to apply for food stamps. Her rent was $550 monthly, and food for herself and her two daughters came to about $450 a month. She moved in with her father-in-law to reduce her living expenses. Yet, she still needed some form of welfare assistance to meet her costs of living. With the food stamps, help from her father-in-law, some child support, and her monthly income of $400, she was able to survive, albeit modestly.

After a period of time with this arrangement, the beauty shop where she worked had to close when one of the owners decided to sell the shop. Ms. Hill was soon out of work. She then decided to enter another career that would provide more income for herself and her two young daughters; however, she would need some help with retraining for a new career. Finally, she applied to the welfare assistance office for a workfare program that would allow her to enter a new career and, hopefully, get off welfare altogether.

This case illustrates how easily people can become "welfare cases" through little fault of their own. An unemployed husband, a divorce, and a shop closing conspired to make Ms. Hill a welfare recipient. Even though she was a hardworking individual, was motivated to produce more income, and was dedicated to providing a better life for herself and her children, she needed help temporarily.

Some Myths About Poor Americans   One of the welfare myths is that recipients lack the motivations and values necessary for seeking and keeping a job and are content with making welfare a way of life. The case above, to the contrary, suggests that welfare recipients are often highly motivated, energetic people who encounter difficulties that make welfare a temporary necessity. Moreover, most welfare recipients are either over 65 or under 18.

A second myth is that welfare recipients are mostly able-bodied men. This is completely wrong. Males generally cannot obtain welfare assistance.

Another myth is that the poor squander their money. In fact, much like the average American, the poor spend most of their money on food, housing, transportation, and medical expenses. Studies suggest that no more than 5 percent of the poor's money goes toward recreation, compared to about 8 percent for the average American.

Yet another myth states that it is easy to get on welfare. However, welfare recipients must fill out long forms to qualify for assistance. In addition, they must submit to home visits, and they must submit to an audit of their income and living expenses.

Another myth is that the poor are "welfare cheats." Studies have found that no more than 1 to 3 percent of welfare program funds go to ineligible persons because of fraud. Thus, the claim that welfare recipients are mostly cheats is grossly exaggerated.

Finally, there is the myth about "once on welfare, always on welfare," which claims that welfare assistance becomes a way of life rather than a second chance. Actually, welfare recipients are a rather fluid group; the average cash assistance recipient received Aid to Families with Dependent Children (AFDC) for only about 20 months. Under the Temporary Assistance for Needy Families (TANF) program, which replaced AFDC, individuals are limited to a total of 60 months of welfare support. Thus, the poor tend to be those who temporarily need help, much as in the case of Ms. Hill, discussed above.

Although these myths persist in the public's mind, the root causes of poverty are not completely understood. One of the most heavily debated issues is the question of why the poor are poor. We now turn to that question.

ALTERNATIVE PERSPECTIVES
ON WELFARE POLICY

Why are the poor poor? As we saw in our earlier discussion, policy makers cannot agree on the scope of poverty in America, or on how it should be measured. Not surprisingly, then, they cannot agree on the root causes of poverty, or on how to solve the problem. In any case, there are two major perspectives or approaches concerning the causes and cures of poverty.

The Liberal (Structural) View

Liberal theories of poverty argue that it is caused by structural or environmental conditions. Thus, poverty results from such conditions as economic stagnation, unemployment, discrimination, or in the most extreme case, "capitalist exploitation."[8] For example, Michael Harrington argues that poverty results from "structural economic change," in that a lack of employment opportunities for the poor was brought about in the past two decades by automation (and the loss of manufacturing jobs) and the importation of cheap (foreign) labor.[9] Marxists, representing a more extreme argument, stress that poverty is maintained by the ruling class to serve its self-interest. Thus, the poor are utilized by the affluent as a source of cheap labor, and welfare policy is designed to maintain poverty. Welfare programs will not be designed to alleviate or end poverty, but to "regulate" the poor.[10] For example, Piven and Cloward argue that the minimal level of welfare in the United States is designed not to help, but to maintain the legitimacy of and support for the political system. In the absence of welfare aid, the argument goes, the poor would be inclined toward rioting, violence, or revolution. Welfare thus creates a calming effect on the poor, and they are less inclined to threaten the political system.

The Conservative (Individualist) View

The conservative view argues that poverty results from conditions within the individual himself or herself. For example, many economists suggest that the poor are poor because their economic productivity is low. They simply do not have the motivation, intelligence, skills, training, or work habits to sell to employers in a free market. For example, authors Richard Herrnstein and Charles Murray suggest that poverty is related to intelligence, or IQ; they argue that 57 percent of chronic welfare recipients are in the bottom 20 percent of intelligence.[11] Others, such as Edward Banfield, argue that a "culture of poverty" exists in which poverty is a way of life that is learned by the poor. This culture of poverty is based on indifference, apathy, irresponsibility, and "present-orientedness" rather than "future-orientedness." These attitudes prevent the poor from taking advantage of opportunities that are available to them.[12]

In its most extreme form, the conservative explanation for poverty is **social Darwinism.** Social Darwinists, such as Herbert Spencer, argue that poverty is a mechanism for the survival of the fittest in the economic arena. Poverty sorts out the weak from the strong. Those who are able to overcome poverty are the strongest members of the society, and this process results in a healthier society overall. Some carry this argument to its logical extreme and argue that the government has no role in this area at all. An illustration of this argument is provided by Charles Murray.[13] For Murray, the welfare system itself is to blame for poverty. Accordingly, he suggested in the mid-eighties that the ideal solution would entail "scrapping the entire welfare and income-support structure for working-aged persons, including AFDC, Medicaid, Food Stamps, Unemployment Insurance, Workers' Compensation, subsidized housing, disability insurance, and the rest. It would leave the working-aged person with no recourse whatsoever except the job market, family members, friends, and public or private locally funded services."[14] Although Murray's position can be criticized on several grounds, it does raise the issue of who is most responsible for causing and correcting poverty.[15]

Table 11.2 illustrates the liberal and the conservative views on poverty.

THE EVOLUTION OF WELFARE POLICY

In the following discussion of welfare policy in America, we see how these alternative perspectives on poverty were the basis for welfare policies in different eras. Welfare policies began with the individualist assumptions that gave rise to a more austere policy in the early history of the country. Then, beginning in the 1930s and continuing through the 1970s, the structuralist assumptions guided welfare policies. Most recently, somewhat of a consensus seems to have been reached that combines both liberal and conservative assumptions about poverty in America.

The Elizabethan Poor Laws

The first recognizable welfare policy may be traced back to the Poor Relief Act of 1601 established by the English Parliament. Prior to the 1930s, the Poor Relief Act was a model for American welfare policy. This early act tended to view poverty as the product of moral or character deficiencies in individuals. Care for destitute persons was to be minimal to discourage all but the most desperate of the poor from seeking aid. It differentiated between the "worthy poor" (including widows, the aged, orphans, and the handicapped) and the "able-bodied poor" (including the unemployed). The former were sent to so-called poorhouses, whereas the latter were sent to county workhouses. Whatever relief was provided by the public could never exceed the value of the income of the lowest-paid person in the community who was not on relief. Poor rolls were made public, and relief was provided only if no living relative could be legally required to support a destitute member of their family. Under Elizabethan law, the care of the poor was the responsibility of the local government rather than the state government. Residency requirements were established for welfare care, so that local governments

TABLE 11.2 Overview of Alternative Perspectives on Poverty

	Structural View (Liberal)		Individual View (Conservative)	
Views on human nature	1.	Optimistic view of human nature	1.	Pessimistic view of human nature
	2.	The individual is shaped by his or her environment	2.	The individual is master of his or her fate
Underlying cause of poverty	1.	Poverty arises from accidents of birth or social injustice	1.	There is a natural distribution of talents, abilities, faculties
	2.	Poverty can be adjusted by a redistribution of resources	2.	Nothing can be done; poverty is inevitable, a state of mind
Measure of poverty	1.	Emphasize relative deprivation	1.	Emphasize absolute deprivation
	2.	The level of poverty is quite significant	2.	The level of poverty is insignificant and/or declining
Role of government	1.	Government should guarantee some level of substantive equality	1.	Government has no real responsibility or should only provide opportunities for the poor
	2.	Make people free and equal; equality should be mandated and results achieved	2.	Government should stop at procedural level; results are not to be mandated
Preferred policy solution	1.	Government should create jobs and/ or train poor	1.	Government should pursue a laissez-faire policy or encourage private sector to create jobs
	2.	Government should provide direct benefits to the poor (income subsidies, services in kind)	2.	Government should encourage trickle-down economics

could make certain they were not caring for the poor of other communities. Support was limited to those who had been born in the area or who had lived there for some time.[16]

The Political Machine

From 1870 to 1920, a number of institutions provided what was, in effect, welfare. The political machine, for example, provided baskets of food, bushels of coal, small loans, jobs, and other favors to those who supported the machine. The political machine essentially traded votes for political favoritism and provided a welfare function for the newly arrived immigrants to the United States in this period.

In addition, private philanthropists, such as the Rockefeller family, provided funds for the poor. State almshouses were set up as well. In short, this period in welfare assistance relied on political machines and private philanthropy to take care of the poor in the United States.

The Great Depression of 1929

The Great Depression brought about significant changes in attitudes toward public welfare as well as changes in the policies and administration of welfare programs. No longer were many people willing to believe that poverty was a product of the individual's moral or character faults. Millions who had previously considered welfare recipients to be unworthy of public concern now joined in the bread lines themselves. One out of 4 Americans was unemployed, and 1 out of 6 was receiving some sort of welfare assistance. This widespread experience with poverty changed public attitudes toward welfare and led to a change away from an Elizabethan-based policy in the United States. In short, welfare was now considered to be a societal and governmental concern rather than an individual one.

In 1935 the Social Security Act was passed, providing the basic framework for welfare policies for all levels of government. The act placed great reliance on a program of social insurance as well as a public assistance program.[17]

Welfare Reforms, 1960–96

The 1960s: The Great Society and the War on Poverty   President Lyndon Johnson (1963–69) undertook a war on poverty itself as his Great Society expanded social service programs. The cornerstone of his program was the Economic Opportunity Act of 1965. This act created the Office of Economic Opportunity in order to conduct experiments in social services and to coordinate all the poverty programs of the agencies in the federal government. In addition, new programs were begun, such as Medicare, Medicaid, and legal services. In 1966, the Model Cities program was created to target federal aid in specific neighborhoods of 150 selected major cities. Community Action Agencies (CAA) were set up in all communities that received federal funds, so that people affected by the programs could participate in designing program plans. These efforts stimulated community organizing efforts in poor neighborhoods and attempted to develop community leadership in black neighborhoods, provide jobs for poor and middle-class blacks, and organize residents of those neighborhoods to pressure local governments for better services.

The social programs of the War on Poverty came under rather severe criticism in the 1980s. Conservative scholars suggested that these programs did not end poverty, may have brought about the urban riots of the late 1960s, and developed welfare dependency among the poor.[18]

The 1970s: Income Maintenance   President Nixon proposed the Family Assistance Plan (FAP), which featured a federally funded minimum-income guarantee to all Americans. A four-person family with no other income would receive $1,600. For each dollar earned beyond this amount, the government's payment would decrease by 50 cents. When the family's income reached $3,920, the government's benefits would be phased out completely. However, this proposal failed to win congressional support for several reasons. First, liberals feared that the FAP would eliminate other programs, such as food stamps. Conservatives felt that FAP would reward poor families for not working. Moreover, the majority of public opinion was opposed to the FAP and the idea of a guaranteed minimum income. Finally, Nixon himself grew cool to the idea when he could not build necessary public support.

President Carter tried to resurrect the idea in the late 1970s by proposing a work benefit and income support program to replace the existing AFDC, Supplemental Security Income (SSI), and food stamp programs.[19] Under his plan, a family of four would receive a cash payment of $2,300 as long as its earned income was less than $3,800. For each dollar earned above that amount, the cash supplement would be reduced by 50 cents until it was completely phased out at $8,400. Thus, every four-person family in the country would be guaranteed a minimum income of $8,400. Carter's proposal faced the same kind of opposition as President Nixon's plan had.

The 1980s: The Reagan Revolution   Following the failure of guaranteed income plans in the 1970s, welfare reform in the 1980s shifted toward reducing the welfare rolls and making the welfare recipients work to earn their grants. President Reagan's approach was to force welfare recipients into the job market by reducing expenditures for most social welfare programs and by tightening up eligibility requirements for the programs.[20]

In 1988, Congress passed the Family Support Act, which had four main components:

1. *The JOBS program.* To qualify for federal AFDC grants, all states would be required, by 1995, to enroll at least 20 percent of their AFDC cases into a program that would develop an employability plan for each participant.

2. *Child support enforcement.* States were now required to provide for automatic withholding of court-ordered child support payments from the wages of noncustodial parents whose children were on AFDC. States were also required to set up regular reviews of child support agreements in AFDC cases, so that the payments could be adjusted upward with inflation and the changing circumstances of the noncustodial parent.

3. *Transitional benefits.* Both Medicaid and child-care benefits would be provided while the participant was in the JOBS program, and for a transitional period of up to a year when the participant left the JOBS program and entered the workforce.

4. *Special provisions for minor parents.* Because some had argued that traditional AFDC allowed a teenage mother to set up a household of her own once her child was born, and to raise that child in circumstances that were believed to

be dysfunctional, the new law permitted states to allow minors to live with their parents and still qualify for AFDC benefits.

The 1990s: Workfare and Welfare Reform   For nearly 60 years, the federal government had essentially guaranteed that most of America's poorest families would receive some form of cash assistance for as long as they needed it. Although originally envisioned as a temporary program of aid, by the mid 1990s Aid to Families with Dependent Children (AFDC) had become an integral part of federal social policy.

That would change in 1996 with the passage of The Personal Responsibility and Work Opportunity Reconciliation Act (PRWORA). Intended to end "welfare as we know it," the legislation dramatically altered the nature of welfare in America. For America's poor this meant a new set of rules and requirements and, perhaps most importantly, an end to the entitlement that had been in place for over half a century. In replacing the decades-old AFDC program with a new program, Temporary Assistance for Needy Families (TANF), federal welfare policy became more clearly focused on moving welfare recipients into the workforce. In doing that, recipients were required to find at least part-time employment within 2 years of receiving aid and were, with some exception, limited to a lifetime total of 60 months of federal cash assistance.

For the American states, welfare reform in the nineties meant a new set of responsibilities and the promise of much more control over welfare within their borders. In replacing AFDC with TANF, the 1996 legislation eliminated what had been an open-ended entitlement program and replaced it with a block grant program to the states. No longer would the amount of federal aid for the poor depend on the number of families that were eligible. Instead, states would receive a fixed amount of federal support. For most states, that shift in funding produced an initial windfall by guaranteeing the states an amount of federal aid pegged to funding levels that had existed during periods of higher poverty and unemployment (so-called maintenance of effort funds). However, as the economy weakened in the late nineties and as the number of Americans in poverty increased, the states began to feel the pressures of having to provide welfare assistance on a fixed federal allocation.

PRWORA also gave the states considerable leeway in dictating the terms of welfare. The result is substantial variation in state welfare programming. For example, while the federal legislation sets a lifetime limit of 60 months on the receipt of cash assistance, the states are allowed to set a shorter lifetime limit, can exempt a percentage of recipients from that limit, and can provide state-funded assistance after recipients have reached the federal time limit. As of 1999, nineteen states had adopted shorter lifetime limits while another 6 states set no limits at all. Similarly, over half the American states required recipients to work sooner than the federally prescribed 24 months.[21] States also have considerable discretion in determining who is exempted from the federal work requirement. Most states exempt individuals responsible for caring for a child under the age of 1 year, but as of 1999 five states

(Georgia, Idaho, Utah, Montana, and Iowa) chose not to exempt mothers of newborns.[22]

State programs also vary in the length and severity of sanctions that are imposed for failing to meet the new requirements. Under the 1996 legislation, states have the option of withholding some or all of TANF benefits for failing to meet work participation requirements. For most states, the severest sanction is the loss of the entire TANF benefit for at least 1 month; and in a handful of instances, failure to comply can result in the permanent loss of benefits. States can also limit who is eligible for aid and the amount of aid a family can receive. Twenty-one states have a family cap provision to limit the amount of assistance to families that have additional children while on welfare.[23] States also have the option of denying benefits to individuals convicted of a drug-related crime and to legal aliens, although few exclude the latter.

Another important way the states vary is in regard to programs of support intended to make getting and keeping a job easier for recipients. Perhaps the most important of these provide child-care assistance to recipients and former recipients. Three-fifths of the states guarantee child care for families on TANF and for those who have left TANF. Nearly every state provides families leaving TANF with transitional Medicaid. States also have used their maintenance of effort and other funds to offer additional programs of support, including programs aimed at reducing teenage pregnancy, services to low-income fathers, programs for teenage parents, homeless shelters, domestic violence programs, and post-employment services and training.[24]

Finally, with its emphasis on work and enhanced state responsibility, PWORA has led a number of states to revisit several fundamental organizational issues, including (1) the degree to which state programs will be centralized; (2) the role of the private sector; and (3) how TANF will be coordinated with other programs of support, including food stamps, Medicaid, child-care programs, and most importantly, programs aimed at moving individuals off of welfare and into work. Most states have chosen a more decentralized structure, often relying on regional boards and local organizations to coordinate and administer TANF and related programs. Increasingly, the states are turning to the private sector to implement welfare programming, including for-profit, not for profit and, in some instances, faith-based organizations. Based on a review of welfare reform in 17 cities in 13 states, analysts at the Urban Institute concluded that:

> Rather than significantly expanding in-house capability to meet the new demands of welfare reform, welfare agencies typically responded to the mandate to make welfare more employment-focused by transferring some or all of their TANF work program responsibilities to different agencies and forging new organizational connections with outside service providers. In particular, workforce development agencies and nonprofit community-based organizations dramatically expanded their role in the TANF service delivery system.[25]

STRUCTURES OF WELFARE POLICY

The Social Security Act of 1935 (and subsequent amendments) constitutes the basic structure of welfare policy in America at both national and state levels.[26] This act promoted two structures of relief for the poor. The first type is more appropriately called **social insurance,** because it is not really based on need. It is provided to everyone who qualifies, regardless of need. It was originally set up to prevent individuals from being poor. The second type is appropriately called **welfare assistance,** because it is need based. Both of these forms of assistance are described below.

Preventive Strategy: Social Insurance

Social insurance includes the following types of assistance:

1. Old Age, Survivors, Disability, and Health Insurance (OASDHI) is given to retired people and the survivors of workers who have died. This is commonly known as Social Security. It is available to people over 65 who have contributed to the system, and to all those over 72, regardless of their contributions and income. It is an entitlement program, in that recipients have a vested right to benefits, usually because of their contributions to the system through compulsory payroll taxes authorized by the Federal Insurance Contributions Act (FICA).

2. Medicare is given to the aged in all income categories after age 65.

3. Unemployment compensation is given to the temporarily unemployed.

Reliance on funding benefits from current contributors to the program means that the Social Security system represents income transfers from younger, employed members of society to the elderly and disabled, whether rich or poor. In 1984, Congress increased program revenues by raising FICA payroll taxes and including federal employees as contributors. The "full" retirement age was raised from 65 to 67. Congress's action in 1984 ensured the fiscal solvency of Social Security through the year 2010, but did nothing to deal with the longer-term financial demands that will occur as the baby boomers reach retirement age.[27] President Bush appointed a national commission to find a solution to the impending crisis in 2001, but it was unable to do much more than encourage working Americans to find ways to supplement their Social Security retirement. The commission did recommend that government offer younger workers the option of a personal savings account, but calls for privatizing Social Security are not likely to bear legislative fruit in the foreseeable future.[28]

Alleviative Strategy: Welfare Assistance

In contrast to the entitlement programs above, welfare is organized as a public charity. The poor have no entitlement to public assistance; rather, access to benefits is based on the recipients' qualifications and specific needs. Welfare requires the application of a means test, in which the poor must prove that they have no income or that their income is insufficient to meet their needs. Welfare assistance includes the following types of programs, which were a part of the Social Security Act of 1935 and the Great Society programs of the 1960s:

1. TANF provides cash assistance to the nonworking poor with children. This includes mostly single, divorced, or widowed mothers and their children.

2. Food stamps are given to the bottom 40 percent of income recipients, which includes both the working and nonworking poor.

3. Supplemental Security Income (SSI) is given to the aged, the blind, and the disabled.

4. General public assistance (excluding TANF and SSI) is given mostly to destitute and homeless people who do not qualify for TANF, SSI, or unemployment compensation.

5. In-kind assistance includes housing assistance, Medicaid and other health programs, legal services, employment programs, and other social services such as child care and family planning.

Welfare recipients can receive assistance from more than one source. For example, a working mother can receive TANF, food stamps, and in-kind assistance, such as day care for her children.

EVALUATING THE IMPACT
OF SOCIAL WELFARE PROGRAMS

What has been the effect of the various welfare programs over the past 70 years? Perhaps the best way to answer that is to look at two waves of welfare research—earlier analyses of the Great Society programs of the sixties and more recent analysis of the reforms enacted in 1996.

With respect to the Great Society programs, it is not surprising that policy makers and policy analysts disagree about the impact of the "War on Poverty." Critics maintain that the poverty programs of the sixties did little to reduce poverty in America and actually may have contributed to its persistence. For example, John Donovan argues that the Great Society programs created hopes for winning the War on Poverty without developing and adequately supporting a program for that purpose.[29] More recent critics include Edward Banfield and Charles Murray. Banfield argues that the programs may have promoted (rather than slowed) urban decline by encouraging dispersion of the urban population to the suburbs through subsidized housing and FHA and VA loans.[30] Similarly, Murray argues that the government welfare programs during the period of 1950–80 only made problems worse by sapping poor people of their initiative and making them dependent on the welfare system.[31]

On the other hand, some argue that the welfare programs of the 1960s produced some positive benefits for the poor. Levitan and Taggart, for example, argue that the Great Society did achieve many of its goals.[32] Similarly, John Schwarz argues that the welfare programs have had some important successes.[33] For the elderly, the welfare programs seemed to have made a clear difference. For others, such as women, blacks, Hispanics, and children, the various programs have provided much-needed relief.

On balance, the most positive view of the Great Society programs suggests several conclusions:

1. These programs stimulated the states and cities to spend significant amounts of money on programs like the Model Cities and Community Action Programs—programs that typically would not have been funded without federal support and encouragement.

2. These programs provided services to the nation's poor with some positive results in income redistribution and increased educational attainment.

3. These programs provided paths to future funds by establishing relationships among federal, state, and local governments.

4. These programs stimulated the local economy through jobs and money.

5. These programs provided a mechanism for the federal government to deal with national problems, such as poverty and transportation, that could not be adequately dealt with at the local level.

A second wave of research looks at the impact of the fundamental changes enacted with the passage of PRWORA in 1996. Here again, the evidence is mixed. On the one hand, it is clear that the effects of the first round of welfare reform have been dramatic. Over the last decade, caseloads nationwide have dropped by half, from around 4 million families in 1996 to just 2 million today. And while wages are low and benefits frequently absent, most of the families that left welfare include a working adult.[34]

But the news is not all good—including the news for those who have left the welfare system. Despite increases in the rate of work, estimates from studies conducted in the 1990s were that anywhere from half to three quarters of those who leave welfare remain in poverty 2–3 years later.[35] In 2002, a total of 26 percent of those who had left welfare within the previous two years had reapplied for cash assistance.[36] There is also concern that reform has created a new class of "disconnecteds"—former recipients who are unemployed, do not have a working spouse, and are no longer receiving TANF or SSI. One estimate places 1 in 7 former recipients in that category.[37] More generally, poverty remains in America and is still on the rise. As an analyst at the Brookings Institution noted in the fall of 2004, "Poverty is up, and welfare is down."[38] In addition, state budget shortfalls over the last few years have led many states to consider and make cuts in cash benefits, transportation assistance, child-care support, and job assistance programs. The reader is also reminded that the national success rates hide substantial variations across the states. While caseloads fell by over 50 percent in the first 5 years of reform, for example, differences across the states were striking. Approximately a third of the states had reduced their roles by 60 percent or more, but ten states could do no better than 40 percent.[39]

WELFARE IN THE NEW CENTURY

The past decade has witnessed a fundamental change in the character of welfare policy in America. For the first time since the 1930s there is no guarantee that if your family is poor, it will receive a cash benefit. Under the new welfare regime, heads of households must work as a condition of aid; and under most circumstances, families can receive federally funded support for only five years. PRWORA draws from both conservative and liberal welfare theories. Requiring recipients to work, setting lifetime limits, and evoking harsh sanctions for failing to meet program requirements reflects the belief among many conservatives that the poor are capable of working but simply lack the incentive to do so. At the same time, state programs that provide child care, transitional Medicaid, and transportation support acknowledge that America's poor often face obstacles in their daily lives that make getting and keeping a job difficult.

That mix of "carrots" and "sticks" apparently has worked for the 2 million or so Americans who have left the welfare rolls. What about those who remain on welfare? Will that same mix of incentives be enough to move additional numbers of the poor into work? For those who have joined the ranks of the working poor, challenges remain. Former welfare recipients often fall between the cracks, ineligible for unemployment insurance or health-care benefits from their employer. Child care remains a major problem. It can be expensive and difficult to obtain.

In assessing where we are a decade after the reforms of the mid-nineties, Olivia Golden, a senior fellow at the Urban Institute, concludes:

> Our challenge now is to build on success. We dismantled the old safety net of welfare, which failed families by not demanding work and by not linking them to the work world. But we have not yet crafted the new safety net needed to replace it, a safety net built around work and the basic benefits, opportunities and protections that parents need to raise healthy children. Until we do, we will be placing the future of America's children and families at risk.[40]

DISCUSSION QUESTIONS

1. To what extent does one's "vision of human nature" (Thomas Sowell) affect one's view about the most appropriate welfare policy? Clarify your own view of human nature before proceeding further with this discussion.

2. To what extent do you agree or disagree with Michael Harrington's view that poverty is "structurally determined," and that poverty in America is a product of "structural economic change" in that a lack of employment opportunities for the poor was brought about by automation and the importation of cheap (foreign) labor?

3. Charles Murray and others maintain that many of the poor in America are poor because they lack the willingness and ability to work. Do you agree?

4. To what extent is the welfare policy debate really a debate between socialism (egalitarianism; redistribution of wealth) and social Darwinism (survival of the fittest; emphasis on individual abilities)?

SUGGESTED READINGS

Blank, Rebecca, and Ron Haskins, eds. *The New World of Welfare* (Washington, D.C.: Brookings Institution Press, 2001).

Dean, Hartley. *Social Policy* (Cambridge, UK: Polity Press, 2006).

Ellwood, David T. *Poor Support* (New York: Basic Books, 1989).

Harrington, Michael. *The New American Poverty* (New York: Viking, 1985).

Mead, Larry. *Government Matters: Welfare Reform in Wisconsin* (Princeton: Princeton University Press, 2004).

Murray, Charles. *Losing Ground* (New York: Basic Books, 1984).

Piven, Frances Fox, and Richard A. Cloward. *Regulating the Poor: The Functions of Public Welfare* (New York: Vintage Books, 1971).

Schwarz, John E. *America's Hidden Success: A Reassessment of Twenty Years of Public Policy* (New York: W. W. Norton, 1983).

NOTES

1. Lawrence M. Mead, "The New Politics of the New Poverty," *The Public Interest* 103 (Spring 1991), pp. 3–20.

2. Bradley R. Schiller and C. Nielson Brasher, "Workfare in the 1980s: Successes and Limits," *Policy Studies Review* 9 (Summer 1990), pp. 665–680.

3. Thomas R. Dye, *Understanding Public Policy,* 7th ed. (Englewood Cliffs, NJ: Prentice Hall, 1991), p. 110.

4. Ibid., p. 111.

5. Charles Murray, *Losing Ground* (New York: Basic Books, 1984).

6. Ibid.

7. Edward C. Banfield, *The Unheavenly City Revisited* (Prospect Heights, IL: Waveland Press, 1990).

8. Paul E. Peterson, "The Urban Underclass and the Poverty Paradox," *Political Science Quarterly* 106 (Winter 1991–92), pp. 617–637.

9. Michael Harrington, *The New American Poverty* (New York: Viking Penguin, 1985).

10. Frances Fox Piven and Richard A. Cloward, *Regulating the Poor: The Functions of Public Welfare* (New York: Vintage Books, 1971).

11. See Richard J. Herrnstein and Charles Murray, *The Bell Curve: Intelligence and Class Structure in American Life* (New York: Free Press, 1994), pp. 127–142.

12. Banfield, *Unheavenly City;* and Mead, "New Politics."

13. Murray, *Losing Ground.*

14. Ibid., pp. 227 228.

15. Sheldon Danzinger and Peter Gottschalk, "The Poverty of Losing Ground," *Challenge* 28 (May–June 1985), pp. 32–38; and David Ellwood and Lawrence H. Summers, "Is Welfare Really the Problem?" *Public Interest* 83 (Spring 1986), pp. 57–78.

16. Dye, *Understanding Public Policy*, p. 127.

17. Ibid., p. 468.

18. See, for example, Stuart Butler and Anne Kondratas, *Out of the Poverty Trap: A Conservative Strategy* (New York: Free Press, 1987); and Murray, *Losing Ground.*

19. See President Carter's message in the *New York Times* (7 August 1977), pp. 1, 40.

20. John J. Harrigan, *Politics and Policy in States and Local Communities* (New York: HarperCollins, 1991), p. 376.

21. National Governors Association, "Round Two Summary of Selected Elements of State Programs for Temporary Assistance," March 14, 1999. www.nga.org/portal/ site/nga/menuitem.9123e83a1f6786440ddcbeeb501010a0/?vgnextoid=3ebb5aa265 b32010VgnVCM1000001a01010aRCRD, accessed June 1, 1999.

22. Heather McCallum, "Welfare as We Know It Now ... State Approaches to TANF," Paper delivered at the annual meeting of the American Political Science Association, August 31–September 4, 1999, Atlanta.

23. Urban Institute, "Welfare Rules Databook: State TANF Policies as of July 2003," at http://anfdata.urban.org/WRD/WRDWelcome.cfm, accessed June 17, 2004.

24. Dana Reichert and Jack Tweedie, "Programs and Services Funded with TANF and MOE," at www.ncsl.org/statefed/welfare/tanfuses.htm, accessed March 1, 2007.

25. Karin Martinson and Pamela Holcomb, "Reforming Welfare: Institutional Changes and Challenges," Urban Institute, published July 31, 2002, at www.urban.org/ urlprint.cfm?ID=7801, p. 2, accessed May 15, 2006.

26. Robert Albritton, "Social Services: Welfare and Health," in *Politics in the American States,* ed. Virginia Gray, Herbert Jacob, and Robert Albritton (Glenview, IL: Scott, Foresman/Little, Brown, 1990), p. 412.

27. Ibid., p. 413.

28. Thomas Dye, *Understanding Public Policy,* 12th ed. (Upper Saddle River, NJ: Prentice Hall, 2007).

29. John C. Donovan, *The Politics of Poverty* (New York: Pegasus, 1967).

30. Banfield, *Unheavenly City.*

31. Murray, *Losing Ground.*

32. Sar A. Levitan and Robert Taggart, "Great Society Did Succeed," *Political Science Quarterly* 91 (Winter 1976–77), pp. 601–618.

33. John E. Schwarz, *America's Hidden Success: A Reassessment of Twenty Years of Public Policy* (New York: W. W. Norton, 1983), especially pp. 57–59.

34. Olivia Golden, "Welfare Reform Mostly Worked," Urban Institute, posted July 24, 2005, at www.urban.org/url.cfm?ID=900824, accessed August 1, 2005.

35. Rebecca M. Blank, "Evaluating Welfare Reform in the United States," *Journal of Economic Literature* XL (December 2002), pp. 1105–66.

36. Golden, "Welfare Reform Mostly Worked."

37. Shawn Fremstad, "Recent Welfare Reform Research Findings," Center on Budget and Policy Priorities, January 30, 2004, at www.cbpp.org/1-30-04wel.htm, accessed March 15, 2007.

38. Margy Waller, "Welfare Reform: Time for Congress to Act," Brookings Institute, 2004, at www.brookings.edu/views/articles/20040915waller.htm, accessed March 15, 2007.

39. U.S. Department of Health and Human Services, Administration for Children and Families, "Percent Change in AFDC/TANF Families and Recipients August 1996—September 2001," at www.acf.hhs.gov/news/stats/afdc.htm, accessed March 15, 2007.

40. Golden, "Welfare Reform Mainly Worked," p. 4.

12

Environmental Policy

"Yet the conservation movement raised a fundamental question
in American life: . . . How can the technical requirements of an
increasingly complex society be adjusted to the need for the expression
of partial and limited aims?"
SAMUEL P. HAYS

"Our political institutions, predicated almost totally on growth
and abundance, appear to be no match for the gathering forces
of ecological scarcity."
WILLIAM OPHULS

"Appreciating the scale of social and economic changes likely in the next
fifty or one hundred years, one can easily be overwhelmed by the
magnitude of the task. . . .
A vital alternative is to accept Camus' simple moral vision—one does
what one can, no more and no less—and one trusts that enough of one's
fellow humans will do the same."
ROBERT C. PAEHLKE

For a variety of reasons, the new century is a particularly exciting time to examine environmental politics and policy. First, state and federal authorities continue to wrestle with how best to implement the range of environmental policies enacted at the federal level over the last four decades. These policies include the Clean Air and Water Acts, Superfund, and the Surface Mining Act. Despite (or perhaps because of) years of congressional debate, litigation in the courts, various amendments to the original legislation, and the comings and goings of successive presidents, the question still remains as what standards should be set and who will enforce those standards and with what vigor. In that sense, the next decade will continue to be an "implementation era" for environmental policy and politics.

Second, **intergovernmental relations** will continue to be a critical element in the formulation and implementation of environmental policy. Beginning in the 1980s, the doctrine of **new federalism** stressed devolution of authority from the federal level to the state and local levels in many areas of public policy. As part of the legacy of the Reagan and Bush presidencies, states and local communities are taking on many responsibilities for protecting the environment. The move to decentralization continued under the presidencies of Bill Clinton and George W. Bush. The question remains as to whether the states and American federalism are up to the task.

Finally, with the emergence of issues that cut across national borders, most notably global climate change, biodiversity protection, and international trade, **international relations** promises to play an ever-increasing role in the debate over how best to protect the nation's air and water.

This chapter reviews the evolution of environmental politics and policy in the United States. Before discussing their present state, it is instructive to review briefly the history of environmental politics and policy in the United States from 1890 to 1990. Next, we review the status of environmental policy and politics since 1990. Finally, we discuss the future of environmental politics and policy in the American states.

THE EVOLUTION OF ENVIRONMENTAL POLITICS AND POLICY

The history of environmental politics and policy may be roughly divided into four periods. These four periods are the **conservation-efficiency movement,** from about 1890 to 1920; the **conservation-preservation movement,** from about 1920 to 1960; the **environmental movement,** from about 1960 to 1990; and the contemporary period of **participatory environmentalism,** starting in the 1990s.[1] However, earlier attempts to protect the environment can be identified as well. For example, during the first part of the 19th century, the federal government took several actions to preserve good mast timber for ships, and President John Quincy Adams's administration even went so far as to establish a program of sustained-yield operations on forest reservations in 1827.[2] However, not much effort was given for environmental protection until some time after the Civil War. Except for the John Quincy Adams administration, no political administration from Washington to Buchanan revealed any concept of natural resources that showed foresight in planning for the nation's future needs.[3] Essentially, the years between 1865 and 1890 may be characterized as a period of resource exploitation by a rising industry, during which time natural resources were subordinated to the political objectives of industrial development, removal of Indians from their native lands for resettlement, homestead settlement, and the promotion of free enterprise.[4] During the Reconstruction era after the Civil War, rebuilding the South and developing the American West required the use of resources rather than their conservation. Nevertheless, by the late 1800s, serious efforts to protect the nation's natural resources had begun.

The Conservation-Efficiency Movement, 1890–1920

The years from 1890 until 1920 saw some of the nation's most bitter conservation battles, as Republicans and Democrats began to take firm positions on the environment. The essence of the conservation movement was rational planning to promote efficient development and use of all natural resources.[5] According to historian Samuel P. Hays, "the modern American conservation movement grew out of the firsthand experience of federal administrators and political leaders with problems of Western economic growth, especially Western water development."[6] Later, federal forestry officials joined hydrographers and campaigned for more rational and efficient use of timber resources. During the 1890s, the organized forestry movement in the United States shifted its emphasis from saving trees to promoting sustained-yield forest management.[7] Action was taken to set aside "forest reserves" within the federal domain by 1891 and to authorize selective cutting and marketing of timber in 1897.[8]

A number of individuals, including W. J. McGee, Gifford Pinchot, John Wesley Powell, Frederick Newell, and George Maxwell, were concerned about natural resources and were employed by the federal government in the late 1800s, many of them for the U.S. Geological Survey. Together, they formulated four basic doctrines for what later became the creed of the conservation movement. These doctrines were (1) conservation is not the locking up of resources; it is their development and wise use; (2) conservation is the greatest good for the greatest number for the longest time; (3) the federal public lands belong to all the people; and (4) comprehensive, multiple-purpose river basin planning and development should be utilized with respect to the nation's water resources.[9]

Gifford Pinchot became an important link between the intellectual and scientific founders of the conservation movement and President Theodore Roosevelt, a Republican. Indeed, the Roosevelt administration is more noteworthy for the drive and support it gave the conservation movement than it is for the initiation of new policies or legislative enactments. A new spirit of law enforcement pervaded the departments and was dramatized to the country at large by the influence of Gifford Pinchot in his role as adviser to President Roosevelt.[10] Under Pinchot's guidance, the Roosevelt administration greatly enlarged the area of the national forests from 41 national reserves to 159.[11] Pinchot, who studied forest management in France and Germany, completely reorganized the U.S. Forest Service and infused it with a new spirit of public responsibility.[12]

The period of 1908 to 1920 saw numerous conflicts over conservation policy. For example, much of the Western livestock industry depended for its forage on the "open range," which was owned by the federal government but was free for anyone to use. Soon, the public domain became stocked with more animals than the range could support. Chaos, anarchy, violence, and destruction were typical of the times. Range wars soon developed between Western cattlemen and sheep operators—and at times, between those groups and farmers, as they all struggled for control of the public grazing lands.[13]

Nevertheless, the deepest significance of the conservation movement, according to Samuel Hays, "lay in its political implications: how should resource decisions be made and by whom?" Should conflicts be resolved through partisan politics, by compromise among various interest groups, or through the courts?[14] To the conservationists, politics was anathema; instead, they believed scientific experts, using technical and scientific methods, should decide all matters of development and use of natural resources, together with the allocation of funds.[15] The crux of the gospel of efficiency, then, "lay in a rational and scientific method of making basic technological decisions through a single, central authority."[16] The inevitable tension that developed between those grassroots interests and the technocratic elites of this conservation-efficiency era raised a question that was to be addressed by future conservationists: how can large-scale economic development be effective and at the same time fulfill the desire for significant grassroots participation?

The Conservation-Preservation Movement, 1920–60

The second form of conservationism, the preservationist movement, was very similar to the efficiency movement, except that this movement was more concerned with *habitat* than sustenance.[17] That is, this preservationist movement developed largely under the pressures of increased leisure and affluence and the growth of outdoor recreation. It drew its support from the upper middle class and had much support from hunting and fishing groups drawn from the working classes. Although conflicts occurred over natural resource policy, they were largely confined to struggles between those who favored "multiple use" of public lands and those who favored "pure preservation."[18] Although the earlier movement was often characterized by conflicts between extractive industries in the West and manufacturing industries in the East, the preservationist movement often included capitalist sponsors, such as Laurence Rockefeller, who facilitated the preservation of major tracts of land surrounding the hotels that he built.[19]

Beginning in 1920, water power, coal, flood control, and even wildlife were given special attention in the major party platforms. Much of the emphasis on natural resources was shifted from conservation of public lands to programs of conservation under private ownership.[20] Another major difference between these two movements was that conservation-efficiency concerns resided with corporations and state agencies, whereas conservation-preservationist concerns resided in local, and especially national, organizations such as the Sierra Club and the National Wildlife Federation.

The period from 1921 to 1950 took on a different look. Much of the federal legislation for natural resources was associated with broad social and economic objectives, such as the Agricultural Adjustment Act of 1938, which was passed to control agricultural production. The legislative history of environmental and natural resource issues suggests that Democrats attained a much better voting record than their Republican counterparts did between 1921 and 1950.[21] By the 1960s, however, the movement began to change dramatically as environmental concern was broadened to include many new groups that had previously been inactive on this issue.

The Environmental Movement, 1960–90

One prominent scholar of environmental politics argues that the conservation movement was an effort by leaders in science, technology, and government to bring about more efficient development of natural resources, whereas the environmental movement was a product of a fundamental change in U.S. public values that stressed the quality of the human environment.[22]

The environmental movement, in contrast to the conservation movement, is more typically viewed as a grassroots or bottom-up phenomenon in which environmental objectives arose out of deep-seated changes in values about the use of nature. Conservation, on the other hand, is viewed as a top-down phenomenon in which technical and political leaders were stirred toward action. Essentially, the environmental movement integrated the habitat and sustenance concerns of the efficiency and preservation movements; but it also covered a broader set of ecosystem concerns.[23] There were new concerns about social welfare issues, growth management, and production expansion decision making.

The environmental movement can also be characterized by the breadth of its constituency and its political strategies. For example, the environmental movement used lobbying, litigation, the media, electoral politics, and even civil disobedience; this in contrast to the more modest mechanisms used by the conservationists, such as technical negotiations, corporate sponsors, and pressure groups.[24] Finally, the base of support for the environmental movement was made up of a larger sector of the public, including the middle and working classes.

Table 12.1 illustrates the four periods in environmental history including the more recent shift to participatory environmentalism. Several observations are in order. First, one can see how the environmental movement steadily broadened its base of support over the 100 years from 1890 to 1990. Specifically, it moved from being largely an elitist concern, involving scientific and government experts, to one with broad-based support including middle-class and even working-class supporters. This broader base of public support has been joined by national environmental groups, such as the Sierra Club, Natural Resources Defense Council, Friends of the Earth, Greenpeace, and Earth First! This tendency toward "opening up" the issue toward greater and more representative participation is also illustrated by the extant literature that seeks to explain the formulation or implementation of environmental policy. Initially, the literature stressed subgovernments as a major explanation for environmental policymaking.[25]

T A B L E 12.1 The Evolution of Environmentalism, 1890–present

	1890–1920	1920–1960	1960–1990	1990–present
Scope of the issues	Preservation issues	Conservation issues	Second-generation issues	Third-generation issues
Dominant policy	Efficient use of resources	Multiple use of resources	Pollution abatement	Pollution prevention
Patterns of participation	Elite-dominated	Subgovernments	Pluralism	Advocacy coalitions
Policy cycle stage	Pre-problem	Agenda setting	Policy formulation	Policy implementation
Level of action	National government	National government	National, state, and local governments	State and local governments
Dominant concern	Environmental science	Technology development	Economics and politics	Philosophy and environmental ethics
Techniques of power	Technical negotiations	Corporate pressure	Middle class politics	Participatory democracy

SOURCE: Compiled by the authors.

More recently, the literature suggests that advocacy coalitions, composed of interests from all three levels of government and the private sector, are now involved in environmental policymaking.[26] Clearly, this suggests a change in the scope of citizen involvement over the past 100 years.

A number of other changes have taken place in environmental policy and politics over just the past 40 years. For example, the way that analysts evaluate the severity of the environmental problem has changed. Specifically, concern has evolved from a primary concern over natural resource issues to environmental issues, or from first-generation problems (e.g., public lands, water rights, park management) to second-generation problems (e.g., toxic waste, groundwater protection, chemical plant explosions) to third-generation problems (e.g., global warming, thinning of the ozone layer, deforestation, acid rain). Along with this change, concern has shifted from purely localized issues involving air and water pollution in communities to the realization that an effective response to these second- and third-generation problems "requires diverse actions by individuals and institutions at all levels of society."[27]

Moreover, public opinion on this topic has changed dramatically over the past 40 years. Initially, in the late 1960s and early 1970s, public opinion reached a high level of support, but it was judged to be "soft support," meaning that it would dissolve in the face of concerns over economic development (e.g., jobs over the environment). Beginning in the late 1980s, on the other hand, public opinion was said to be both strong and salient.[28] The American public indicated that it wanted stringent environmental protection regulations, and it was willing to pay for it in new taxes.

Finally, a growing involvement of states, cities, and grassroots organizations in environmental management has occurred. After the advent of new federalism in the 1970s and 1980s, states and communities are increasingly being asked to assume more of their environmental responsibilities that were previously handled by the federal government. Yet, not all of the states are able to muster the economic and institutional wherewithal to meet their new responsibilities.[29] Indeed, the states vary greatly in their capacities to assume environmental management.

Table 12.2 lists the major environmental legislation enacted during the era that we have labeled the environmental movement. As the reader can see, much of the nation's environmental laws were originally enacted in the seventies during the administrations of Richard Nixon and Gerald Ford. Over the next few decades, that legislation was renewed and amended and new areas and issues were added to the scope of federal policy, including the surface mining of coal, nuclear energy, and hazardous wastes. Interestingly, the nation's first piece of legislation on global warming was enacted in 1987 and directed the U.S. Department of State and a newly created intergovernmental task force to develop a national strategy for addressing the problem of global warming. Twenty years later, critics maintain that the United States still lacks such a strategy.

ENVIRONMENTAL POLICY AND POLITICS IN THE NEW CENTURY: A NEW FEDERALISM?

While the bulk of environmental policy in the United States is of national origin, American states play the preeminent role in implementing those standards on a day-to-day basis, albeit under the supervision of the federal authorities listed in Table 12.2. Evidence reported by Barry Rabe indicates that state governments issue more than 90 percent of all environmental permits, conduct over three-fourths of all enforcement actions, and receive less than one-fourth of their total funding for environmental policy from the federal government. According to the Environmental Council of the States, by the late nineties the U.S. Environmental Protection Agency (EPA) had granted the states authority over 757 federal environmental programs, including 82 percent of programs under the Clean Air Act.[30]

Several developments contributed to the increase in the states' environmental policy role in recent decades. First, beginning with the Nixon, Reagan, and Bush administrations, presidents and Congress returned power and authority to the states and cities under the rubric of a "new federalism." The new federalism, beginning with the State and Local Fiscal Assistance Act of 1972 (and accelerated by President Reagan in 1981), mandated a greatly expanded role for state governments. Among other things, states would become less subject to fiscal control by the federal government. Initially, the new federalism involved a number of short-term inducements, such as programmatic flexibility, elimination of de facto dual planning requirements for categorical grant applications, and increased consultation with state and local decision makers prior to the initiation of "direct development" activities. By 1981, however, the objectives of President Reagan's new federalism were to *decentralize* and *defund* federal environmental protection

TABLE 12.2 Major Federal Environmental Legislation: 1969–92

Nixon Administration	Implementing Agency
National Environmental Policy Act of 1969, PL 91-190	All Federal Agencies
Resources Recovery Act of 1970, PL 91-512	HEW, later EPA
Clean Air Act Amendments of 1970, PL 91-604	EPA
Federal Water Pollution Control Act Amendments of 1972, PL 92-500	EPA
Federal Environmental Pesticides Control Act of 1972, PL 92-516	EPA
Marine Protection Act of 1972, PL 92-532	EPA
Coastal Zone Management Act of 1974, PL 92-583	Commerce Department
Endangered Species Act of 1973, PL 93-205	Interior Department
Ford Administration	
Safe Drinking Water Act of 1974, PL 93-523	EPA
Toxic Substance Control Act of 1976, PL 94-469	EPA
Federal Land Policy and Management Act of 1976, PL 94-579	Interior Department
Resource Conservation and Recovery Act of 1976, PL 94-580	EPA
National Forest Management Act of 1976, PL 94-588	U.S. Forest Service
Carter Administration	
Surface Mining Control and Reclamation Act of 1977, PL 95-87	Interior Department
Clean Air Act Amendments of 1977, PL 95-95	EPA
Clean Water Act Amendments of 1977, PL 95-217	EPA
Public Utility Regulatory Policies Act of 1978, PL 95-617	Energy Department, states
Alaska National Interest Lands Conservation Act of 1980, PL 96-487	Interior Department, Agriculture Department
Comprehensive Environmental Response, Compensation, and Liability Act of 1980, PL 96-510	EPA
Reagan Administration	
Nuclear Waste Policy Act of 1982, PL 97-425	Energy Department
Nuclear Waste Policy Amendments Act of 1987, PL 100-203	Energy Department
Resource Conservation and Recovery Act Amendments of 1984, PL 98-616	EPA
Food Security Act of 1985, PL 99-198, Renewed in 1990, 1996, and 2002	Agriculture Department
Safe Drinking Water Act of 1986, PL 99-339	EPA
Superfund Amendment and Reauthorization Act of 1986, PL 99-499	EPA

TABLE 12.2 Continued

Clean Water Act Amendments of 1987, PL 100-4	EPA
Global Climate Protection Act of 1987, PL 100-204	State Department
Ocean Dumping Act of 1988, PL 100-688	EPA
George H. W. Bush Administration	
Oil Pollution Act of 1990, PL 101-380	Commerce Department, Transportation Department
Pollution Prevention Act of 1990, PL 101-508	EPA
Clean Air Act Amendments of 1990, PL 101-549	EPA
Intermodal Surface Transportation Efficiency Act of 1991, PL 102-240	Transportation Department
Energy Policy Act of 1992, PL 102-486	Energy Department
The Omnibus Water Act of 1992, PL 102-575	Interior Department

SOURCE: Compiled from Appendix 1, "Major Federal Laws on the Environment, 1962–2002," Norman J. Vig and Michael E. Kraft, eds. In *Environmental Policy: New Directions for the Twenty-first Century*, 6th ed. Copyright © 2006 CQ Press, a division of Congressional Quarterly Inc. Reprinted with permission of Congressional Quarterly Press.

activities. Seen most favorably, the Reagan administration thought that the states were now in a position (due largely to their enhanced institutional capacity) to assume greater responsibilities than ever before. States and cities would simply make difficult choices about what programs they wanted to retain (and thus replace the federal cuts with their own-source funds) and which ones they wanted to terminate. In this sense, public pressures would thus force state decision makers to take responsive actions that reflected localized policy preferences. Critics, on the other hand, argued that the administration used the shift of responsibilities to the states, at least in the environmental area, for another reason—as a way to eliminate particular functions altogether.[31]

Despite radically different environmental ideologies, both Bill Clinton and George W. Bush have continued to support the decentralization of regulatory authority to the states. During his presidency, Bill Clinton proved much more supportive of the environment than his predecessors had, but he still managed to disappoint environmentalists. Nonetheless, Clinton is given considerable credit for, among other things, his environmental appointments, reversing many of the Reagan and Bush executive orders that had been challenged by environmentalists and his support and leadership for restoration of the Everglades, various land legacy initiatives, sustainable development, and spending increases for environmental protection and alternative energy use.[32] Regarding the states, Clinton's major initiative during his two terms in office was the creation of the National Environmental Performance Partnership System (NEPPS) in 1995. NEPPS was part of the Clinton administration's effort to reinvent government and sought to give state governments more flexibility in carrying out federal policies as they demonstrated their ability to administer polices in an innovative manner. The program included "partnership grants" that allowed states to focus resources on innovate programs. Although over forty states chose to participate in NEPPS, little innovation resulted because officials at EPA proved reluctant to allow states the flexibility they needed. For their part, the states proved less innovative than anticipated.[33]

While the administration of George W. Bush has been much less supportive of the environment, administrative officials have supported an enhanced state role in environmental policy. Evidence of that is found in (1) the president's appointment of two governors—Whitman of New Jersey and, in 2003, Leavitt of Utah—to head the EPA, and (2) his support for plans that would shift more authority for environmental regulation to the states. While there were few formal initiatives to decentralize environmental management, the Bush administration's preoccupation with the war in Iraq, attempts to roll back federal standards, and reluctance to address global climate change have created a vacuum that many states have been willing to fill.

The second development that has contributed to the states' enhanced environmental role is the transformation of their institutional capabilities in recent decades. On the demand side of state government, a variety of reforms including reapportionment, civil rights policy, the use of initiatives and referendums, the resurgence of the states' political parties, and greater diversity of interest groups has accelerated the rate at which women and minorities serve in government, increased the rate of citizen participation, and, on balance, strengthened statehouse democracy. On the supply side of government, legislatures are more diverse, professionalized, and assertive; governors now have more power and are more willing to lead; and state courts have structurally reformed themselves and often play a more active role in governing their states. The net result is that state governments are generally more capable of producing coherent, effective policies than they were a half-century ago. Over the last several decades, the resurgent states have frequently become the policy laboratories where the nation develops and tests new policy ideas.[34]

Of course not all the news from the states is good. In the first place, states vary considerably in terms of institutional reform. Not all state legislatures are professional, and not every state has reformed its courts.[35] Moreover, many of the reforms can have negative consequences as well. Some worry that the mix of more assertive legislatures, stronger governors, more active interest groups, and increased electoral competition has produced conflict, stalemate, and policy incoherence.[36] One veteran observer of state politics, Alan Rosenthal, has warned of a "deinstitutionalization" of state legislatures as the result of a dramatic decline in the institutional loyalty of members and a tendency for legislatures to become captured by organized interests.[37]

A third set of reasons for the states' growing role reflects changes in the states' environmental politics. First, scholars have noted an increase in "civic environmentalism" at the state level occasioned by broad public support for environmental protection and grassroots policy development independent of federal initiatives. Second, over the past decades networks of environmental professionals have emerged that bring together experts from state agencies, environmental groups, and industry. Increasingly those networks play an influential role in setting the environmental agenda and identifying innovative policy solutions. Third, some groups and policy actors are taking advantage of the opportunities for "direct democracy" in the thirty states that allow citizens to use the initiative and referendum to pass legislation at the ballot box. In recent years, voters have approved ballot measures concerning nuclear plants, the mix of fuels used to produce electricity, and the acquisition of public land.[38]

The States' Response to a New Environmental Federalism

As we have seen, state governments have enjoyed a dramatic resurgence in recent decades. Today, statehouse democracy is stronger than ever, and the states have often taken the lead in fashioning innovative solutions to the nation's most pressing problems. Some analysts have gone so far as to hail the states as the "new heroes" of American federalism. Nowhere is that more evident than in the area of environmental policy. On balance, most scholars would agree that the states are doing a good job in protecting the environment. State environmental agencies have been modernized, and the states continue to seek solutions to environmental problems. But there are limits to the states' capacity to manage the environment, most notably the often-substantial variation in state performance. We discuss each of those points below.

One important way the states have signaled a commitment to the environment is by creating agencies whose sole mission is environmental protection. Originally, responsibility for environmental policy was placed in state health departments, and environmental protection competed with other health programs for agency dollars and attention. Today many states rely on a single state agency to coordinate environmental programs. As one observer notes, "These agencies have sweeping, cross-programmatic responsibilities under a single organizational umbrella."[39]

Some states have also taken the lead in enacting innovative ways to protect the environment. Several states have attempted to streamline the regulatory process. Permitting is one area where states have worked to reduce the amount of paperwork and delay for regulated firms. States typically issue permits to control the amount and nature of pollution allowed within an industry or firm. All too often, companies find themselves mired in a bureaucratic maze where they are required to obtain multiple permits from several different agencies covering multiple environmental standards and mediums. One solution is to integrate the issuance of permits within a single agency or division through "one-stop" permitting systems. One of the more successful efforts at reforming the permitting process took place in New Jersey, where environmental officials worked with several manufacturing firms to integrate the inspection and permitting process so that firms would end up with a single comprehensive permit that regulated several areas of compliance. Some states are also relying on economic incentives, including emission fees and tax breaks to reduce pollution.[40] The most recent round of state innovation concerns global climate change. Despite considerable agreement within the scientific community that carbon dioxide emissions and other "greenhouse" gases are the principal cause of global warming, policy makers at the national level have proven unable to enact policies that address in any serious way what may be the most pressing environmental challenge facing the planet.

Instead, a number of states have taken action to deal with the problem, either on their own or as part of a regional compact. In 2005, for example, seven Northeastern governors signed an agreement that aimed at reducing carbon dioxide emissions from power plants within the region. The governors also agreed to allow companies to trade emission allowances. According to the Pew Center on Climate Change, over half the American states provide incentives for alternative fuels and alternative fuel or low-emission vehicles. Twenty-two states and the District of Columbia require that electric utilities generate at least some of their electricity from renewable sources.[41] In 2006 the state of California passed the nation's first law to set limits on greenhouse gas emissions. Under the California legislation, carbon dioxide emissions must be cut by 25 percent by the year 2020.

Over the last several decades, various organizations have attempted to assess the states' record on environmental protection. The Resource Renewal Institute provided the most recent assessment in 2001.[42] Drawing upon a variety of sources, Institute analysts created a 100-point index of state efforts on behalf of the environment. In creating the "Green Plan Capacity" index, state efforts were assessed in four critical areas—environmental management, environmental policy innovation, fiscal and program commitment, and governance. We have summarized the Institute's results in Table 12.3. On balance the evidence indicates that the states are doing pretty well in protecting their environments. Over 3 states in 4 are implementing most of the federal programs they have been entrusted with; half had either adopted or were drafting a program to address global warming; and several states, including Oregon, New Jersey, Minnesota, Maine, Washington, Massachusetts, Vermont, Connecticut, Illinois, and Florida, are given high marks for their efforts to fund innovative environmental programs.

Unfortunately, the evidence in Table 12.3 and elsewhere also points to a major limitation of a new environmental federalism—the often sizable variations in state environmental efforts. As the data in Table 12.3 indicates, for example, eleven states—including Arizona, California, New Jersey, and Pennsylvania—had still not been delegated authority for at least 50 percent of delegable programs under federal air, water, solid, and hazardous waste legislation by 2000.[43] That uneven performance is seen in several other instances. An increasing number of states have passed legislation that prohibits state agencies from exceeding federal air and water standards and thus restricting efforts to limit greenhouse gas emissions. States have also been slow or negligent in implementing many federal standards. Only one state, for example, had issued the permits necessary for compliance with Title V of the Clean Air Act amendments enacted in 1990. One EPA study found that several states had failed to report major environmental violations, ignored permit deadlines, and failed to conduct required emission tests.[44]

States' institutional capabilities to protect the environment vary as well. In 1988, in 1990, and again in 1992, the Council of State Governments studied the fifty states' institutions for environmental management, their expenditures for environmental and natural resource programs, and the numbers of state government employees with environmental or natural resource responsibilities.[45] The data suggested some potential problems in the states' abilities to manage the environment effectively, no matter how progressive or innovative they may be.

T A B L E 12.3 The States' Green Planning Capacity: 2001, Selected Indicators

Rank	State	Overall GPC Score[a]	Federal Delegation %[b]	Innovation Rating[c]	Global Climate Plan[d]
1	Oregon	73	79%	4	Y
2	New Jersey	71	29	4	Y
3	Minnesota	64	68	4	D
4	Maine	59	64	4	D
5	Washington	57	64	4	Y
6	Massachusetts	57	54	4	D
7	Vermont	55	71	4	Y
8	Connecticut	45	79	3	N
9	Illinois	45	79	4	Y
10	Florida	43	64	3	N
11	Maryland	43	54	2	N
12	California	42	50	4	Y
13	Georgia	42	62	3	N
14	Pennsylvania	42	46	4	Y
15	Indiana	41	71	3	N
16	Delaware	40	68	3	Y
17	Texas	40	61	3	N
18	New York	39	61	4	D
19	Utah	39	96	1	Y
20	North Carolina	38	79	1	Y
21	Wisconsin	37	57	3	Y
22	South Carolina	37	79	3	N
23	Kentucky	36	39	2	Y
24	Missouri	36	86	2	D
25	Michigan	36	68	3	N
26	Iowa	34	39	3	Y
27	Idaho	31	57	2	N
28	New Hampshire	31	50	2	D
29	Montana	30	50	2	Y
30	Virginia	29	46	1	N
31	Arizona	29	50	3	N
32	Rhode Island	28	61	2	N
33	Tennessee	28	64	2	Y
34	Hawaii	28	25	1	Y

(Continued)

TABLE 12.3 Continued

Rank	State	GPC Score[a]	Overall Federal Delegation %[b]	Innovation Rating[c]	Global Climate Plan[d]
35	Ohio	26	79	2	N
36	Colorado	25	71	3	Y
37	Kansas	24	64	1	N
38	Mississippi	23	68	4	N
39	South Dakota	22	82	2	N
40	Louisiana	22	75	1	N
41	Nebraska	20	75	1	N
42	Nevada	18	61	2	N
43	Alaska	17	50	2	N
44	West Virginia	17	75	1	N
45	North Dakota	17	75	1	N
46	Oklahoma	15	82	1	N
47	Arkansas	15	71	1	N
48	New Mexico	11	68	2	D
49	Wyoming	10	71	1	N
50	Alabama	8	79	1	Y

[a]Index can range from 0 to 100, where higher values indicate greater state green capacity.

[b]Percentage of delegable federal programs delegated to the state

[c]Summary rating of state innovativeness: 4 = high level of innovation, 3 = above average level, 2 = below average, 1 = low level of innovation

[d]Whether state has or is drafting a global climate plan: Y = yes, D = draft, N = no

SOURCE: Compiled from Table 1, "Overview of Research Results—Selected Indicators, GPC Index," in *The State of the States to Achieve Sustainable Development Through Green Planning.* Copyright © 2001 by Resource Renewal Institute. All rights reserved. Reprinted with permission of Resource Renewal Institute.

Some environmental problems, such as toxic waste, cannot be effectively managed without enormous sums of money and highly trained staff. Yet these data, and interviews with environmental personnel at both federal and state levels, suggest that the states suffered from inadequate fiscal resources, inadequate numbers of staff, inexperienced staff, staff turnover, and other problems that affect these states' abilities to implement federal directives.[46]

THE FUTURE OF ENVIRONMENTAL POLITICS AND POLICY

Although attempting to predict the future is always risky, it is nevertheless useful to focus on the variation in state capabilities in an effort to predict state environmental management in the near-term future. This is especially appropriate due to the current decentralization of federal environmental programs under the new federalism. If one assumes that the trend toward decentralization of environmental programs will continue in the new century, then it seems safe to predict that environmental management will be governed by two fundamental considerations that are *internal* to the states themselves. The first consideration concerns the question of *state government capability,* and the second consideration concerns the question of *state commitment to environmental protection.* Based on those considerations, James Lester developed a typology of the states in the mid-1990s that suggests four possible responses to the new environmental federalism in the 21st century.[47]

The Progressives

The first group of states is composed of those with a high commitment to environmental protection, coupled with strong institutional capabilities. These include California, Florida, Maryland, Massachusetts, Michigan, New Jersey, New York, Oregon, Washington, and Wisconsin. In these states, substantial improvements in the quality of the environment and in the implementation of federal environmental legislation are expected. As these states move ahead with regard to environmental quality, they may adopt policies that are independent of federal mandates. Environmental conditions will likely get better, not worse.

California, for example, considers the natural environment an important issue. For almost four decades, "air pollution bills have been winning approval in Sacramento, well ahead of the national government."[48] For states such as California, the major issue will be the extent to which the private and public sectors can reach a consensus on the strong environmental policies that these states will likely pursue. Significant tensions may arise in the course of these deliberations.

The Strugglers

A second category of states includes those with a strong commitment to environmental protection, but with limited institutional capacities. These states are Colorado, Connecticut, Delaware, Hawaii, Idaho, Iowa, Maine, Minnesota, Montana, Nevada, New Hampshire, North Carolina, North Dakota, Rhode Island, and Vermont. These states are willing, but often structurally unable, to implement federal environmental programs effectively. They have the will, but not the resources (fiscally and institutionally) to pursue aggressive environmental protection policies. Progress probably will be made in these states, but it will be slower and possibly less innovative than in the progressive states. The "strugglers" will do the best they can within the constraints imposed on them. The major issues in these states will revolve around finding the means to implement aggressive environmental protection policies. Much of the debate will focus on issues associated with tax increases as these states seek to increase their resource base for environmental protection.

Vermont, for example, is staunchly protective of its environmental assets but historically has been described as a "low service, high unemployment, communal" state.[49] That is, it has kept the costs of government low and has preferred a decentralized, "town-meeting" approach to its problems as opposed to the development of strong, state-level institutions that are necessary for effective environmental policy.

The Delayers

The third group of states is composed of those with a strong institutional capacity but a limited commitment to environmental protection. These include Alabama, Alaska, Arkansas, Georgia, Illinois, Louisiana, Missouri, Ohio, Oklahoma, Pennsylvania, South Carolina, Tennessee, Texas, Virginia, and West Virginia. They will probably maintain the status quo with respect to the environment and move very slowly in implementing federal legislation. Whatever progress is made will be painstakingly slow.[50]

States that are dominated by the energy industry, such as Louisiana, Oklahoma, Texas, and West Virginia, are in this group. West Virginia, for example, has been characterized as "still struggling," which means that it has few if any areas of exceptional program management, save for welfare policy.[51] It is a state that depends heavily on the federal government for intergovernmental aid, and one that has not been able to build up its political institutions in a way that would sustain innovative environmental policies.[52] The major issue in the delaying states will be apathetic state bureaucracies that seem unwilling to respond effectively to state environmental crises.

The Regressives

States with weak institutional capacities as well as a limited commitment to environmental protection include Arizona, Indiana, Kansas, Kentucky, Mississippi, Nebraska, New Mexico, South Dakota, Utah, and Wyoming. For these states, decentralization of environmental programs will likely be a disaster. They may fail to implement federal laws in this area, and they are unlikely to take independent actions. The quality of life may deteriorate so much that large numbers of the population may move to other states (especially to the more progressive ones). Dirty industries may continue to move into these regressive states, making them even more unattractive to the inhabitants. These states will continue to promote economic development at the expense of environmental quality. At some point a catastrophe may turn the states in this category around, but at present they seem to be captured by an obsessive optimism that prevents their taking necessary precautions against further damage to the environment.

Mississippi, for example, has been described by Neal Pierce and Jerry Hagstrom as a state in which the federal cutbacks in the early 1980s made the "road ahead bleaker than anytime since the Great Depression."[53] All too often, Mississippi is singled out as the state that lags behind all the other Southern states in the area of environmental protection. The "Mississippi syndrome," as it is called, describes the situation when a state cannot, or will not, move ahead in implementing its programs to protect the environment.

SUMMARY

In this brief review of environmental policy under the doctrine of new federalism, we have described changes in federal–state relations and reforms of state institutions. We also have examined environmental policy innovations in the states, including their commitment to and capacity for environmental policy-making. Implementation in the states is discussed, and we have suggested four possible classifications of the states in the new century: progressives, strugglers, delayers, and regressives. These scenarios range from extremely optimistic (the progressives) to extremely pessimistic (the regressives) regarding how effectively states will address environmental problems. The scenarios assume no major changes in state commitments or institutional capabilities; but public opinion, recent tendencies toward participatory democracy, and attention by the media could cause some legislators to adopt very different strategies if conditions become intolerable.

The policy implications of this discussion are significant. If it is found that federal-level factors are crucial influences on state environmental management, then the argument for centralization of environmental management would once again acquire enhanced credibility. That is, if federal inducements (i.e., federal legislation and intergovernmental aid) are necessary conditions for successful state environmental management, then a policy of decentralization probably will not work effectively for all states. On the other hand, if state-level conditions strongly influence state environmental management, then arguments about decentralization of environmental management would acquire even more credibility. Decentralization may work well in some states (e.g., the innovative states), but poorly in others (e.g., the regressive states). Thus, "selective decentralization," a policy in which some programs are decentralized for some states and other programs for other states are not, may be a more appropriate strategy.[54]

In any case, policy makers need to reconsider intergovernmental relations as they affect state environmental management. The federal government may or may not be the most appropriate governmental institution to tackle environmental pollution, but the fifty states are not equally able to muster the necessary resources to deal with environmental problems. Novel approaches will thus be required and are particularly appropriate in the era of "regulatory federalism" that will likely characterize the new century.

DISCUSSION QUESTIONS

1. Given the evolution of environmental politics and policy over the past 100 years or so, where do you think we are going in the future? In other words, what does the environmental future look like?

2. Given the "devolution revolution" that has occurred in recent decades, are the states and cities up to the tasks before them as far as responsible management of the environment is concerned? Are state and local governments

the appropriate levels of governments for environmental issues that are both global and national?

3. Why are some states so much more effective than others when it comes to protection of the environment?

4. Given the variation among the states in terms of environmental management, what role should the national government play vis-à-vis the states?

5. Do you think that decentralization of environmental management (a shift in power and authority to the states and cities) is a good idea? Why or why not?

SUGGESTED READINGS

Lester, James P., ed. *Environmental Politics and Policy: Theories and Evidence,* Second Edition (Durham, NC: Duke University Press, 1995).

Rosenbaum, Walter A. *Environmental Politics and Policy*, Seventh Edition (Washington, D.C.: Congressional Quarterly Press, 2007).

Vig, Norman, and Michael E. Kraft, eds. *Environmental Policy: New Directions for the Twenty-First Century,* Sixth Edition (Washington, D.C.: Congressional Quarterly Press, 2006).

NOTES

1. Not all scholars are in agreement as to the exact dates of these movements, but these dates are generally acceptable as benchmarks for each movement. See Samuel P. Hays, *Conservation and the Gospel of Efficiency* (Cambridge, MA: Harvard University Press, 1959); Alan Schnaiberg, "The Environmental Movement: Roots and Transformations," in *The Environment: From Surplus to Scarcity*, ed. Alan Schnaiberg (New York: Oxford University Press, 1980); and Henry P. Caulfield, "The Conservation and Environmental Movements: An Historical Analysis," in *Environmental Politics and Policy: Theories and Evidence*, 2d ed., James P. Lester, ed. (Durham, NC: Duke University Press, 1989).

2. Ernest A. Engelbert, "Political Parties and Natural Resources Policies: An Historical Evaluation," *Natural Resources Journal* 1 (November 1961), p. 226.

3. Ibid., p. 233.

4. Ibid., p. 227.

5. Hays, *Conservation,* p. 2.

6. Ibid., p. 5.

7. Ibid., p. 28.

8. Caulfield, "The Conservation and Environmental Movements," p. 16.

9. Ibid., pp. 20–21.

10. Engelbert, "Political Parties," p. 245.

11. Hays, *Conservation,* p. 47.

12. Ibid., pp. 28–46.

13. Ibid., p. 53.

14. Ibid., p. 271.

15. Ibid.

16. Ibid.

17. Engelbert, "Political Parties," p. 380.

18. Schnaiberg, "Environmental Movement," p. 386.

19. Ibid.

20. Engelbert, "Political Parties," p. 240.

21. Ibid., p. 244.

22. Hays, *Conservation,* p. 13.

23. Schnaiberg, "Environmental Movement," p. 382.

24. Ibid., p. 383.

25. Phillip O. Foss, *The Politics of Grass* (Seattle: University of Washington Press, 1960).

26. Paul A. Sabatier and Hank Jenkins-Smith, "A Symposium of Public Policy Change and Policy-Oriented Learning," *Policy Sciences* 21 (1988), pp. 123–278.

27. John Carroll, ed., *Environmental Diplomacy: The Management and Resolution of Transfrontier Environmental Problems* (Cambridge, UK: Cambridge University Press, 1988); and Norman Vig and Michael Kraft, *Environmental Policy in the 1990s* (Washington, D.C.: Congressional Quarterly Press, 1990), p. 4.

28. Robert C. Mitchell, "Public Opinion and the Green Lobby: Poised for the 1990s," in Vig and Kraft, *Environmental Policy,* pp. 81–99; and Riley Dunlap, "Public Opinion and Environmental Policy," in Lester, ed., *Environmental Politics and Policy,* pp. 87–134.

29. James P. Lester, "Federalism and State Environmental Policy," *Publius* 16 (Winter 1986); Charles E. Davis and James P. Lester, "Decentralizing Federal Environmental Policy: A Research Note," *Western Political Quarterly* 40 (September 1987); James P. Lester and Emmett N. Lombard, "The Comparative Analysis of State Environmental Policy," *Natural Resources Journal* 30, no. 2 (Spring 1990), pp. 301–319; and David Hedge and Michael Scicchitano, "Devolving Regulatory Authority: The State and Federal Response," *Policy Studies Review* (Summer 1992).

30. Barry Rabe, "Power to the States: The Promise and Pitfalls of Decentralization," in Vig and Kraft, eds., *Environmental Policy: New Directions for the Twenty-First Century* (Washington, D.C.: CQ Press, 2006), pp. 34–56.

31. J. Clarence Davies, "Environmental Institutions and the Reagan Administration," in *Environmental Policy in the 1980s: Reagan's New Agenda,* ed. Norman J. Vig and Michael E. Kraft (Washington, D.C.: Congressional Quarterly Press, 1984), p. 150.

32. Michael E. Kraft and Norman J. Vig, "Environmental Policy from the 1970s to the Twenty-First Century," in Vig and Kraft, eds., *Environmental Policy,* pp. 1–34.

33. Rabe, "Power to the States."

34. See Advisory Commission on Intergovernmental Relations, State Government Capability; and Advisory Commission on Intergovernmental Relations, *The Transformation in American Politics* (Washington, D.C.: U.S. Government Printing Office, 1986); Ann O'M. Bowman and Richard C. Kearney, *The Resurgence of the States*

(Englewood Cliffs, NJ: Prentice Hall, 1986); and more recently David M. Hedge, *Governance and the Changing American States* (Boulder, CO: Westview Press, 1998).

35. See Ann O'M. Bowman and Richard C. Kearney, "Dimensions of State Government Capability," *Western Political Quarterly* 41 (June 1988), pp. 341–362.

36. Hedge, *Governance and the Changing American States*.

37. Allan Rosenthal, "The Legislature: Unraveling of Institutional Fabric," in Carl E. Van Horn, ed., *The State of the States*, 3d ed. (Washington, D.C.: CQ Press, 1996).

38. Rabe, "Power to the States."

39. Ibid., p. 36

40. Ibid., pp. 39–41.

41. Pew Center on Climate Change, "Climate Change 101: State Action," at www.pewclimate.org/docUploads/101%5FStates%2Epdf accessed March 10, 2007.

42. Resource Renewal Institute report, "The State of the States: Assessing the Capacity of States to Achieve Sustainable Development Through Green Planning," (San Francisco: Resource Renewal Institute, 2001).

43. Resource Renewal Institute, "The State of the States," pp. 16–18.

44. Rabe, "Power to the States."

45. R. Steven Brown and Edward Garner, *Resource Guide to State Environmental Management* (Lexington, KY: Council of State Governments, 1988), pp. 2–96.

46. Interviews with staff at the U.S. Environmental Protection Agency, Office of Solid Waste, State Programs Branch, July 1987.

47. See Lester, "Federalism and State Environmental Policy."

48. Neal Pierce and Jerry Hagstrom, *The Book of America: Inside the Fifty States Today* (New York: Warner Books, 1984), p. 766.

49. Ibid., p. 199.

50. Donald G. Schueler, "Southern Exposure," *Sierra* 77 (November–December 1992), pp. 44–49.

51. Pierce and Hagstrom, *Book of America,* p. 345.

52. Ibid., pp. 338–347.

53. Ibid., p. 456.

54. Paul E. Peterson, Barry Rabe, and Kenneth K. Wong, *When Federalism Works* (Washington, D.C.: Brookings Institution, 1986).

PART IV

Conclusions

Utilizing Policy Analysis

"In principle, everyone is for analysis; in practice, there is no certainty
that it will be incorporated into the real-world decision process."
JAMES SCHLESINGER

A newcomer to the analysis of public policy might assume that once a policy analysis has been carried out and the findings have been reported to the decision makers, the analysis will be used in designing new policies or in changing old ones. However, in most cases nothing at all seems to happen after the analysis is delivered to those who commissioned the study in the first place. One might then assume that the policy analysis was not utilized by the decision maker because it was flawed. In fact, the quality of the methodology used in the policy analysis has very little to do with the actual use of that analysis. Many other factors influence the utilization of policy analysis, most of them beyond the analyst's control.

This chapter discusses the factors influencing utilization of policy analysis by the consumers of that analysis, usually governmental decision makers. Understanding why analysis is not used, as well as the factors that influence utilization, can perhaps help to increase the use of policy analysis in the future.

USING POLICY ANALYSIS

The study of the utilization of policy analysis is "concerned with understanding and improving the utilization of scientific and professional knowledge in settings of public policy and professional practice."[1] It has benefited from periodic reviews of research, and some of this research has examined the effects of factors that influence the utilization of research by decision makers.[2] Because much of contemporary public policy research is directed toward discovering ways to improve policy outcomes in substantive issue areas such as those covered in this book, it is important to understand the knowledge utilization process. This includes developing both an understanding of the degree to which research findings are utilized by policy makers and the circumstances under which use typically occurs.

As we noted in Chapter 1, there has been a tremendous growth in policy analysis over the previous three decades, yet early utilization research suggests that governmental decision makers make little direct use of this research.[3] Recent studies are somewhat more optimistic about the utilization of policy analyses by decision makers.[4]

Research findings are inconsistent for a number of reasons, many of them stemming from conceptual and methodological problems identified by Downs and Mohr and others.[5] Moreover, knowledge utilization research is still in its infancy, and a well-defined framework does not yet exist that attempts to explain the full range of conditions under which policy analysis is useful. In this chapter, we synthesize and critique research on knowledge utilization as well as present a conceptual framework for future testing at the level of federal, state, or local government policymaking. We define what is meant by the utilization of policy analysis and discuss recent efforts at synthesizing this research. Second, we review the major obstacles to and predictors of knowledge utilization. Finally, we offer some summary observations and discuss the implications of the framework for knowledge utilization by decision makers and others.

DEFINING KNOWLEDGE UTILIZATION: PREVIOUS RESEARCH

Most of the literature examining knowledge utilization by political decision makers has been concerned with answering the question, "What are the characteristics of social science research studies that make them most 'useful' for decision making?" According to Weiss and Bucavalas, "useful" involves (1) whether or not the content makes an intrinsic contribution to the work of an agency; and (2) whether or not officials say they would be likely to take that research into account in decision making.[6] Among the several meanings of *utilization* employed by researchers, Weiss identifies the knowledge-driven model, the problem-solving model, and the enlightenment model.[7] Bulmer identifies the empiricist model, the engineering model, and the enlightenment model.[8] In the empiricist model, the researcher's task is to produce facts that, when fed into the policy process, will enable policy makers to reach the best decisions based on the information available. This model posits a one-way, linear relationship between the researcher and the policy maker. That is, the researcher produces policy-relevant information, and the decision makers use it in reaching their decisions. The engineering model sees the social scientist as a technician who provides the evidence and conclusions to help solve a concrete problem. Therefore, the task of the basic researcher is to develop and test a logical list of hypotheses explaining use and to communicate their findings directly to policy makers. The enlightenment model also seeks specific answers to policy problems, but its emphasis is on creating the intellectual conditions for problem solving.[9]

To a large extent, the research utilization literature has adopted the two-communities theory, which suggests that direct use of policy research by decision makers is unlikely because of the competing worldviews and belief systems of policy researchers and policy makers.[10] The usual recommendation for increasing the use of policy research by policy makers is that both communities should undertake changes so that the two groups are more likely to communicate and interact. Specifically, (1) users of knowledge must become better consumers of knowledge by being more open to research and looking for applications to policy problems; and (2) researchers must become more assertive and/or more sensitive in their dissemination of knowledge. Recently, for example, Bolton and Stolcis argued that the gap between practioners and scholars could be reduced by increasing agency involvement in schools of public administration, expanding practitioner experiences for academics, and improving the accessibility of scholarly information for those in government.[11]

Although it is recognized that both producers and users of policy analysis must become more sensitive to the concerns of each other, it is useful at this point to understand the criticisms directed at this area of policy analysis. Some of those criticisms are described below.

Some Criticisms of Previous Research

Empirical research on knowledge utilization has been the subject of much criticism by the research community. At least three main criticisms are directed toward the literature. First, previous research on knowledge utilization has relied on survey questionnaires or case studies with unknown or unreported reliability and validity.[12] One cannot be sure that the information reported on the surveys by decision makers accurately reflects the reasons for nonuse of policy analysis. Second, knowledge use has not been adequately defined. There is still no mutually agreed-upon definition of knowledge use. Finally, empirical support for claims that particular classes of factors affect the utilization of knowledge in decisive ways has not been consistent.[13] Much more research will be needed to confirm that specific sets of variables are crucial to knowledge use by decision makers.

This latter criticism stems from the fact that researchers do not agree about the set of variables existing in the literature to predict knowledge use by decision makers.[14] In many cases, these models are merely a "checklist" of variables presumed to influence knowledge utilization, rather than a formal heuristic device. Moreover, there has been little rigorous research on the ability of these models to predict knowledge use.[15] Finally, these models have been developed largely in response to the two-communities perspective on knowledge utilization, in which attention is directed toward bridging the gap between knowledge producers and knowledge consumers. Thus, these models attempt to identify variables that can be manipulated by either of these two sets of actors in such a way that knowledge transfer is facilitated.

However, most of the previous models fail to take into account the context or external political environment that affects both producers and consumers of knowledge. That is, modifications in both the policy-maker community and the researcher community still leave use open to impact by a number of variables. As a consequence, a large portion of the explanation for knowledge use by decision makers may have gone unexamined. Researchers too often ignore the comparative importance of competing sets of explanatory factors by focusing primarily on two sets of variables that relate either to the analysis itself or to the users of that analysis. Research over the past several years suggests that additional explanations can be found in some of the obstacles to knowledge use among policy makers and others. We discuss those obstacles below.

OBSTACLES TO KNOWLEDGE USE

The research on knowledge utilization suggests a number of empirical variables that are helpful in developing a more comprehensive framework for examining the determinants of utilization of policy analysis by decision makers. More particularly, that research identifies a series of obstacles to the more complete use of policy analyses in making public policy. Those obstacles can be categorized into three groups of factors: (1) **contextual factors,** or factors having to do with the political environment within which the policy analysis takes place; (2) **technical factors,** or factors having to do with the methodology employed in the policy analysis; and (3) **human factors,** or factors having to do with the psychological makeup of the users of the policy analysis.

Contextual Factors

Some scholars have suggested that the research utilization literature needs to include the political context into which analytic projects enter as a key set of variables that affect utilization.[16] An examination of the context in which policy research use takes place permits a more complete appreciation of the causes of research utilization.[17] One characteristic of the political context is the nature of the problem itself. For example, what exactly are the intended effects of a policy? Rossi and Wright suggest that "the intended effects of a social policy are often so vaguely stated that almost any evaluation of it may be regarded as irrelevant because it missed the problem toward which the policy was directed."[18] Thus, the goals of the policy to be analyzed must be clearly stated so that an effective evaluation of its intended effects can be carried out.

Second, policymaking often involves the weighing of competing claims on communal resources. Achieving a balance among various claims may be more important to policy makers than enacting an effective social policy. Thus, the "political feasibility" of different courses of action is a constraint on utilization of policy analysis.[19] Furthermore, to be useful in policymaking, research has to occur in a timely manner. Research is more likely to be used, for example, when an immediate decision is needed to resolve a specific problem, and technical advice is provided early in the process.[20]

In addition, the amount of group conflict generated by the policy problem and the issue salience of the problem are factors that affect use. More specifically, greater use follows greater conflict and greater salience.[21] Lehne and Fisk point out several other factors that tend to influence utilization, including whether the issue under analysis is a single-agency issue, whether a funding change is proposed, and whether an immediate decision is needed.[22] Others propose that centralized decision making is crucial to use.[23]

Technical Factors

Scholars have often argued that a major constraint on the application of social research to policymaking is methodological in character. For example, Meltzner highlights the problems associated with designing research capable of answering the questions posed by policy makers.[24] Indeed, "serious difficulties exist in the design and implementation of each evaluation research study."[25] One of the earliest studies of the impact of policy analysis on decision making identified several technical variables affecting use. These variables included study size (small, medium, large), study timing (good to poor), and methodological adequacy (superior to poor).[26] These authors discovered that one of the strongest factors influencing use was whether there was good timing in performing the analysis, as well as a narrow focus.[27]

Moreover, policy research often produces findings that are ambiguous or equivocal and, hence, of little apparent use to policy makers.[28] Thus, the more unequivocal the results, the greater the use. Finally, another factor influencing utilization of the findings is credibility   of the analysis itself and of the analyst's organization.[29]

Human Factors

A number of other scholars have found knowledge utilization to be related to some of the personal characteristics of the users. For example, utilization has been found to be related to the cognitive skills of users, their ability to understand the findings, and their socioeconomic background.[30] Moreover, others have identified various personal motivations in decision makers (such as interest, enthusiasm, commitment, caring, ideology, or determination) as being crucial to successful utilization.[31]

One of the most salient variables believed to influence policy makers' use of policy analysis is the decision-making style adopted by the decision maker. Webber identifies three styles of decision makers: the arbitrators, the messengers, and the evaluators. He concludes that arbitrators and messengers may be enlightened by policy research, but it is only the evaluators who will actively send for it.[32] Still others suggest that interest and participation by the decision maker in the policy analysis are crucial factors affecting use, as well as the policy maker's worldview and the resultant commitment to specific solutions to policy problems. Finally, Rein and White suggest that use depends on a clear definition of objectives by policy makers.[33]

An understanding of the obstacles to knowledge use provides a wider understanding of the range of factors that presumably affect use and permits development of a more comprehensive model of knowledge utilization. That model may help to predict better the conditions under which policy analysis will or will not be used.

KNOWLEDGE UTILIZATION: A CONCEPTUAL FRAMEWORK

Knowledge utilization is a function of (1) inducements and constraints provided to or imposed on the user from the **context** within which analysis takes place; (2) the **analysis** itself; and (3) the decision makers' own **predispositions** toward policy analysis (see Figure 13.1).[34] A model of knowledge utilization must also recognize the interdependence of each of these three categories of factors. Figure 13.1 illustrates the model of knowledge utilization used in this discussion. In examining the components of the model in Figure 13.1, one needs to distinguish between conceptual and instrumental uses of knowledge. Generally,

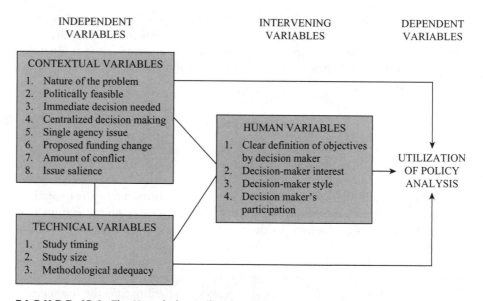

FIGURE 13.1 The Knowledge Utilization Process.

SOURCE: James P Lester and Leah J. Wilds, "The Utilization of Public Policy Analysis," *Evaluation and Program Planning* 13(3), p. 316. Copyright © 1990. Elsevier Science Ltd. Reprinted with permission of Elsevier Science Ltd.

T A B L E 13.1   Seven Standards of Utilization

1. *Reception*
   Utilization takes place when policymakers or advisors receive policy-relevant information. When the communication comes to rest in the "in-basket," so that the data "reach" the policymaker rather than remain on an analyst's desk or in the files of a distant consultant firm, utilization is complete.

2. *Cognition*
   The policymaker must read, digest, and understand the studies. When he has done so, utilization has occurred.

3. *Reference*
   If frame of reference is the criterion, then utilization somehow must change the way the policymaker sees the world. If information changes his preferences, or his understanding of the probabilities or magnitudes of impacts he fears or desires, utilization is a reality.

4. *Effort*
   To make a real difference, information must influence the actions of policymakers. If they fight for adoption of a study's recommendations, we know a real effort was made even if political forces or other events block it.

5. *Adoption*
   What is essential is not whether policy-relevant information is an input to the policy process...but whether it goes on to influence policy outcomes. Policy results, not inputs, are the proper standard.

6. *Implementation*
   Policy adoption is critical but, if adopted policy never becomes practice, information has no chance to affect action. Adoption without implementation is a hollow victory.

7. *Impact*
   A policy may be implemented but fail to have the desired effects. Hence it may be (and is) argued that only when policy stimulated by information yields tangible benefits to the citizen has utilization taken place.

SOURCE: Jack Knott and Aaron Wildavsky, "If Dissemination Is the Solution, What Is the Problem?" *Knowledge: Creation, Diffusion, Utilization* 1. Copyright © 1980 by Sage Publications, Inc. Reprinted with permission of Sage Publications, Inc.

conceptual use refers to changes in the way the users think about problems, and instrumental use refers to changes in actual behavior, especially changes that are relevant to decision making.[35] A useful approach to understanding knowledge utilization is to "see it as the flow of information to decision-makers in which levels of utilization are conceived as stages in which each is a link in the chain of utilization."[36] Table 13.1 presents such a continuum.

Contextual Inducements and Constraints

The first set of predictor variables is concerned with the policy and political environment within which policy analysis is undertaken. The nature of the problem obviously affects utilization, because some problems are more intractable than are others. Many problem types, such as the effects of low-level radiation on human health, are subject to widely different interpretations by equally reputable scientists.[37] Highly intractable problems that are subject to diverse and conflicting interpretations tend to make utilization of knowledge much more difficult than problems for which there may be more definitive solutions. Second, the political feasibility of any policy alternative (no matter how convincing the argument) will affect the ultimate use of a policy solution. Third, the immediacy of the need for a decision will affect use, because urgency creates a greater demand for analysis. Fourth, centralized decision making lends itself to utilization of policy analysis as well as a proposed funding change. Finally, the amount of conflict involved in the policy issue as well as its salience to decision makers will affect utilization.[38]

Technical Inducements and Constraints

The model also suggests that characteristics of the analysis itself will affect utilization. Specifically, the quality of the policy analysis itself will affect use. For example, such considerations as a study's timing, size, and methodological adequacy will affect usage. These are the only variables under the direct control of the analyst, yet they are only a few of the kinds of variables that might affect use.

User Attitudes as Inducements and Constraints

Finally, the model suggests that characteristics of the recipient of the policy analysis will ultimately affect utilization. For example, if the decision maker has a clear definition of objectives to be pursued by the policy analysts, then the chances of utilization are enhanced. Also, the greater the interest and participation by the decision maker in the subject and scope of the policy analysis, the better the chances of utilization. In addition, a decision maker's style has been shown to be related to knowledge utilization.[39]

The findings cited above suggest a basic applicability of this framework to an explanation of utilization of policy analysis by decision makers. In the remainder of this chapter, we discuss some implications of this framework and an agenda for future work in this area.

SOME SUMMARY OBSERVATIONS AND IMPLICATIONS FOR FUTURE RESEARCH

In this chapter we have reviewed some of the literature on knowledge utilization in an effort to develop a more comprehensive model for explaining such behavior. The model suggests that utilization of policy analyses by decision makers is affected by three categories of variables: (1) contextual inducements and constraints, (2) technical inducements and constraints, and (3) human (user) inducements and constraints.

The most obvious implication of the framework is that variables in addition to those related to the "two communities" need to be considered in future attempts to explain knowledge utilization by decision makers. Previous approaches have been, for the most part, limited to variables related to the producer of knowledge (i.e., the policy analyst or the analysis itself) or the consumer of knowledge (i.e., the decision maker). In doing so, other important conditions, such as the political context within which analysis takes place, may have been neglected as far as understanding the determinants of utilization.

A second major implication of the framework is that most of the variables affecting knowledge utilization are outside the control of the policy analyst. Thus, it is no surprise that much of the early research found knowledge utilization to be limited. Some of the variables (e.g., methodological or technical) can be controlled by the analyst, and manipulation of these variables by the analyst may enhance future use. Indeed, some of the variables identified in the framework can be controlled by the analysts, whereas others cannot.

A number of questions need to be answered about research on the utilization of policy analysis by decision makers. First, policy analysts need to know which category of variables has the most influence on utilization. Are contextual variables more important than technical or human variables? Second, analysts need to discover which variables in the framework are most important in determining utilization. Which individual variables are most important in the framework? Which are unimportant? Are important variables left out of the model? Third, the relationships between and among these variables need to be identified. That is, what are the interactive effects (if any) of these variables on utilization? Finally, as Beyer and Trice suggest, "researchers should employ methods that discriminate between partial and complete use by collecting data on a range of utilizing behaviors; they will then be able to investigate factors associated with greater or less utilization and with different patterns of incomplete utilization."[40] It would be instructive to explore the determinants of use in each of these various stages of knowledge use. Are contextual factors more important in the impact stage or in the implementation stage? Are technical factors more important in the reception stage or in the impact stage? Are human factors more important in the cognition stage or in the implementation stage? These kinds of questions have not yet been answered by research on knowledge use.

In the future, researchers will need to examine the utilization of policy analysis by federal, state, and local government decision makers in several functional areas including agriculture, alcohol and drug abuse, child labor, corrections, economic development, environmental protection, higher education, highway safety, mass transportation, public utility regulation, public welfare, telecommunications, and vocation education. In conducting this research, analysts will need to address three different sets of questions:

1. What are the sources of information for these decision makers? Do the sources vary by type of decision maker?

2. Do these decision makers use policy analyses in reaching policy decisions in these functional areas? If so, is this usage primarily conceptual or instrumental?

Do some types of decision makers (or functional areas) utilize policy analyses more so than others?

3. What are the determinants of knowledge utilization? Do these determinants vary by type of decision maker?

Future research in the utilization of policy analysis will need to answer these questions as well as to further refine the model of knowledge utilization presented here.[41]

DISCUSSION QUESTIONS

1. What do we mean by "knowledge utilization"? Are there various levels of knowledge use by decision makers?
2. Discuss the factors that are believed to affect the use of policy analyses by decision makers.
3. What are some of the criticisms directed toward research on knowledge utilization?
4. What can be done to increase the use of policy analyses by decision makers?
5. Why doesn't policy analysis have a greater effect on decision makers' choices of policy?

SUGGESTED READINGS

Bulmer, Martin. *The Uses of Social Research* (Boston: Allen and Unwin, 1982).

Macnaghten, Phil, Matthew B. Kearnes, and Brian Wynne. "Nanotechnology, Governance, and Public Deliberation: What Role for the Social Sciences?" *Science Communication* 27 (2005), pp. 268–291.

Rothman, J. *Using Research in Organizations* (Beverly Hills, CA: Sage, 1980).

Weiss, Carol. *Using Social Research in Public Policy-Making* (Lexington, MA: Lexington Books, 1977).

NOTES

1. William N. Dunn, Burkhart Holzner, and Gerald Zaltman, "Knowledge Utilization," in *The International Encyclopedia of Education,* ed. T. Husen and T. N. Postlethwaite (Oxford, UK: Pergamon Press, 1985).

2. See, for example, Michael Huberman, "Steps Toward an Integrated Model of Research Utilization," *Knowledge: Creation, Diffusion, Utilization* 8 (1987), pp. 586–611.

3. See, for example, Carol H. Weiss, "Knowledge Creep and Decision Accretion," *Knowledge: Creation, Diffusion, Utilization* 1 (1980), pp. 381–404.

4. David Whiteman, "The Fate of Policy Analysis in Congressional Decision-Making: Three Types of Use in Committees," *Western Political Quarterly* 38 (June 1985), pp. 294–311; David Webber, "Legislators' Use of Policy Information," *American Behavioral Scientist* 30 (July–August 1987), pp. 612–631; Thomas E. Backer, "Knowledge Utilization: The Third Wave," *Knowledge: Creation, Diffusion, Utilization* 12 (1991), pp. 225–240; Nabil Amara, Mathieu Ouimet, and Rejean Landry, "New Evidence on Instrumental, Conceptual and Symbolic Utilization of University Research in Government Agencies," *Science Communication* 26 (2004), pp. 75–106; and John Hird, "Policy Analysis for What? The Effectiveness of Nonpartisan Policy Research Organizations," *Policy Studies Journal* 33 (2005), pp. 83–105.

5. C. W. Downs and L. B. Mohr, "Conceptual Issues in the Study of Innovation," *Administrative Science Quarterly* 21 (December 1976), pp. 700–713; and Paul A. Sabatier, "The Acquisition and Utilization of Technical Information by Administrative Agencies," *Administrative Science Quarterly* 23 (September 1978), pp. 396–417.

6. See Carol H. Weiss and Michael Bucavalas, "The Challenge of Social Research to Decision-Making," in *Using Social Research in Public Policy-Making,* ed. Carol H. Weiss (Lexington, MA: Lexington Books, 1977).

7. Weiss, "Knowledge Creep."

8. Martin Bulmer, *The Uses of Social Research: Social Investigation in Public Policy-Making* (Boston: Allen and Unwin, 1982).

9. Ibid.

10. Nathan Caplan, "The Two-Communities Theory and Knowledge Utilization," *American Behavioral Scientist* 22 (January–February 1979), pp. 459–470.

11. Edward M. Glaser, "Knowledge Transfer and Institutional Change," *Professional Psychology* 4 (November 1973), pp. 434–444. More recently, see Michael J. Bolton and Gregory B. Stolcis, "Ties That Do Not Bind: Musings on the Specious Relevance of Academic Research," *Public Administration Review* 63 (2003), pp. 626–630.

12. Sabatier, "Acquisition and Utilization."

13. Dunn, Holzner, and Zaltman, "Knowledge Utilization."

14. There have been, however, some attempts to develop analytical frameworks of the variables purported to affect the utilization of knowledge by decision makers. See, for example, Sabatier, "Acquisition and Utilization."

15. Jeffrey Bedell et al., "An Empirical Evaluation of a Model of Knowledge Utilization," *Evaluation Review* 9 (April 1985), pp. 109–126.

16. Thomas R. Dye, *Understanding Public Policy,* 7th ed. (Englewood Cliffs, NJ: Prentice Hall, 1991), p. 10.

17. To the contrary, one study found state contextual factors, such as population, mean family income, percent of labor force in agriculture, percent urban, and so on, not to be associated with the use of policy analyses. See Robert D. Lee and R. J. Staffeldt, "Executive and Legislative Use of Policy Analysis in the State Budgetary Process," *Policy Analysis* 3, no. 3 (Summer 1977), pp. 395–406.

18. Peter Rossi and Sonia Wright, "Evaluation Research: An Assessment of Theory, Politics and Practice," *Evaluation Quarterly* 1, no. 1 (February 1977), pp. 5–51.

19. Arnold Meltzner, "Political Feasibility and Policy Analysis," *Public Administration Review* 32, no. 6 (December 1972), pp. 859–867.

20. Edward Suchman, "Action for What: A Critique of Evaluation Research," in *Evaluating Action Programs,* ed. Carol Weiss (Boston: Allyn and Bacon, 1972).

21. D. Whiteman, "The Fate of Policy Analysis in Congressional Decisionmaking," *Western Political Quarterly* 38 (1985), pp. 294–311.

22. Richard Lehne and D. M. Fisk, "The Impact of Urban Policy Analysis," *Urban Affairs Quarterly* 10, no. 2 (December 1974), pp. 115–138.

23. See Jerry Mitchell, "The Utilization of Policy-Relevant Information in State Government" (paper presented at the annual meeting of the Southern Political Science Association, Atlanta, Georgia, 1986); and Martin Rein and Sheldon White, "Can Policy Research Help Policy?" *The Public Interest* 49 (Fall 1977), pp. 119–136.

24. Meltzner, "Political Feasibility."

25. Rossi and Wright, "Evaluation Research."

26. Not all researchers agree that methodological sophistication leads to greater use. On this point see Peter DeLeon, "The Influence of Policy Analysis on U.S. Defense Policy," *Policy Sciences* 20, no. 2 (1987), pp. 105–128.

27. Lehne and Fisk, "Urban Policy Analysis."

28. Rossi and Wright, "Evaluation Research."

29. Barry Bozeman, "The Credibility of Policy Analysis: Between Method and Use," *Policy Studies Review* 14 (June 1986), pp. 51–57.

30. Webber, "Legislators' Use of Policy Information," pp. 612–631.

31. Evelyn Florio and Joseph R. Demartini, "The Use of Information by Policymakers at the Local Community Level," *Knowledge: Creation, Diffusion, Utilization* 15 (1993), pp. 106–123.

32. Webber, "Legislators' Use of Policy Information."

33. Reinand White, "Can Policy Research Help?"

34. See James P. Lester and Leah J. Wilds, "The Utilization of Public Policy Analysis: A Conceptual Framework," *Evaluation and Program Planning* 13, no. 3 (1990), pp. 313–319.

35. Dunn, Holzner, and Zaltman, "Knowledge Utilization."

36. Jack Knott and Aaron Wildavsky, "If Dissemination Is the Solution, What Is the Problem?" *Knowledge: Creation, Diffusion, Utilization* 1 (1980), pp. 537–578.

37. William W. Lowrance, *Of Acceptable Risk* (Los Altos, CA: William Kaufman, 1976).

38. Whiteman, "Fate of Policy Analysis."

39. Webber, "Legislators' Use of Policy Information."

40. Janice M. Beyer and Harrison M. Trice, "The Utilization Process: A Conceptual Framework and Synthesis of Empirical Findings," *Administrative Science Quarterly* 27 (December 1982), pp. 591–622.

41. See James P. Lester, "The Utilization of Policy Analysis by State Agency Officials," *Knowledge: Creation, Diffusion, Utilization* 14 (March 1993), pp. 267–290.

14

Taking Stock: The Evolution of Public Policy in America

"All is ready if our minds be so."
SHAKESPEARE

As the title of this book suggests, public policy in America and how we study public policy in America have changed considerably over both the long and short term. Various chapters have examined both the evolution of research on the policy process and the evolution of public policy in the areas of education, welfare, and the environment. By tracing both the evolutionary development of the study of public policy and the evolutionary development of selected public policies, we hope to convey the amount of intellectual growth and development that has taken place over the past three or four decades. Too often, students fail to understand how earlier conceptual developments pave the way for later ones. Our understanding of the policy process is constantly evolving as policy scholars develop new conceptual tools to increase their knowledge of how policies are made, implemented, evaluated, and changed. Similarly, policy analysts continue to learn more about the substance of policy and try to develop solutions that remedy pressing public policy problems in any number of policy areas. In addition, students need to understand that the analysis of policy problems has provided a better understanding of the policy process. For example, research on environmental policy, welfare reform, and education and politics has added a great deal to the understanding of public policy implementation and change. In this chapter, we briefly summarize the major changes that have occurred in American politics and policy and consider the implications of those changes for future research and governing.

CHANGES IN AMERICAN PUBLIC POLICY

Over the last 200 years, politics and policy in America have changed considerably. While scholars disagree about the nature and course of those changes, it is clear that the scope and content of American public policy has shifted on a regular basis through much of the nation's history. In the past century, politics and policy in America moved from the Progressive era of the early 1900s to the New Deal politics of the 1930s to what some hail as a new conservative era that began with the presidency of Ronald Reagan in 1980. As the nation moves into the 21st century, it will be interesting to see how governments and their citizens address the critical issues we identified in Chapter 2—*Should government act? What values should governments pursue? What actions should government take? Which level of government should govern?* Recent developments and trends suggest several tentative answers to those questions.

Should Government Act?

Despite the rhetoric of both Democrats and Republicans about curbing the growth of government and putting our fiscal houses in order, the evidence to date suggests that the rate of government will continue to grow as old problems persist and new problems emerge. One needs only to look at the federal government's budget deficits as evidence of that. Among other things, the war on terrorism, continued demands to reform education, global warming, America's health-care crisis, and an aging population guarantee that governments will continue to be active participants in solving the nation's problems. But as we saw in Chapter 5, not all problems reach the government's agenda. Models of agenda setting suggest that various considerations having to do with the nature of the problem, potential solutions, and the nation's politics determine which issues governments attend to and, equally important, which issues governments will ignore. Just as important, how those in and out of government define problems will shape the kinds of solutions governments consider and which aspects of the problem will be addressed.

Chapter 9 adds a few twists to the question of whether government should act. Often the decision is not simply whether governments should do something, but whether governments should continue doing things—and, if so, what changes (if any) are warranted. Policy termination is and will continue to be a vital part of the policy process as problems, priorities, and resources change. Moreover, as we note in Chapter 9, several models have been developed in recent years to account for policy change, a development that attests to the importance of the issue.

What Values Should Governments Pursue?

The most fundamental issue citizens and their governments will face over the next several decades concerns which values governments will address. Former Colorado governor Richard Lamm and Richard Caldwell have argued that between the 1950s and the 1990s, Americans moved from a "we" to a "me" society that places less value on achieving equality and protecting the poor and disadvantaged and more on individual freedom, opportunity, and personal responsibility. In recent years there have been renewed efforts to introduce private values on social issues (gay rights, abortion, prayer in schools, the role of faith-based organizations) onto the public agenda, and market values (competition, choice, work, efficiency) are increasingly the benchmarks by which we judge and prescribe public policies.

What Actions Should Government Take?

As we have seen, governments have a full arsenal of tools they can use in carrying out public policy, among them direct action, tax expenditures, subsidies, and regulation. The decisions concerning which tools are used often have a substantial impact on the effectiveness of public policies. Increasingly, policy makers at all levels of government are drawing on market values, principles, and mechanisms to "do the peoples' business." In some instances, policies fold market principles into substantive programs. The use of effluent charges to regulate pollution levels and educational schemes that promote choice and competition are just two examples of that way of thinking about public policy. In other instances, governments simply "outsource" responsibility for public policy to private for-profit and not-for-profit organizations. As we have seen, private firms play a major role in the war in Iraq. Private firms and non-profit organizations are also responsible for administering welfare programs, operating prisons, and running schools across the country. More and more, those organizations are faith-based groups.

Decisions by policy makers regarding which tools the government will use reflect how problems are defined and brought to the agenda as well as the values governments seek to advance. But those decisions also reflect the kinds of individuals and groups who make policy and the considerations they bring to the table. As we saw in Chapter 6, there is no shortage of models that seek to explain who and how decisions are made. Sometimes decisions entail a careful weighing of costs and benefits; but just as often they reflect, among other things, the tugging and pulling of partisan politics, groupthink, or something akin to garbage can politics. Not surprisingly, which model operates in a particular instance will determine the kinds of programs that will be adopted and, in all likelihood, their effectiveness.

Which Level of Government Should Govern?

One of the most important characteristics of American government is its federal nature. Political power has historically been divided between the national, state, and local government. Beginning in the 1930s, the role and influence of the national government grew dramatically; and over the next 50 years, federal policy increasingly usurped state and local law. Beginning in the 1970s, efforts have been made to restore power to subnational governments, particularly state governments. A decentralization of authority is seen in a number of instances. Currently, states have primary responsibility for enforcing the nation's environmental standards, and they make the critical decisions concerning who will receive welfare and under what conditions. Often, the states are the first level of government to respond to emerging problems. In the 1980s it was state governments that first responded to the AIDS epidemic. More recently, several states have taken the initiative in responding to the challenges of global warming and the seeming inability of Congress and the White House to address the issue. The flow of authority has not always moved from federal to state governments, however. In the wake of the No Child Left Behind Act, states must now meet education standards set in Washington, D.C., or risk losing federal funding. The demands of homeland security have also added to the demands placed on state and local authorities. The citizens of New Orleans learned that lesson the hard way when they waited in vain for relief from FEMA, an agency that had recently been folded into the Department of Homeland Security. In 2007, several states were challenging a federal requirement that driver's licenses not be issued without two forms of identification; it will cost states millions to comply with this seemingly simple idea.

A BLURRING OF LINES

In considering how politics and policy have changed in recent years, the authors of this book have been struck by how much the lines of governing have blurred. When we think about the institutions of government, we normally envision a separation of powers in which each branch of government is primarily responsible for performing certain functions. Legislatures are tasked with the responsibility of drafting and funding legislation, presidents and governors are responsible for faithfully executing those laws, and the courts are responsible for making sure everyone is playing by the rules. Federalism provides a similar, if frequently changing, division of labor. The lines are evident in other areas as well. Take the line between church and state. The First Amendment to the U.S. Constitution builds a wall that separates church and state. More generally, most of us think of the public and private sectors as two separate spheres of activity, each with its own rules, structures, and dynamics. And in considering what governments do, a basic distinction is made between foreign and domestic policy. Of course, students of American politics have long understood that these divisions have never been absolute, and much of the debate and controversy that takes place in and near government is where those lines should be drawn. But in recent years it seems that those lines are becoming even more blurred, so that it makes much less sense today to talk about a division of activity and authority between institutions and levels of government, church and state, foreign and domestic policy, or public and private spheres. As we have seen, governments are increasingly turning to the private sector to administer public policies, and issues like global warning, immigration, and homeland security make the distinction between foreign and domestic policy less meaningful. The allocation of responsibilities between levels of government also seems to operate without much of a rationale for who does what within a federal system. Problems that are supposedly national in scope— for example, pollution and poverty—are increasingly being turned over to the states. Meanwhile, policies that have generally been seen as the province of local authorities, most notably education, are increasingly subjected to federal and state mandates. And, if there is one lesson that emerges from studies of the policy process, it is that the line between the stages of the policy process are at best heuristic devices for isolating processes that occur continuously and at various venues in the life of pubic policies. In the real world of government, policy-making frequently takes place at the implementation stage; and increasingly, policy makers are as concerned with how (and by whom) policies will be implemented as they are with the content of policy itself.

The challenges for governments from this blurring of lines are several. In the case of markets and market mechanisms, governments need to attend to a number of issues. Does the drive for efficiency come at the expense of equality? Are there things the private sector should *not* be doing? How do those who work in the private sector differ from those who work in the public sector? Does the increasing use of private organizations to implement public policies change the nature of what government bureaucracies do? Is political control less or more problematic? Where faith-based organizations are involved, additional questions are raised. Some of those questions revolve around constitutional issues. But greater reliance on faith-based organizations also raises the more practical question of whether such institutions are actually capable of providing education and social services on a large scale. With respect to federalism, additional issues emerge. Is there a set of principles or rationales for deciding which levels of government should have which responsibilities? Do state and local governments have the capacity to govern, and govern wisely? What are the implications of globalization for federalism in the United States? Does it make sense, for example, for the states to take the lead in addressing global warming?

Finding answers to these and other questions will keep public officials busy for the foreseeable future. Those same issues provide an agenda for policy scholars. As we have seen, scholars have made enormous strides in learning how governing proceeds. There is now a large body of empirical research that examines what occurs at various stages of the policy process. There is also no shortage of rigorous models that draw from multiple disciplines to explain agenda setting, policymaking, implementation, evaluation, termination, and policy change. In short, we now know more than ever before about what governments do, how they do it, and with what effects.

As the business of governments changes, however, policy scholars will need to adjust their research agendas to reflect those changes. As governments embrace markets, for example, increasing attention will need to be paid to the nexus between the public and private sectors. Globalization suggests that policy analysts might also consider the influence of international considerations in examining what are ostensibly domestic policies. In a related fashion, policy scholars should also look more closely at how other nations provide public goods and how federalism works in other contexts. And as the lines between various stages of the policy process, levels and institutions of government, and the public and private sector continue to blur, policy analysts might reconsider what are the most appropriate units of analysis for policy research. The most recent models of policy change, most notably Sabatier and his associates' advocacy coalition framework and Baumgartner and Jones' punctuated equilibrium theory, do just that. In each model, policies are created, changed, and implemented by policy subsystems consisting of elected officials, interest groups, implementing officials, and others who share basic beliefs. Little attention is given to the stages of the policy process or to the distinctions between public and private, elected and unelected officials. For the authors of those models, the critical units of analysis are policy change and stability, subsystem actors, and conditions in the larger political, social, and economic environment.

SUMMARY

The previous chapters have discussed the nature of public policy, the evolution of public policy and policy studies, several phases of the policy cycle, and several substantive policy areas. As a final comment, we return to our original point of departure for this book—that the student should be aware of how understanding of the policy process, as well as substantive policy, has evolved over time. Hopefully the reader can better appreciate how knowledge develops, and the extent to which it may inform policy choices. As policy scholars better understand the policy process, as well as problems such as poor educational performance, poverty, and environmental pollution, perhaps they can design better substantive policies to remedy those public problems.

The study of public policy involves an understanding of the public policy process, the methods policy scientists use to study this process, and the substance of policy in areas of interest. All three areas interact with one another and are crucial to the ability to improve the system's performance in remedying public problems. Moreover, as we said at the outset, we can better understand where we are today by looking backward to where we have been. An understanding of historical context is fundamental to designing more effective policies in the future.

Finally, all of us are involved in the policy process whether we choose to be or not. Therefore, we must gain an appreciation of public policy, its challenges, and its opportunities. Whether we find ourselves in the governmental bureaucracy, in policy institutes, in colleges or universities, or in the voting booth, all of us are policy analysts.

Index